Caring Hearts &
Critical Minds

Caring Hearts & Critical Minds

Literature, Inquiry, and Social Responsibility

Steven Wolk

Stenhouse
PUBLISHERS

www.stenhouse.com
Portland, Maine

Stenhouse Publishers
www.stenhouse.com

Credits
Page 58: From *The Hunger Games* by Suzanne Collins. Copyright © 2008 by Suzanne Collins. Reprinted by permission of Scholastic Inc.

Library of Congress Cataloging-in-Publication Data
Wolk, Steven.
  Caring hearts and critical minds : literature, inquiry, and social responsibility / Steven Wolk. 1st ed.
      p. cm.
  Includes bibliographical references and index.
  ISBN 978-1-57110-859-3 (pbk. : alk. paper) — ISBN 978-1-57110-973-6 (ebook)
  1. Affective education. 2. Social learning. 3. Social justice--Study and teaching. 4. Citizenship—Study and teaching. 5. Children's literature—Social aspects. 6. Inquiry (Theory of knowledge) I. Title.
  LB1072.W65 2012
  370.15'34—dc23
                                                                    2012023037

Cover design, interior design, and typesetting by designboy creative group

Manufactured in the United States of America

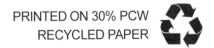
PRINTED ON 30% PCW
RECYCLED PAPER

19 18 17 16 15 14 13   9 8 7 6 5 4 3 2 1

For my mom
Wilma Joy Wolk
1932–2002
who loved to read

Contents

Acknowledgments

Without the six teachers featured in this book there would be no book. My unending gratitude and appreciation go to Laura Meili, Leslie Rector, Ron Sledge, Karen Tellez, Mary Tripp, and Natalie Tyrell. They not only welcomed me into their classrooms but also trusted me with their students. These are passionate, committed, smart, and creative teachers. I am forever grateful. Thank you.

A special thank-you to teachers Ben Kovacs and Sara Ahmed at Burley School in Chicago, who also gave me the privilege of spending time in their wonderful classrooms and shared some of their magnificent work with their middle schoolers in this book. And a big round of applause to Barbara Kent, the former principal at Burley, as well as the rest of the teachers, administrators, and staff at that very special school that my son, Max, was lucky enough to attend.

Over the years other teachers have opened their classroom doors to me as they spun their magic with their students. My thanks go to Mary Kovats, Gina Laino, Shelly Leland, Ivette Loza, Kari Rowe, and Katie Welsh.

See this book in your hands? Thank my editor, Holly Holland. I had a book in my head; Holly made that book a reality. Like an exceptional teacher, she knew just when to step to the side and give me some space and when to step back in and give me a nudge (and sometimes a little push). I will be forever grateful for her patience, which I surely tested at times. We all know about helping a student find the "just right" book. Well, lucky for me, I was given the "just right" editor. Holly also had a few "mystery reviewers" give me some written feedback, and let me tell you, they took that task seriously, so a huge thank-you goes to them.

There would also be no book without Philippa Stratton at Stenhouse, as well as their entire talented production, editing, and marketing team, including Chris Downey, Jay Kilburn, Rebecca Eaton, Jill Cooley, and Laurel Robinson.

My students at Northeastern Illinois University make this calling of teaching a special pleasure. Interacting with them inside our classes and schools challenges my mind, feeds my intellect, nurtures my creativity, and gives me plenty of good times. I consider it a privilege to collaborate with so many talented educators on this remarkable endeavor of transforming our schools and classrooms. I also want to extend my thanks to my colleagues and the staff in the Teacher Education Department, as well as throughout NEIU. And here's a special shout-out to our College of Education leader, Maureen Gillette. Thanks for your support (and all the good talk) over the years.

I have had the honor to be associated with Mary Hicks and the rest of the amazing staff at the nonprofit Chicago literacy organization Boundless Readers. They conduct literacy workshops for teachers, facilitate teacher study groups inside schools, and award grants for teachers to put books inside their Chicago Public School classrooms, bringing one of the greatest gifts of all to children: easy access to lots of good books.

And there is my family, Laura and Max. You guys are the best support team any writer could wish for. Sometimes my writing this book must have felt to Laura as if my computer had swallowed me and then spit me out five hours later. Yet there she was, with that shining smile on her face and the endless warmth in her heart. And what a lucky dad I am to have Max in my life. You are more than a great kid who loves baseball and knows how many strikeouts Tim Lincecum has; you are a great person with a soaring mind and caring heart. Thank you both for your wholehearted encouragement. I am a very lucky guy. I love you.

Learn everything you can—everything. And then use all that you have learned to grow up to be a wise and good man.

—*The Wednesday Wars* (Schmidt 2007)

Matthew had called her harmless. Harmless. And being with him made her feel squashed into a box—a box where she was expected to be sweet and sensitive (but not oversensitive); a box for young and pretty girls who were not as bright or powerful as their boyfriends. A box for people who were not forces to be reckoned with.

Frankie wanted to be a force to be reckoned with.

—*The Disreputable History of Frankie Landau-Banks* (Lockhart 2008)

Dare I disturb the universe? Yes, I do, I do. I think.

—*The Chocolate War* (Cormier 1972)

Teachers, people on the block, Mama, Neeka—everybody was always talking about me being smart, how I'd leave them and go away to some fancy college. And maybe I would and maybe I wouldn't. I read all those books and watched those educational shows and peeped the newspapers and people's biographies and autobiographies because I was trying to see some tiny bit of myself up in those books.

—*After Tupac and D Foster* (Woodson 2008)

That's what I'm into. Questioning. It's how you learn. Even when you don't get the answers, you get the heat to find them. Right now my heat is turned on high.

—*Deadline* (Crutcher 2007)

"Thank you!" said Maltcassion, reaching to lick the wound with a tongue the size of a mattress. "That's been annoying me for about four centuries. You may help yourself to some gold or jewels by way of payment, Miss Strange."

"I require no payment, sir."

"Really? I thought all mankind gravitated toward things that are shiny. I'm not saying that's *necessarily* a bad thing, but when it comes to species development, it could be limiting."

"I'm not here for money. I'm here to do the right thing."

—*The Last Dragonslayer* (Fforde 2012)

Introduction

The ability to read awoke inside me some long dormant craving to be mentally alive.
—Malcolm X (Haley 1964)

Let's begin with my mistakes. Actually, first let me share the backstory and then the mistakes. After nine years teaching elementary and middle school and another twelve years at the college level, I was itching to get back inside middle school classrooms so I could put into practice ideas that I had been writing about and breathlessly advocating as a teacher educator. I wanted to teach in ways that I had not done before. Back then, I had loved and used children's literature and project-based learning to teach across the curriculum, but I had not tied these approaches together. Nor had I articulated a comprehensive mission and philosophy of inquiry-based teaching. In a sense, I would be returning to the classroom as a rookie.

I started by contacting some middle school teachers in the Chicago area. Most were former students of mine at Northeastern Illinois University, and all of them were dedicated teachers, striving to make learning and thinking thrive in their classrooms. They loved using good books with their students, wanting the words and ideas on the pages to clamor into their hearts and minds. They were more than happy to allow me into their classrooms to try out some new ways to engage students and stimulate deeper reading.

Figures 1 through 6 show the teachers in action. Natalie Tyrell and Leslie Rector teach sixth grade, Ron Sledge and Mary Tripp teach seventh grade, and Karen Tellez and Laura Meili teach eighth grade. Natalie works in a suburb of Chicago, and all the others work in the Chicago Public Schools. Unfortunately, because of space limitations, the units with Mary and Laura could not fit into this book. But I have included some of the activities and teaching we did, as well as some of the resources we used, as examples throughout these pages.

Our plan was to design and coteach units that combined four elements:

Figure 1 Natalie Tyrell enjoys reading to her sixth graders.

Figure 2 Students read one of their unit books with their teacher Leslie Rector.

Figure 3 Ron Sledge and his students are engaged in a shared reading of *The Adoration of Jenna Fox*.

Figure 4 Mary Tripp discusses *Black and White* with some of her seventh graders.

Figure 5 Eighth graders still appreciate picture books that are part of Karen Tellez's inquiry units.

Figure 6 Students in Laura Meili's class take notes about the themes in *The Hunger Games*.

- Strong middle-grades and young adult literature
- Inquiry-based teaching
- Interesting and vibrant real-world resources
- Teaching for social responsibility

Most of the teachers had limited experience designing this type of curriculum—especially integrating specific content about social responsibility—so they let me take the lead. We were in contact throughout the designing and teaching of our units, sometimes coming up with an idea the night before (or even as I walked into the classroom). Contrary to the assumption of many new teachers that instructional units are complete before you begin the unit, we did what real teachers usually do, which is shape these units as we went along. I cotaught about three days a week. On the other days, the teachers usually taught the units on their own. Figure 7 shows the units I designed with each teacher, as well as the books we used as the anchor texts.

Now, here are some of the mistakes I made on my sojourn back into the classroom. These were entirely my own. Some of the faults are perfectly acceptable; others border on embarrassing. Of course, failure is a necessary and important part of learning, for students and teachers. I have tried

Chapter	Teacher	Grade	Unit Focus	Anchor Books	Length
7	Ron	7	Media and Technology	*The Adoration of Jenna Fox*	6 Weeks
8	Leslie	6	The Environment	*The City of Ember*	7 Weeks
9	Natalie	6	Empathy and Caring	*The Tiger Rising* *Leon's Story*	3 Weeks
10	Karen	8	Global Awareness Personal Journeys	*Red Glass*	5 Weeks
11	Leslie	6	U.S. and Global Poverty Historical Consciousness	*Esperanza Rising*	7 Weeks
Not a separate chapter	Mary	7	Race and Racism Friendship	*Black and White*	3 Weeks
Not a separate chapter	Laura	8	Violence Flipping Our "Life Scripts"	*The Hunger Games*	6 Weeks
Not a separate chapter	Ron	7	Current Social Problems: Teenage Pregnancy American Criminal Justice System Illegal Immigration	*Make Lemonade* *Monster* *La Linea*	7 Weeks

Figure 7 Inquiry units referenced in the book.

to reframe the missteps as insights that will further our growth and, I hope, provide some valuable lessons for other educators. Here's a short list:

- Sometimes we did too much. Most of the units were overly ambitious for the time frame and the students' understanding. Lesson learned: usually less is more. We never want the scope of a unit to interfere with our students' enjoyment of good literature.

- The quality of the students' work was inconsistent, sometimes poor. Their thinking often showed maturity, but we didn't do enough to help them create sufficient high-quality work. If we want and expect excellence, we must provide models and time for producing works of excellence. This requires us to slow down. With a vast curriculum to cover and a ticking clock, making space for deep learning and high-quality work is never easy, but we need to find time to help kids create beautiful work.

- We overdid journal writing. In hindsight, I wish we had guided students through the fuller writing process at times so they could learn how to revise and refine their thinking and improve their writing.

- It's easy to get pulled away from the literature. I'm aware of the irony, considering these are *literature-based* inquiry units, but we struggled to find the right balance between the books and other connected texts and resources.

- I wish we had included more ways for students to ask and explore questions about the books and unit topics. It's always a challenge to juggle your goals as a progressive and creative teacher with the interests of students. Sometimes we must have the courage and humility to step away from our own plans and let students' inquiries lead the way.

- We did too much shared reading. For some of these units, we read the entire book and nearly all of the connected short texts (such as newspaper articles) collectively. I'm a huge fan of shared reading (more on that in Chapter 6), but we must also regularly engage students in reading these texts on their own.

I have come to realize that the first time teaching a unit is a practice run. Like a Broadway play in the preview stage, we are not finished tweaking the production. Of course, we want to do a great job with our students the first time and every time. Yet the process of our learning encourages us to keep adapting and revising. The inquiry units shown in Chapters 7–11 were our "first-runs." Looking back, I see clearly that good teaching is *reteaching*. Designing a great unit involves more than gathering and organizing terrific resources; it also requires a conscious commitment to *learn* from the first-run and refine the unit for the next time and on and on.

What I want to focus on for most of the book, however, is what worked well with these inquiry units. My colleagues and I did indeed cultivate caring hearts and critical minds in these middle school classrooms. As I look back at our experiences with six groups of young adolescents, I have many memories of thoughtful learning, important conversations, good laughs, a few tears, stimulating reading, exciting creativity, and profound moments of wonder. That's why I've spent the past twenty-four years in education. The extraordinary possibilities never end.

Chapter 1

Why Read?

When I was near shelves of books, I came alive, almost as if I were picking up emanations.
I felt a sense of perspective, of scale, the solace of the idea of generations,
as well as a great desire to do things on my own, to achieve.

—Sven Birkets (2007)

Grab a pencil and jot a list of all the reading you've done in the past week, including everything from cereal boxes to novels. Start scribbling.

Finished? I bet most of the items on your list match the items on mine:

- bills (online and paper)
- Web sites
- newspapers (online and hard copy)
- magazines
- books
- online documents
- work-related documents
- grocery list
- e-mails (personal and work)
- food labels
- mail (junk mail, flyers, etc.)
- road signs
- my son's baseball information
- recipes

There are more items that I could include, but you get the idea. Nancie Atwell (1998) refers to this list as our "reading territories," all of the different reading we do—in all forms and for all purposes—throughout our daily lives. At the start of the school year, Atwell asks her students to make a graphic organizer of their own reading territories, categorizing the specific texts they read.

Needless to say, we read a lot in our lives, much more than most of us realize. A great deal of that reading is functional—that is, reading that allows us to survive in daily life. We don't necessarily want to do some of this reading, but we have to. (Work memos can make my eyes glaze over.) In addition, many of us read books, poetry, magazines, newspapers, Web sites, and candy wrappers. We don't have to read them; the routine machinations of our lives would work just fine without these texts.

As educators, we want our students to devour skateboarding Web sites, video game manuals, vampire novels, sports magazines, and whatever authentic text catches their interest. But we don't want them to limit their reading territories to popular texts or what they might need to function in life. We want them to read widely, read texts that will open their hearts and challenge their minds, and read critically and wisely. We want students to *own* these habits of mind so they will use them outside of our classrooms, over the summer, and throughout their lives.

We know that such knowledgeable reading makes us smart—not just "school smart" but life smart and world smart and smart in ways that help us connect seemingly disparate ideas. We want such inquiry to be a central part of the lives of all adolescents because it teaches them how to be thoughtful and caring as well as intellectually robust and capable of anticipating and responding to change in all facets of life, from our families and the country to technology and politics.

Recently, I interviewed a principal of a Chicago public school. Some of my questions focused on her school's professional development needs. I asked her what would help her faculty most with their literacy teaching. She didn't hesitate a moment. Her thoughts burst out in a flow of passion and dedication. She said that her teachers already know how to improve their students' reading skills; they're well versed on strategies to improve comprehension and fluency and the like. What they need, she said, is to learn how to take it to the next level. They need ideas on how to use reading and writing to help their students to *think* and to *care*. They need to know how to make students' reading relevant to the real world. They need to help their kids develop real purposes for reading a wide variety of texts beyond a test score and a grade, and to learn how reading can be used to engage students in intellectual debate. That's what this book is about.

Reading for Pleasure

Although critical purposes for reading are essential, I would argue that the single most important reason to read is for pleasure. We read books and other texts simply because we enjoy them. There's nothing like getting lost in a good story. Books take us places we can't go: the Amazon in Peru, the Hogwarts School of Witchcraft and Wizardry, a hundred years into the future, inside boxcars filled with Jewish people on their way to Auschwitz. They also take us into the stories of the joy and turmoil in our own lives, families, and communities. As educators we cannot promote reading for pleasure enough; we know that a lifetime of reading for pleasure makes us happier people and better readers, including on standardized tests (Gallagher 2009; Krashen 2004).

So, I want to be clear that what I'm advocating in these pages is not meant to be the entire reading curriculum. Independent reading with self-chosen books and daily silent reading time should be the foundation of any reading curriculum. I agree with Nancie Atwell (2003), who writes in *The*

Reading Zone that what we want are "skilled, passionate, habitual, critical readers," and the best way to achieve that is to immerse children in a culture of books that allows them to connect with reading on a personal level.

Yet we also need people who use reading for thinking, self-improvement, and acting to make the world a better place. For the past four years, I've been working with Leslie, the sixth-grade teacher whose Chicago classroom is the focus of Chapters 8 and 11. Figure 1.1 shows the class library in Leslie's sixth-grade classroom. Walking through a school and seeing libraries like this—filled with the best and most exciting children's and young adult literature—speaks loud and clear to visitors: We *love* books here, and we use books not only to cultivate a love for reading but also to help students think about ideas and issues and questions that matter.

Figure 1.1 Books overflow in Leslie Rector's classroom library.

In Figure 1.2 you can see some of the results of Leslie's classroom reading routines. When her sixth graders finish reading a book independently, they make a "book card" that Leslie adds to the wall display. Each card includes the book title, author, student's name, and date. Students also add a tiny picture and either a short written response or a quote from the book. At the end of each quarter, Leslie totals the cards. If you want students to read as Leslie's do, you need to do four things: give them easy access to lots of good books they want to read, introduce them to many great authors,

Figure 1.2 Leslie Rector's "Books We've Read" wall shows how frequently and widely her students read.

model being a passionate reader, and give them regular time to choose and read books. Mix these four ingredients together and you have created a powerful classroom reading and book culture.

Reading for a Better World

Cris Tovani (2000) writes that when it comes to reading, "purpose is everything" (24). When students are given something to read in school—a book, an essay, a poem, or a textbook—how do they see the purpose of that reading? When my graduate students interview adolescents about their reading in school, virtually none can articulate a purpose other than to "get the assignment done" or to "read the textbook" or to learn a skill. There's no mention of reading for pleasure or reading to stay informed about current events or reading to shape their political, moral, or cultural identities. They don't see any connection between the books they read in school and improving their "self" or the world, or reading as an intellectual and moral engine of democracy. As Tovani writes, "When I ask students why they read in school, they say their teacher makes them: Read chapter 10. There will be a test on Monday" (24).

Reading has vital purposes beyond improving reading skills or learning subject content. Living in a democracy gives us the opportunity, indeed carries the responsibility, of reading to support and improve society. Whereas our national economy depends on workers who *can* read, our democracy depends on people who *do* read and think and act in response to their reading. Our schools were originally created with the vital mission of educating Americans to be the caretakers of our democracy. Somewhere along the way our schools and our nation lost this purpose. Books and inquiry-based teaching can help bring this mission back to our classrooms.

If we want young adolescents to take their reading in school more seriously, then we as their teachers need to take it more seriously too. Deborah Appleman writes that adolescents want their school experiences to *matter*. They don't want school to dwell on fluff and endless facts and a curriculum sanitized of interesting and provocative ideas. They want to read a wide variety of texts that confront the complexities of life and adolescence head-on and challenge them to think and see in new ways. They want their readings to be honest about the world we live in and bold enough to explore the world we *could* live in. Appleman writes:

> Constructing significance in their work is not simply a matter of having them read more contemporary texts. It is a matter of creating and re-creating fresh and unrehearsed opportunities to make discoveries about texts, about language, about the world, and about themselves. (2007, 144)

We cannot undervalue the abilities of adolescents to meaningfully engage in this journey. They are more than capable of tackling important ideas. Many lack the sophistication or the background knowledge and the vocabulary to tackle these complex texts and topics on their own, but that does not hinder their ability to engage with ideas and questions that matter. And reading these authentic texts for important aims is the best way for them to develop that sophistication, learn that background knowledge, and expand their vocabulary.

Teaching for civic literacy, for social responsibility, goes to the heart of what we want to do as teachers. And if we accomplish that while also deepening our students' inquiry and comprehension skills, we give them the tools and habits of mind they will need to make the world a better place, both as children and adults. Teaching for social responsibility and what Maxine Greene (1988) refers to as a "wide-awakeness" to the world goes beyond a basic citizenship class, however. It focuses on shaping human beings with intellectual curiosity as well as caring hearts. More than getting students to follow the party line, to become the embodiment of political correctness, we must show students that it is safe—in fact, a civic responsibility—to engage in authentic debate, to use their reading and analytical skills to discuss and dissect texts and social issues as they examine multiple perspectives and divergent choices.

Teaching with middle-grades and young adult literature is a creative, powerful, and exciting experience of guiding students on this journey. Because we have so many books that wrap vital ideas into good stories, we can use them in pleasurable and meaningful ways to bring learning to life. No longer are students reading just to pass a quiz, or to write an essay, or to answer factual comprehension questions. Teaching for social responsibility through contemporary young adult literature awakens civic consciousness and gives authentic purpose to reading.

Rethinking Teaching with Books

In these pages, I'm focused on using literature to invite students to explore vital issues and questions. Why do we have racism? Do I have prejudices? Why is there so much violence and war? Does our nation have an ethical responsibility to stop genocide? How do other people live around the world? Is all technology good? What are our responsibilities to the poor? Who should get my vote? Why? How does my way of life affect the Earth and its ecosystems? Should I care? Who am I? Can I make a difference?

We can use good books as catalysts for young adolescents to think about these topics, create their identities, engage with others about important ideas, and learn to critique, as well as to inspire them to create a better world. These qualities, I believe, form ethical and educated human beings. Environmental educator David Orr (1994) wrote, "We must remember that the purpose of education is not mastery of knowledge but mastery of self *through* knowledge" (125). And while students are immersed in this authentic and purposeful literacy to shape their selves, they are also becoming better readers.

It would be naïve for me to ignore the complexity and difficulty of teaching for social responsibility today. I am all too aware—as both an educator and a parent—of our intense national focus on teaching to the test. Facts and skills are quantifiable; when it comes to education, our schools and our society love numbers: test scores, grades, GPAs, class ranks, reading levels, and stanines. To teach against this torrent of quantification can be a staggering task. Yet many teachers not only have found a way to teach a more comprehensive approach to literacy but also have found that teaching for social responsibility through literature is one of the best ways to integrate content standards and skills in authentic and meaningful contexts. Rather than seeing state and district requirements as insurmountable hurdles, good teachers see them as challenges to creatively rise above.

Leslie Rector embodies that philosophy. Early in her teaching career, she ended an e-mail message to me with this news:

Just a side note: the 6th grade had the best overall test scores. We had the most kids move from meet to exceed standards. It is interesting because we were the team that did the least amount of test prep and we were all on the same page as using authentic literature in our classrooms. Good research data. So, finally after 4 years of teaching I'm not so crazy when it comes to testing.

Stories like this dispel the myth that purposeful and authentic teaching through literature and good test scores are mutually exclusive. They are not! There are similar stories in classrooms around the country. Like all the educators I respect, I'm certainly no fan of standardized tests. They inhibit real learning, reduce knowledge and humanity to simplistic multiple choices, and hinder the teaching of critical thinking and social responsibility. But as long as these tests are a part of schools and society, teachers have a responsibility to help students do well on them. The more we help kids to care and think about important and relevant ideas, the more meaningful their learning becomes. As Leslie alluded to in her e-mail, the best "test prep" is good teaching, great resources, and a dynamic and interesting curriculum that matters.

Teaching from a Critical Perspective

We are living in the Enlightenment of middle-grades and young adult literature. Teachers never have had so many remarkable books to invigorate their instruction and introduce themes that reinforce social responsibility. However, it's not enough to have students read relevant and engaging books; we must also use these books to teach authentic inquiry (Friedman 2000; Wilhelm 2007). Through this shift, says English teacher Phyllis Muldoon, "the definition of knowledge changes from something learners extract from a text to something they create in collaboration with each other" (1990, 34). Muldoon has a spectacular way to describe her literature classroom. It is, she says, a "brawl of ideas."

Imagine two seventh-grade classrooms. Both teachers are passionate about using good contemporary literature and are reading the popular middle-grades novel *The Breadwinner* (Ellis 2001) with their students. *The Breadwinner* tells the story of a thirteen-year-old girl, Parvana, who is struggling to survive under the Taliban in Afghanistan. The first teacher in this example emphasizes the "facts" of the book: plot, characters, and setting, as well as some comprehension skills and strategies. Yet the teacher also strives to create a constructivist classroom, helping her students make connections from the text to their lives. She values her students' opinions and ideas and honors their interpretations of the book's themes. If we were to represent her teaching through five key questions, the list might look like this:

1. Why can't Parvana go to school?
2. How would you feel if you were in Parvana's shoes?
3. Who do you know that is similar to Parvana's mother?
4. What are the similarities and differences between your and Parvana's lives?
5. Imagine Parvana ten years later. Where is she? What is she doing?

Now let's look inside the classroom of the second teacher. She is also teaching the important facts of the book. She certainly wants her students to understand the plot, characters, and setting, and to develop good inference skills, because she knows her students will not become good readers without them. But she does not stop with those comprehension strategies; she also addresses different aspects of social responsibility and helps her students connect themes in the book to issues in their lives and around the world. Being student-centered is not enough; we need classrooms that are also community-centered and world-centered and democracy-centered. As students make their way through *The Breadwinner*, this second teacher challenges them with more complex questions:

1. Why would a country or a culture deny its girls and women equal rights?
2. Is it okay for a country to treat males and females differently because of cultural beliefs?
3. How do you see and interact with the opposite sex?
4. Do wealthy countries have a responsibility to help poor countries?
5. Are there are any parallels between what is happening in the book in Afghanistan and life in the United States, either in the past or at the present?

The second set of questions does not exclude the first set; the key is to ask *both*. As we prepare to teach a book, we make choices: how to organize the reading of the book, what activities and projects to do, what questions to ask, and so on. With just one novel, teachers make literally hundreds of instructional decisions. Before teaching a book, teachers should ask themselves how they want their students to be *different* once they have completed the book. Good books have the power to change us; they can be transformative experiences. Books can certainly improve students' reading skills, but that is not why Deborah Ellis wrote *The Breadwinner*. I'll let her speak for herself:

> I've been doing antiwar work since I was 17, in one form or another, and the Taliban takeover of Kabul in 1996 fit into what I was doing. It brought together issues of women's rights, foreign intervention, and war. I got together with some women in Toronto and we started to raise money for women in the camps. I thought that I could be useful by going over and interviewing women about their lives over the course of this terrible war, what [they were] like both now and in the past. But I hadn't planned to do a children's book until I met the mother of a daughter who was still back in Afghanistan masquerading as a boy in order to feed her family. As a writer, sometimes you just get bolts of lightning through your brain that tell you that this is really important and you need to pay attention. I knew at that point that I'd write the book, *The Breadwinner*. (O'Brien, n.d.)

Patrick Shannon (1995) writes that schools are in the "identity creation business." Do we want to inspire our students to come to school each day waiting for their teachers and textbooks to give them the answers? Or do we want to embolden original and creative thinkers with wonder in their hearts and questions on their minds and compassion in their souls to work for a better life and the common good? As teachers, what "bolts of lightning" do we want our students to experience to help them look at themselves and the world and truly pay attention?

Good books are filled with lightning bolts—ideas and stories that cause readers to look at the world with amazement and pay attention to what is happening all around them. Consider Gary

Schmidt's remarkable novel *The Wednesday Wars*. Set in 1967, the book features seventh grader Holling Hoodhood (yep, that's his name), who is stuck in Mrs. Baker's classroom each Wednesday afternoon while his classmates attend religious school. One day, when an awful odor permeates the classroom, Mrs. Baker takes Holling on a field trip. As they drive through town, she shares a magical history of local architecture. Here's a snippet of that:

> And on the west, on the far outskirts of town, we drove past what looked like a garden shed. "The first abolitionist school," Mrs. Baker said, "where Negro children could come to learn to read and write and so escape the ignorance that slavery wanted to impose. Right there, Holling, is the true beginning of the end of slavery." I never knew a building could hold so much inside. (222)

Holling would probably never look at a building—and the memory it holds—quite the same way again. The same could be true of a sixth grader who reads Holling's story and then gets an assignment to choose a local building, learn its history, and give voice to its memory. Projects like this bring relevancy to students' lives and cultivate creativity and imagination.

Reading Makes Us Human

In his book *Why Read?*, Mark Edmundson (2005) writes about what he calls "Final Narratives," which he defines as "the ultimate set of terms that we use to confer value on experience. It's where our principles are manifest" (25). Edmundson, a humanities professor, believes that reading literature is one of the most important ways for us to develop our Final Narratives. Through reading good books we excavate, interrogate, debate, and give shape to who we are, what we believe, and how we want to live. He continues: "Get to your students' Final Narratives, and your own; seek out the defining beliefs. Uncover central convictions about politics, love, money, the good life. It's there that, as Socrates knew, real thinking starts" (28).

This notion of Final Narratives does not end with having your students write one thematic essay or complete a related project or read a particular book. Rather, it supports an ongoing process of inquiry of the self and society and the human condition. This process is neither neat nor linear; on the contrary, it can be a messy and meandering endeavor. Done honestly, it is a courageous act, requiring time and a caring, empathic classroom community. Perhaps this is what reading and exploring books with ideas that matter gives us most—a connection to others, a reminder that as different as we are, we have so much in common.

Making Purposes for Reading Explicit

Imagine creating a poster for a classroom with the title "Why Read?" We would need one list that works as well for an eighth-grade class reading *The Chocolate War*, a vacationer reading a trashy novel on the beach, a harried professional reading a newspaper on the train to work, and a fourth grader reading *MAD* magazine. This can be a great activity for the first week of school. Rather than dancing around the question with students, we should make our reading purposes and passions explicit.

Break the class into small groups, give students a piece of chart paper, and ask them to list every reason for reading they can think of. Afterward, display the sheets on the wall. Take some time to talk about what's up there. Be sure to add your ideas that the kids did not mention. This is very important. As teachers we most certainly want to honor students' ideas—that's why we *begin* with their ideas—but there are pieces of knowledge and perspectives they do not know, and it's our job to make those an important part of our classrooms.

Then, working together, place all the ideas into categories, creating a concise yet comprehensive final list. Turn that list into your classroom poster and hang it in a prominent place at your students' eye level where you refer to it again and again throughout the school year. When Elisa, who is reading Matt de la Peña's superb novel *Mexican WhiteBoy* (2008), mentions to you that the friendship between Danny and Uno reminds her of the emotional connection with her best friend, link that insight to the list and celebrate it with the class. We need to make the usually invisible purposes for reading very visible.

Leslie used a similar process with her sixth graders. Here's what they came up with for their final list of why people read:

1. To know what's happening in our world
2. To pass time
3. To block out the world and relax
4. To be successful
5. Expand your mind
6. Connect with others
7. To learn facts, information, and history
8. To be a better person
9. To learn new vocabulary
10. To have meaningful conversations
11. To survive
12. To be confident
13. Step inside someone else's shoes
14. To "visit" new places
15. To be a better writer
16. To be a better reader
17. Spark your imagination
18. For fun and entertainment
19. To answer questions that we wonder about
20. To manage our feelings
21. For gossip
22. To fall asleep
23. Sometimes you have to

I'd condense this list a bit and add a few other items to make social responsibility more explicit:

♦   To improve our democracy and society
♦   To understand people who are different and to reduce racism and prejudice
♦   To cultivate compassion and empathy
♦   To become critical, independent, and creative thinkers
♦   To shape our moral identity

Yes, such lists give us many ideas to consider, and teachers are already expected to cover mountains of content. But we don't need to address these themes in one unit or a single lesson; we can weave them into our teaching over the course of the entire school year. For example, if your students are already building literacy skills by reading Paul Volponi's *Black and White* (2006), you can also use the book to explore racism, the criminal justice system, and the complexities of friendship. If some of your book groups are reading *The Heaven Shop* (Ellis 2007), let them also use the book to study poverty in Africa, the devastation of AIDS, and the moral and political questions arising from these issues. Even fantasy novels like Gabrielle Zevin's wonderful *Elsewhere* (2007) can help students explore identity-building questions such as "What is happiness?" and "What should matter most in my life?" right along with helping them become better readers.

Engaging ideas are right there in the pages of books. As teachers, we need to pluck out these themes and invite our students to question them, to relate to them, and to make sense of them. We can do better. We want to do better. Our students are desperate for us to do better.

Chapter 2

Good Books

Stories can help teenagers look at their feelings, or come to emotional resolution,
from a safe distance. If, as an author, I can make an emotional connection with my reader,
I have already started to help him or her heal. I have never met a depressed person,
or an anxious person, or a fearful person who was not encouraged by the knowledge
that others feel the same way they do. I am not alone *is powerful medicine.*

—Chris Crutcher (1992)

Books surround me. The walls in my home office where I sit typing these words are lined with bookshelves. Sometimes piles of books on the floor form rolling hills. The world of middle grades and young adult literature is extraordinary, even enthralling. *Ender's Game, The Skin I'm In, Between Shades of Gray, Freak the Mighty, Perfect, Spite Fences, Delirium, Never Fall Down, I Am the Cheese, You Don't Know Me, Love That Dog*—these books explore the issues and stories that matter to adolescents, the writing qualities that excite teachers, and the thematic ideas that can transform self and society.

Walk into a good middle school classroom and you will see books stacked in bins on classroom library shelves, grasped in students' hands during silent reading, held aloft during a teachers' read-aloud or book talk, circulating in book groups or literature circles, integrated through interdisciplinary units, and shared as a whole-class reading. Adolescent and young adult literature should be as ubiquitous in twenty-first-century middle school classrooms as chalk dust was in twentieth-century classrooms.

Yet this transformation continues from textbook-based teaching to literature-based teaching, sometimes against daunting odds. Teachers must confront the realities of life in the classroom: lack of resources, large class sizes, pressure to raise test scores and conform to obsolete instructional practices, limited time and ever-more content to teach, mandates to offer a sanitized curriculum, and a society that does not really value reading and thinking. And we don't do our students (or ourselves) any favors by turning a good book into a regimen of unimaginative exercises. If students see our practices with literature as little more than a phone book of monotonous lessons, then what students are really learning is to hate reading. This is what Kelly Gallagher defines as *readicide*: "The systematic killing of the love of reading, often exacerbated by the inane, mind-numbing practices found in schools" (2009, 2).

The opposite of readicide is emphasizing reading for pleasure, surrounding students with a diverse sea of books they want to read while using good books to engage them in purposeful and relevant explorations of real issues and "hot topics" (Groenke, Maples, and Henderson 2010). This approach turns kids on to the astonishing wonders and powers and emotions of reading and a life spent inside books.

The Universe of Middle-Grades and Young Adult Literature

Middle-grades and young adult literature have at least three key characteristics:

- ♦ Books written and published for intermediate and young adult audiences between the ages of eight and fourteen (intermediate) and twelve and eighteen (young adult)
- ♦ Books with main characters within the age range of the audience
- ♦ Books with captivating plots, stories, and issues that are relevant to adolescents

These are the books I'm writing about on these pages. These are the books that should fill students' lives. Besides the realistic fiction that takes up the bulk of our teaching, the breadth of genres we can use to teach those big ideas and hot topics is wide: historical fiction, science fiction, fantasy, dystopian fiction, graphic novels and graphic memoirs, and the wide world of nonfiction, from history to biography to science. There are also edited collections of children's poetry and short stories. (See Appendixes C and D, along with the companion Web site, stenhouse.com/caringhearts, for book lists.)

Some students love romance and others love fantasy; some love sports books and others can't get enough thrilling action and adventure. Consider the most popular genres since 2000 or so: dystopian fiction such as *The Hunger Games* and *Divergent*, fantasy, the Harry Potter series (practically a separate genre), paranormal romance (thank you, *Twilight*), and "graphic" books such as *Diary of a Wimpy Kid*, as well as graphic novels and even Japanese manga. We need to give students wide and easy access to these books because they're *entertaining* and *they like them*.

But books can also have more enlightening aims, including helping to reverse the flood of civic illiteracy and cultivate social responsibility. Want to engage kids in a study of real war as opposed to sanitized textbook war? Have them read *Lord of the Nutcracker Men* or *Tree Girl* or *Fallen Angels*. Want to take your students to Africa? Have them crack open *The Heaven Shop* or *Child of Dandelions* or *Chanda's Secrets* or *A Long Walk to Water*. How about exploring social issues today by looking through a lens of the past? Read *The Loud Silence of Francine Greene*, *The Evolution of Calpurnia Tate*, *Elijah of Buxton*, or the extraordinary *Between Shades of Gray*, which is about Joseph Stalin's brutal purges. Want to explore issues of sexual orientation and bullying? Read James Howe's wonderful

Totally Joe or *So Hard to Say.* Want to blow students' minds with works of staggering imagination? Dip into *A Monster Calls* or *Unwind* or *Mortal Engines* or *Leviathan* or *Railsea*.

As we read these books, we can use particular scenes to delve into specific ideas of social responsibility. In Chapter 4, I'll go into more detail on social responsibility, but for now here's a quick example: Two central habits of mind of social responsibility are thinking for yourself and speaking your mind. These themes resonate in *The Loud Silence of Francine Greene*, Karen Cushman's (2006) novel of the friendship between two girls during the "Red Scare" of McCarthyism. Francine was raised to never question authority, whereas her friend Sophie was raised to challenge the use and abuse of power. After dinner at Sophie's house one evening, her dad has a chat with Francine:

> "Now that Russia has the bomb," he went on, "should we develop a bigger one? And what if Russia develops an even bigger one? A K-bomb or a U-bomb or a Z-bomb? What should we do then?" He took another noisy sip of his coffee. "Speak up, Francine."
>
> Speak up? What a notion, coming as I did from the land of "Sit down, Francine" and "Be quiet, Francine." What did I think? "I don't know," I told him.
>
> "It's important to know what you think, my dear, or else you will be so hemmed in by other people's ideas and opinions, you won't have room for your own." (97–98)

Eloquent moments like this beg to be explored by young adolescents. These three short paragraphs carry vital ideas about living in a democracy: As active citizens, we must stay informed, ask questions, form our own opinions, think for ourselves, and let our voices be heard. If students were to read *Francine Greene* on their own, they may not think about these compelling topics. That is why we must make our teaching of social responsibility explicit. Learning this content in school does not happen by magic; teachers make it happen.

Some of these books also contain controversial content: sex, drugs, violence, strong language, mental illness, suicide, and child abuse, as well as issues that often (and tragically) get books banned from school, including homosexuality and abortion. What should teachers do about this content? That's for you to decide. Teachers have their own comfort zones and personal beliefs about what content is right for their students. And teachers work in their own school and community contexts. A book that is problematic in one school could be perfect in a school six blocks away.

I will add, however, that we should not be so quick to discount a book because of its content. The American Library Association Web site has a long list of books that have been challenged or banned in schools. Every September the organization promotes Banned Books Week (which makes it a particularly great time to read a banned book in your classroom). I heard young adult author David Levithan speak at a National Council of Teachers of English conference on the censorship of children's and young adult literature. He said that when people attempt to censor books or limit the titles allowed in a classroom, and teachers and librarians do not speak up and fight for the books, they are participating in a "complicity of silence." We must be the ambassadors for bringing good, diverse, even provocative books into our classrooms. Be bold. Greatness rarely springs from being ordinary.

Stuck in the Classics

As children enter adolescence, as they climb the ladder of middle school, books written for adults soon monopolize their school reading lists. We call these books "classics." The trickle often begins in seventh or eighth grade, and then the floodgates open as they step into high school and encounter *The Great Gatsby, The Scarlet Letter, Animal Farm*, and lots of Shakespeare. This canon of reading has held remarkably steady for decades. I surveyed students in my undergraduate Young Adult Fiction class on the books they were assigned in school. Their top ten assigned titles were nearly identical to the top ten books cited more than twenty years earlier by Arthur Applebee (1992) in his survey of reading in grades seven through twelve in 500 schools.

Not one book listed in both of these top ten lists was written and published for children or young adults. Only one, *To Kill a Mockingbird*, was published after 1960. Think back to your own school days and ask yourself what books you were assigned to read. How many were published in the last twenty years? How many were written by females or nonwhite authors? How many were set in Asia, Africa, or South America? As we push our way deeper into the twenty-first century, it is shameful how homogeneous and "old" the reading is that children do in school.

My Young Adult Fiction class of thirty students was shocked by the lack of diversity of the authors they were assigned to read. They had a combined total of 210 years in grades six–twelve, yet only *six* books written by female authors and authors of color were mentioned by more than two students: *To Kill a Mockingbird, The Giver, The Diary of Anne Frank, The House on Mango Street, The Outsiders*, and *Speak*. On the entire list how many were written by African American and Latino men? *Zero*. How many books did they list with a gay protagonist? *Zero*. This will change only when teachers make it change.

Donald Gallo, who has edited terrific collections of short stories for young adults, writes:

> When I look back at that phenomenon now, it all makes perfect sense to me. I wasn't READY for classical literature when I was 13, 14 . . . 17, 18 . . . I was a typical teenager interested in teenage things. *The classics are not about TEENAGE concerns!* They are about ADULT issues. Moreover, they were written for EDUCATED adults who had the LEISURE time to read them. (2001, 34)

Gallo nails it. I could not have stated the issue better. Many of the classics in the canon are wonderful works of literature, and good teachers craft creative and thoughtful units for these books. But that does not make them good school reading material for adolescents or for life in the twenty-first century. Unless we make contemporary literature an important part of students' reading, we will never help them see language arts or reading as truly relevant to their lives.

My own high school reading serves as Exhibit A. I "fake-read" my way through high school because nearly every book assigned was written for an adult, and all it did was turn me off to reading. The only book I really read—actually, the only novel I read in my entire life through high school—was *The Pigman* by Paul Zindel (1968) because it was the only assigned book written for young adults like me. I came to love reading as an adult, when I had the freedom to find books that connected to my interests and passions. Cris Tovani writes that she was a "fake reader" too:

> I started to "fake-read" in sixth grade and continued doing so for the next twenty years. In high school, I fooled everyone by attending classes, reading first and last chapters, skimming through Cliffs Notes, and making Bs or better on essays and exams. (2000, 4)

Students today know about Cliffs Notes and SparkNotes. The only difference now is that they can read them online for free! Cliffs Notes also has apps they can download, including "cramcast," an audio story summary they can listen to. SparkNotes has "video SparkNotes" that students can watch. The SparkNotes video for *To Kill a Mockingbird* is seven minutes long, a lot less time than it takes to read the book.

A greater concern for middle school students is the very limited scope of adolescent literature they're taught in school. Far too often when teachers do use contemporary children's literature, they restrict the choices to a de facto canon of authors, such as Lois Lowry, Louis Sacher, Jerry Spinelli, Karen Hesse, and Walter Dean Myers. Don't misunderstand me. I greatly admire the work of these writers. But the universe of good books has massively expanded, and we need to make sure that our classrooms aren't hitched to a coal-fired train. Having students read good books is not enough; they need to read a wide variety of books with cultural, economic, and geographic diversity, as well as books from across genres.

Expanding What We Read

Over the years, I must have interacted with thousands of teachers. Virtually every K–8 teacher tells me they have the freedom to choose the books they teach to students. In other words, their school administrators are not requiring them to teach specific books. If they want their kids to read, for example, *Leepike Ridge* by N. D. Wilson (2007), they would be able to do that. The hindrances to making that happen are more often limited financial resources and the unquestioned canon of authors and books and less often teachers' autonomy in making these decisions. Granted, with the Common Core State Standards, many teachers will have to make the case that these books are "complex texts." (For more information on this, see Appendix A of the Common Core State Standards.)

Teachers and librarians need to be advocates who persuade school officials to buy good literature for young adolescents, for both class sets of novels and classroom libraries. If they don't do this, who will? There are ways for teachers to get more books. First, make your case to your principal. When Ron and I wanted to design a unit with *The Adoration of Jenna Fox* for his seventh graders (see Chapter 7), he went to his principal with the cost of a class set of the book and argued that most of his students had never read a science fiction novel. The principal approved the purchase. Teachers should go further and advocate for their school to create an expansive library of class sets of literature. This would give grade-level teams the flexibility to change the books they use over the years. Figure 2.1 shows the lending library I helped Shelly Leland create at her school in Chicago.

Figure 2.1 A school literature-lending library, such as this one built by Shelly Leland, gives teachers the power to create a widely diverse literature-based curriculum.

Teachers can also apply for local grants or post their needs on DonorsChoose.org in the hope that it will be funded. And if all else fails and you really want books, sometimes we do what Natalie did for our unit discussed in Chapter 9: she paid for thirty copies of *Leon's Story*.

Yes, expanding the high school canon is a more difficult mountain to scale, but it is certainly not impossible. Needless to say, high school reading lists are set in significantly deeper cement. But that just requires teachers to work harder to crack that cement to expand the world of what their students read. Surely we can argue that high schoolers, especially in their first few years, should also read young adult books featuring protagonists with whom they can identify. Why do we return to the same tired list when we can find fresher inspiration in books written specifically for adolescents and young adults that are wonderfully diverse and extremely well written? Shouldn't that be part of educating children for the twenty-first century?

We know so many of these books: *Life as We Know It, The Moves Make the Man, Any Small Goodness, Bamboo People, One Crazy Summer, Thirteen Reasons Why, Flipped, The Outsiders, The Disreputable History of Frankie Landau-Banks, Copper Sun, Scrawl, Deadline.* These books can take your breath away. Really, they can. Walk into a classroom with fifth graders quietly lost in the world of an author's imagination or sixth graders briskly debating a character's actions or eighth graders connecting a book to a war raging on the other side of the planet, and you can feel the energy pulsating around you. You know good things are happening. During the Chapter 7 unit, as I was reading aloud *The Adoration of Jenna Fox* and we were racing toward a climax in the story, Lisa started pounding on her desk in anticipation. Then, just after the truth of the main character emerged from the text, Anthony screamed to the class, "She's a cyborg! She's a cyborg! She's a cyborg!" Teaching doesn't get more dramatic than that.

The more we can shape our teaching around books that truly excite students, the more we can use the same books to promote reading for pleasure, help kids become better readers, and teach socially responsible habits of mind. The idea that books for pleasure and books for "serious learning" are somehow mutually exclusive is a dangerous assumption; it runs the risk of our teaching being overwhelmed with books students have little interest in reading and limiting the purposes of their reading to getting higher test scores.

Let's be honest: every student is not going to love every book he or she reads. We teach in schools, after all, and we're different people with different tastes. This isn't necessarily bad: by reading a wide variety of books students expand their repertoire of texts that might enlarge their reading interests. How exciting is it for a teacher when a student says she *hates* science fiction (maybe announcing that sentiment to the class), and then tells you four days later (most likely in private) how much she *loves* reading *Ender's Game*? It goes without saying that if we want to cultivate lifelong readers and readers who use books to expand their thinking, they must read many books that excite them (see Figure 2.2).

Figure 2.2 Benjamin is engrossed in *The Adoration of Jenna Fox*.

How to Find Good Books

We need to search every literary nook and cranny to find the gems like *Ender's Game*. How do we do that? Most important, we need to read widely. The more we read, the better prepared we'll be to help students get hooked on books. The more we read, the more we can engage students with current books that resonate with their lives. The more we read, the more we will experience firsthand the incredible pleasure and quality of these books. And the more we read, the more respect adolescents will give us for our book authority, especially if we can sit and chat with Joshua or Jennifer about the latest novel by Chris Crutcher or Lois Lowry or Matt de la Peña. In the world of YA literature, that gives us "street cred."

It's true there are more books that we can reasonably read and review in our busy lives. So, we need to be able to extract the gold. Here's how to do that:

Visit bookstores. Spend regular time in a bookstore. Take time to peruse. Pull books from the shelves and look at the covers and read the first few pages. Most children's books have a very helpful one-sentence summary on the copyright page. (Those book lists in Appendixes A–F can also help you get started.)

Read blogs. A great blog on middle-grades and young adult literature is like having a children's librarian living in your house. (Librarians write some of them.) Some bloggers get advanced reader copies before a book is published, so you'll know good books before they're released. See Appendix G (also included on the companion Web site, stenhouse.com/caringhearts) for a list of good blogs.

Use blurbs. Like adult books, the covers of adolescent literature use blurbs to praise and promote the books. There are many highly respected children's review publications, such as *School Library Journal*, *The Horn Book*, *Booklist*, *Voice of Youth Advocates* (*VOYA*), and the Young Adult Library Services Association (YALSA). There are also reviews from the *New York Times Book Review*, *Booklist*, *Kirkus Reviews*, and *Publishers Weekly*.

Know awards. If you search for "children's literature awards" on your Internet browser, you will see links to Web sites of the many book awards. These include the Newbery Medal, the Michael Printz Award (for YA literature), the Coretta Scott King Award (African-American authors and illustrators), the Boston Globe–Horn Book Awards, and the National Book Awards. There are also the Batchelder Award (translated children's book), Pura Belpre Award (Latino/Latina author and illustrator), and the Jane Addams Book Award, for books that "promote peace, social justice, and world community." Another great source is the Children's and Young Adult Bloggers Literary Awards (the Cybils). Be sure not to limit your search to award winners. There are so many good books and so few awards. And the list of nominated books is far more comprehensive than just the winners.

Go online. Blogs are great, but the wider Internet is an invaluable resource. I use Amazon as a kind of books-in-print listing to find books by genre, author, or topic. When you look up a book on Amazon, you will see reviews written by readers and professional reviewers. I have spent hours reading book reviews on the excellent Web site goodreads.com. Teenreads.com and Teenink .com have book reviews written by teens. And each year the Center for Children's Literature at Bankstreet College of Education publishes a terrific list of their "Best Books of the Year." You can access them at bankstreet.edu/center-childrens-literature.

Read journals. Besides offering terrific articles, professional journals such as *The Journal of Adolescent and Adult Literacy*, *The English Journal*, *Language Arts*, *The Reading Teacher*, and *Social Education* are outstanding sources for books. If you love children's and YA literature, I strongly encourage you to subscribe to *The Horn Book*, one of the most-respected review publications. They also have an excellent Web site at hbook.com.

Ask people. The world is full of book experts. Librarians, teachers, booksellers, parents, and especially students can keep us up to date on hot new titles and authors.

The more we explore the universe of adolescent and young adult books, the more titles we'll discover that resonate with students and work well with the themes and issues of social responsibility. In *The Queen of Water* by Laura Resau and Maria Virginia Farinango (2010), an impoverished native *indigena* Ecuadorean girl is sold by her parents to a middle-class mestizo family to be their housekeeper. (The book is a novel based on the coauthor's life.) Needless to say, there are connections to economic class, poverty, global awareness, culture, and personal empowerment. And although that book may be set in Ecuador, teachers can use the book as a lens through which students can look at similar issues in our country and in their own lives.

We can often find important themes inside books such as the insightful, funny, and wonderfully written *Stupid Fast*. A sports book on the surface, *Stupid Fast* probes beneath that layer to examine empathy, family, stereotypes, friendship, mental illness, the culture of sports, and a boy's journey into what really matters in life. Fantasy novels such as *Incarceron*, *Elsewhere*, *The Last Dragonslayer*, and Neil Gaiman's *The Graveyard Book* can also spark discussions related to social responsibility.

Graphic Novels and Graphic Nonfiction

The world of graphic books, both fiction and nonfiction, has exploded. Graphic nonfiction includes biographies, memoirs, history, science, and journalism. Don't think of them as "comic books," but rather as a wholly different form of storytelling, combining words and often dazzling images. Some graphic novels, like Shaun Tan's masterpiece, *The Arrival*, which tells the universal story of immigration, have no words. These books can be exciting additions to an inquiry unit, offering students opportunities to engage with a different medium and tap into their interest in visual storytelling.

Let's say you love Brock Cole's wonderful novel *The Goats* (1989) and want to design a unit based on the theme of survival. In the book, two young teens, a boy and girl, are away at camp when they are cruelly tricked by their peers, stripped of their clothes, and stranded on an island in the middle of a lake. They need each other to survive, not as much physically as emotionally. A unit such as this can go beyond the book to explore different kinds of survival, and we can use graphic novels and nonfiction to do that. Here are five examples:

♦ *A.D. New Orleans: After the Deluge* uses graphic nonfiction to tell the true stories of six people who survived Hurricane Katrina.
♦ *I Kill Giants* is a graphic novel about a girl who is struggling to survive the overwhelming grief over her terminally ill mother.
♦ *It Was the War of the Trenches* is a graphic novel originally published in France about the horror of trench warfare during World War I.
♦ *Smile* is a graphic novel that tells the story of Raina, a sixth grader, who is trying to survive, well . . . being a sixth grader. She falls and breaks some teeth and has to wear a variety of devices that do not exactly make her popular in middle school.
♦ *Yummy: The Last Days of a Southside Shorty* is the true story of Robert "Yummy" Sandifer's very short and violent life as a gang member in Chicago.

This brief list offers just a glimpse of the remarkable scope and quality of graphic books available for teachers to use. See Appendix F (also included on the companion Web site, stenhouse.com/caringhearts) for a list of graphic fiction and nonfiction books.

Books and Memories

Do you know what happens when you surround kids with an abundance of good middle-grades and young adult literature, lavish the books with praise, give the students the freedom and choice to be real readers, let them see you as an adoring reader, and use those books to invite students to think and feel and talk? They read. In her book *The Reading Zone,* Nancie Atwell writes that her middle school students each read at least thirty books a year (2007). Another teacher devoted to YA literature, Jeannette Haskins, writes that on average her students read thirty-eight books a year (2011, 101). Our job is to help students fall in love with books, but we don't want to stop there. We also want to inspire caring people, critical thinkers, active citizens, and bold and imaginative minds. Good books really can help make that happen.

When I scan my bookshelves, I see memories. That's one reason I love owning books. I hold these memories close like prize photographs in my pocket.

I remember in *Heartbeat* by Sharon Creech that Annie's art teacher gives her an assignment to draw the same apple a different way for each of 100 days. I remember that her art teacher, Miss Freely, says, "No apple is ordinary."

I remember in *Mexican WhiteBoy,* when Danny and his new best friend Uno wrap their arms around a train trestle as the train roars above so they can *feel* the energy of the train. After it passes, Uno shouts, "Hell yeah, boy! That's some *power*!"

I remember the first page in *Crossing Jordan* when twelve-year-old Cass, who is white, hears her mom say that a "black family" is moving in next door. Cass's dad slams his fist on the dinner table and says, "I'll just have to build a fence." A hundred pages later, after Cass has secretly become best friends with her new neighbor, Jemmie, Cass's baby sister, Missy, becomes very ill. Jemmie's mom, a nurse, races to help. I remember her coming through the front doorway of a racist's home to save a child. It is as if she is breaking through a barrier a thousand years thick.

I remember in *Tree Girl* when Gabriela must hide in a tree for *two days* to keep from being shot by Guatemalan soldiers.

I remember reading *Parrot in the Oven* and being awed by Victor Martinez's luscious words. When Manny stands before his lifeless grandma at her wake, Martinez writes, "She will flake away into dirt, I thought, just as the sun does at the bottom of a pond during a drought. Her shadow will be erased, and her soul will drift to heaven like the fluff of a dandelion in the wind. And then it will blossom in another garden, so bright the colors will hurt your eyes."

I remember crying while reading Robert Newton Peck's autobiographical novel of growing up on a Vermont Shaker farm and discovering why it was *The Day No Pigs Would Die.*

I remember (and will never forget) the last sentence in *The Book Thief.*

I remember ten-year-old Auggie in R. J. Palacio's *Wonder.* Born with severe facial abnormalities, he explains why Halloween is his favorite holiday: "I wish every day could be Halloween. We could all wear masks all the time. Then we could walk around and get to know each other before we got to see what we looked like under the masks."

I remember in *Lord of the Nutcracker Men*, Iain Lawrence's historical novel of life in the trenches during World War I, how Johnny's dad, the "finest toy maker in London," wrote to his son from the trenches. "The truth is, Johnny, that I'm crouched in the mud like an animal, and the man at my side is crying and holding himself, and there is nothing between us and the Boche but fifty yards of the most haunted ground I have ever imagined." As he sits in the trenches day after day, he carves toy soldiers and mails them to Johnny. The longer he fights, the more horrific his toy soldiers become.

I remember *Feed*, M. T. Anderson's dystopian story of people getting their media "feed" directly into their brains from implanted microchips. The main character, Violet, says, "Because of the feed, we're raising a nation of idiots. Ignorant, self-centered idiots." I remember knowing *Feed* is not about the future. It's about our lives today.

And I remember Junior, in Sherman Alexie's masterful *The Absolutely True Diary of a Part-Time Indian,* who is growing up amid the human and social wreckage of his Native American reservation. Junior is fifteen years old. He's attended forty-two funerals. In his "rez" high school one morning he's handed a new textbook. But it's not new. It's very used. He opens it and sees the inside cover listing the former students who used the book. One of them is his mother. He is outraged by the injustice of his life:

> And let me tell you, that old, old, old *decrepit* geometry book hit my heart with the force of a nuclear bomb. My hopes and dreams floated up in a mushroom cloud. What do you do when the world has declared nuclear war on you? (31)

I own these memories because I read these books. We must help our students form their own book memories. The experiences will give them endless joy, make them better people, and shape a better world.

Chapter 3

Learning Through Inquiry

Teach with questions, not with answers.

—Sam M. Intrator (2003)

Want to plant a garden? Play the saxophone? Make homemade pasta? Understand the Vietnam War? You need information. Chances are you don't begin your investigation with written questions, but you could:

- How do I prepare the soil for my garden?
- Which kind of saxophone should I play?
- What ingredients do I need for good homemade pasta?
- Who was responsible for the Vietnam War?

These questions help you begin your search for knowledge. If your neighbor has a beautiful garden, you might start with her. If a local music school has a good reputation, you'd probably give some teachers a call. If you don't know a pasta-making expert, you'd most likely check a good-quality Web site, find a good book, or perhaps watch a video. If your uncle fought in Vietnam, you might interview him about his experiences.

We can also ask existential and ethical questions:

- What is the purpose of life?
- Why is there so much pain and suffering in the world?
- What does it mean to be good?
- Do I have a responsibility to help others?

These questions require a different kind of exploration. You certainly could still do more typical forms of research, such as interviewing a philosophy professor, reading a book, or participating in a debate. But your inquiry could also include an inward investigation about your beliefs.

The questions we ask may change as our lives change. For example, when my son, Max, was born, I had many questions about babies and parenting. And now I have many questions about teenagers and parenting!

A thoughtful and thorough investigation is rarely easy. It's often a meandering journey with successes and failures. There's a good chance your first batch of pasta will be lousy. But because you *want* to make it and your inquiry is *purposeful,* you will probably consider missteps a natural part of the learning process. You may experiment with various pasta recipes, adding a little of this or subtracting a little of that—in a sense, exploring different opinions and conflicting ideas. You need to weigh options and make decisions.

These processes—questioning, thinking, analyzing, tinkering, deciding, and doing—lie at the heart of inquiry learning. Some people may equate these skills with traditional school "research," which students have been doing since the days of clapping erasers. Well, yes and no. Teaching through inquiry can involve research but it is *much more* than research.

Many people see the investigation part of the process as the sole focus of inquiry. But this view ignores the time before and after the investigation, as well as the social and collaborative aspects of students' work, most of which is done inside the classroom when teachers can facilitate and monitor learning. During this entire process students are engaged in intellectual, dialogue-rich, idea-exchanging experiences, including working with short texts and other authentic resources. The energized classroom space—picture it as a combined workshop, studio, and think tank—becomes an incubator for learning and creating new knowledge. Sam Intractor describes an inquiry-based literature classroom he studied as a "busy, industrious workshop" (2003, 143).

Viewing through this broader spectrum, inquiry becomes far more than kids just "doing research." It represents the entire process and experience of planning, discussing, debating, reading, connecting, rethinking, and creating and presenting beautiful projects. Too often "research" in school means that students browse the Internet or plumb a few books in a library. Yes, these resources are still indispensable tools, but there are many more ways for us to investigate the world, such as interviewing people; writing, conducting, and analyzing surveys; listening to music; watching videos; engaging in debate; and of course, reading good books, including fiction, which gives us insight into the human condition through stories.

Just as we can ask students to investigate the laws of atoms in science class and racism in social studies, we can use inquiry to teach social responsibility with literature. Let me make an important distinction here. Teaching for social responsibility through inquiry is not synonymous with encouraging kids to simplistically save the world. Adolescents are far too savvy and cynical to accept pat answers. Exploring the complexity and messiness of life motivates them. This requires genuine experiences for discussion and debate. It also means teachers must give students the space to speak their minds and to disagree with our own views. Inquiry, democracy, and critical thinking all require the free interchange of ideas and perspectives. By living genuine inquiry in the classroom, we cultivate inquiry in society.

Inquiry from Past to Present

Teaching through inquiry and its partner, project-based teaching, are certainly not new approaches. Throughout the twentieth century, teaching through projects and child-centered inquiry were foundations of progressive education. William Heard Kilpatrick, a student of John Dewey's and later his colleague at Columbia University, wrote a prominent article, "The Project Method," way back in 1918. (My grandma Gertie was in seventh grade then.) Kilpatrick wrote, "The purposeful act is thus the typical unit of the worthy life in a democratic society, so also should it be made the typical unit of school procedure" (325).

Today, inquiry-based teaching and engaging projects are considered vital to a twenty-first-century education. Prominent educators such as Richard Beach and Jamie Myers (2001), Michael Smith and Jeff Wilhelm (2007), and Harvey Daniels and Stephanie Harvey (2009) are passionate promoters of bringing together inquiry and literacy. There is a quickly growing chorus of educators urging the use of literature to engage adolescents in open and critical inquiry of life and the world (Groenke, Maples, and Henderson 2010; Petrone and Gibney 2005; Sawch 2011; Stallworth 2006). The distinguished Stanford professor Linda Darling-Hammond frames the book *Powerful Learning* that she coauthored with an opening chapter on inquiry- and project-based teaching (2008). Teaching with inquiry and projects are cornerstones of George Lucas's respected education organization, Edutopia (see edutopia.org and read about the organization's work in Milton Chen's 2010 book, *Education Nation*.)

There is also a robust presence of inquiry in science education. Major science education organizations, such as the American Association for the Advancement of Science and the National Science Foundation, advocate inquiry-based science teaching. In fact, that phrase is redundant, because doing science is inherently doing inquiry.

The American Association of School Librarians (part of the American Library Association) also has enthusiastically embraced inquiry. The organization's new set of standards is titled Standards for the 21st-Century Learner. Here is standard 1.1.1: "Follow an inquiry-based process in seeking knowledge in curricular subjects and the real-world connection for using this process in their own life." In Standard 3 the group connects inquiry to citizenship and democracy—in other words, to social responsibility: "Share knowledge and participate ethically and productively in our democratic society" (AASL 2007).

As you read through these past and current writings, you keep seeing the same key ideas: inquiry, projects, authentic literacy, critical thinking, vibrant and interesting resources, reading great books, real talk and debate, relevant curriculum, integrating technology, and teaching for a caring and participatory democracy. Separately, each of these is a powerful idea, but together they create a dynamic learning process that redefines the purpose of school and what it means to be an educated human being. As Smith and Wilhelm write:

> Inquiry is not simply thematic study, but the exploration of a question or issue that drives debate in the disciplines and the world. Our work shows us that kids need to find both personal connection and social significance in the units and texts we offer them. (2007, 233)

A Culture of Inquiry

More than just creating units of inquiry we really want to permeate classrooms with a *culture of inquiry*. Bob Peterson (2002) wrote about a notebook hanging in his fifth-grade classroom titled "Questions We Have" so that his kids can constantly add questions that arise from their classroom studies and discussions. Ben Kovacs, a sixth-grade teacher at the Burley School in Chicago, had a bulletin board for writing workshop that he titled "Essay Itches We Might Want to Scratch." Ben added this text: "Some questions students are adding to their writing territories lists. Students came up with topics that mattered to them. They are the problems in their world that need investigating." On the board are some of the questions his students asked:

What is global warming?
Is HIV/AIDS everywhere?
How do they come up with gas prices?
Why does the bad guy always lose in the movies?
Why is Illinois so corrupt?
What it is like to be part of a military family?
Why is there discrimination against atheists?
How do they rate movies? Why is it PG-13 and not PG-12?
How can we solve violence in Chicago?
Are redheads going extinct?

Ben took his classroom culture of inquiry further by having his students frame their own "common curiosities" into inquiry projects. Stephanie Harvey and Harvey Daniels refer to these as "open inquiries" (2009). Ben created an exhibit in the hallway outside his classroom to show his process of inquiry (see Figure 3.1).

In their book *Make Just One Change*, Dan Rothstein and Luz Santana advocate for what they believe is one of the most important changes needed in classrooms: teaching students to ask their own questions. They point out that the purpose is not simply to inspire curiosity and cultivate inquiry but also to teach students how to ask *good* questions, a skill they have found that most children (and many adults) lack. Rothstein and Santana directly connect the asking of questions to democracy and the critical-thinking skills of social responsibility:

Even in our own democratic society, we have not done a particularly good job of investing in developing our citizens' ability to think independently and ask their own questions. We need to make a stronger, more deliberate effort to build the capacity of all our citizens to think for themselves, weigh evidence, discern between fact and myth, discuss, debate, analyze, and prioritize. (2011, 153)

Although the word *inquiry* is technically a noun, the root word, *inquire*, is very much a verb. So, inquiry is wholeheartedly about *action*. Having students spend the vast majority of their school day anchored to desks while their teacher lectures is a relic from the Industrial Revolution. We need

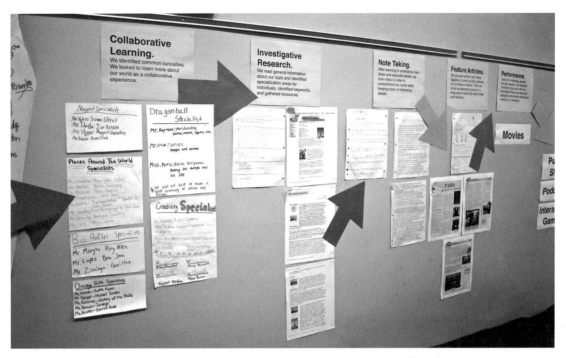

Figure 3.1 Ben shows the process his sixth graders used for their independent inquiry projects.

to transform classrooms into spaces with the pulse of active adolescents, engaged in learning that is purposeful, meaningful, and relevant for the twenty-first century, not for the days of Model Ts and Prohibition, when my grandma Gertie was walking her school hallways.

Teachers of middle-grades students and young adults know how shrewd they are; students recognize how irrelevant most of school is because they see the real world every day on their smartphones, computers, and 400 cable channels. They want that world inside their classrooms, and they want to interact with it; they don't want to sit still all day, both literally and metaphorically. Emily Pilloton and Mathew Miller are designers who created their program Studio H to engage high school students in designing and building projects to improve their local community. They call this "humanitarian design," and their mantra is "Design. Build. Transform." On a video, a boy in Studio H says, "It's not like regular class where you just sit and write down on a piece of paper; you actually get to do stuff" (Project H Design). There you have it: the wisdom of a young adult. He wants to go to school and really *do stuff*.

Inquiry with Books

In an inquiry-based literature unit, the book is the "anchor text," not the central focus. Ideally, the unit would not even be titled after the book. Consider Lois Lowry's classic young adult dystopian novel *The Giver*, a book often taught in middle school. A related unit could be titled with a question, such as one of these:

- How important is individuality?
- Should we feel joy and pain and love?
- Do we have free will?
- Does government control truth?
- What is a perfect world?

Because of the thematic nature of *The Giver*, these questions tend to be more existential. If you prefer not to use questions, you can just use the topics of individuality, human emotion, love, free will, or government power, or a combination of questions and issues.

Designing a unit strictly about a novel is a "school thing"; exploring one of the previous questions or topics is a *life thing*. Such learning experiences situate reading in the real world. This is exactly what Jeff Wilhelm and Bruce Novak (2011) mean when they refer to *life-centered teaching*. Rather than design curriculum around a specific school subject or a particular book, we design teaching around a relevant issue, question, or topic. Reading *Everybody Sees the Ants* by A. S. King during a unit about bullying or *No Ordinary Day* by Deborah Ellis during a unit on global poverty would situate those issues in a good story while humanizing them and making literature come alive.

Ethical Inquiry

Human beings are by nature moral animals; we make daily decisions that stake moral positions. Helping students develop their moral selves can be directly connected to teaching through inquiry. Pamela Bolotin Joseph and Sara Efron have written about *ethical inquiry*, which they offer as an alternative to traditional "character education" programs. It involves engaging students in discussion and debate about real moral dilemmas. They see a natural role for using literature in this exploration:

> Teachers guide discussions on the moral dilemmas embedded within subjects across the curriculum. Springboards for ethical inquiry include literature, history, drama, economics, science, and philosophy. In particular, students learn the consequences of making moral decisions and how fictional characters and real people make choices when aware that a moral question is at stake. (2005, 531)

For decades the preeminent child psychologist Robert Coles taught a course at Harvard called A Literature of Social Reflection. Coles considers reading literature to be one of the most important experiences for our moral development. In his book *The Call of Stories: Teaching and the Moral Imagination*, he writes that in his class "we read fiction in the hopes of doing moral and social inquiry" (1989, xvi). He also writes, "I can still remember my father's words as he tried to tell me, with patient conviction, that novels contain 'reservoirs of wisdom,' out of which he and our mother were drinking . . . 'Your mother and I feel rescued by these books'" (xii).

When students use books to inquire into challenging questions, our classrooms become ethics think tanks. Consider Julia Alvarez's historical novel *Before We Were Free*. Moral inquiry can play an important part in a unit with *Before We Were Free*, with questions such as these:

- Is it ethical to assassinate a dictator?
- Do democratic countries have a moral responsibility to help free people in dictatorial countries?
- Do we have more responsibility to our family or to our country?
- Where does evil come from? Are people born good?
- What does it mean to be a good person?
- When is war ethical?

Skills Are Still Important

Schools spend too much time teaching reading skills and not enough time actually reading as a purposeful activity. Imagine if kids went to gym class and spent the majority of time learning how to play soccer by reading about drills on paper instead of actually experiencing them on the field. We would probably have a rebellion, because often the most authentic and experiential learning in school happens in gym, art, and music. Why should it be different with reading?

This does not mean that when teaching through inquiry we toss away the literacy skills we know adolescents need to be good readers and writers. (Playing soccer is essential, but so is learning soccer skills.) By teaching those skills within inquiry units that explore the real world, we make learning those skills truly meaningful. As kids work their way through an inquiry unit, we are also taking the time to do carefully selected mini-lessons, demonstrations, and activities to teach necessary skills, from comprehension and inference, to vocabulary and writing conventions. This is also how we can integrate required standards into a unit. One inquiry unit can cover many standards from across the curriculum.

Inquiry in Interdisciplinary Teaching

All of the inquiry units presented in Chapters 7–11 were taught in language arts classrooms, yet they would also be ideal for interdisciplinary inquiry. You do not need to have every teacher on a grade-level team participate. Most books and topics don't work for every subject, and what matters most is committed teachers who believe in the process. Most likely, two or three teachers, such as the language arts and social studies teachers, will partner for an inquiry unit or perhaps just one part of a unit (see Chapter 11 for an example).

Teaching literature in science, or connecting a book in language arts to a science class, can create powerful learning experiences. My friend Chuck Cole taught middle school science for more than thirty years. When his seventh graders studied atoms, he also had them read John Hersey's famous nonfiction book, *Hiroshima,* about the dropping of the atomic bomb from a Japanese perspective. In an e-mail to me he wrote:

On one level [reading *Hiroshima*] was an attempt to illustrate and explain a science concept. But then I realized that there was also a total disconnect in my students between hearing about the atomic bomb being dropped and an awareness of what that actually meant in real lives. I saw enormous teaching opportunities and possibilities in it. They just jumped out of every page—the scientific and the social, but also all sorts of other connections. There's vocabulary, history, geography, the math (what does 20 kilotons mean?). But underneath it all, emerged the unimaginable horror of the event. The kids always wanted to know if dropping the bomb could have been avoided. And that allowed me to help them discover a bit of the nature of political leadership, and what awesome responsibility leaders really have—that they're people just like us in some ways, who have to make huge decisions. Someone had to give the OK to drop that bomb. All of the goals and reasons for reading it in class couldn't have been clear and obvious from the start. I had to discover them too, although, I knew there was a lot of potential for examining the politics and ethics of the event. Reading that book was like jumping into another universe. (Wolk 2008)

Chuck's point about not knowing all of his goals and purposes for reading *Hiroshima* before he began is important. As teachers we like to plan; we like to know what we're going to do and how we're going to do it. We have a lot to do, materials to gather, a ticking clock, and thirty kids with raging hormones. But too-specific planning can also be a detriment to learning that grows naturally out of the experience. We need to build the space into our teaching for spontaneity and happenstance. We also run the risk of losing the mind-set that the teacher must be open to learning from the experience too. Brenda Kraber, a veteran teacher who embraces teaching through inquiry, said, "I've learned about things I never knew existed. Because I'm learning along with the kids, there is a real air of excitement" (Owens, Hester, and Teale 2002, 618).

Personal Inquiry

Although it is not a part of the units presented later in this book, I'd like to suggest another idea for our literature teaching. Imagine giving middle school students a chunk of time to design their own literature-based inquiry studies. We have all heard of independent reading; this would be *independent inquiry*. Jessica Singer did something similar with her ninth graders (2006). Beginning with the theme of activism, she allowed her students to choose a book and shape a meaningful unit. I suggest taking personal inquiry further, empowering students to choose a personally meaningful and purposeful topic or question in collaboration with their teacher, choose a book (fiction or nonfiction) as an anchor text, find some related resources and short texts, conduct their own exploration, and then create a culminating project.

Imagine how amazing it would be to have an entire class of students discuss diverse readings and exhibit their work. While one student read *Freak the Mighty* (Philbrick 1993) and explored friendship, another might read *Whirligig* (Fleischman 2000) to study forgiveness and redemption; while one student read Geoff Herbach's fantastic *Stupid Fast* (2011) to explore sports in American culture, another could read *Yellow Star* (Roy 2006) to investigate the Holocaust and genocide. If we could find the time to do a unit like this just once a year, it would be a giant leap away from school today, which gives students almost no ownership of their learning. Perhaps this is the greatest hope of teaching through inquiry. We can give students the freedom to ask their own questions, read their own books, and express their own ideas. Wouldn't that be a great reason to go to school?

Chapter 4

Teaching for Social Responsibility

Because it involves the richness of human connection, the breadth of human diversity, the complexity of human conflict, and the inspiration of human hope, social responsibility is truly a heartfelt responsiveness to the world. It's not just a tool we give to students or a skill we help them develop, it is a gift we offer them of their human birthright.

—Sheldon Berman (1997)

Why go to school? What is the purpose of school? What knowledge should we teach? These questions are the most important in education. They have been written about since Plato walked the streets of Athens and were fiercely debated during the creation of our modern school system by educators such as John Dewey and John Franklin Bobbitt (Kleibard 1987). These defining questions should guide education policies and the practices of every teacher.

When I ask people why they teach, no one ever says, "To increase our gross domestic product" or "To raise the Dow Jones Industrial Average." Yet, listen to a political speech, read a magazine or newspaper article on education reform, or hear the education ideas of corporate leaders, and just one purpose of school is mentioned: creating future workers. Consider the mission statement of the Common Core State Standards, which ends with this sentence: "With American students fully prepared for the future, our communities will be best positioned to compete successfully in the global economy" (commoncore.org). In fact, the Common Core State Standards are built entirely on the premise of school being all about college and career readiness (which is why I have a love/hate relationship with the Common Core).

Rather than schooling primarily for work and the economy, how about schooling for *life*? This is not to say we should ignore the economic purposes of school. All teachers want their students to have the knowledge and skills needed for future education and employment, yet I wonder how many of us have ever questioned the notion that this is our major goal as educators. Nel Noddings writes:

It is as though our society has simply decided that the purpose of schooling is economic—to improve the financial condition of individuals and to advance the prosperity of the nation. Hence students should do well on standardized tests, get into good colleges, obtain well-paying jobs, and buy lots of things. Surely there must be more to education than this? (2003, 4)

Teaching for social responsibility redefines the purpose of school. Rather than simply preparing children to "win the twenty-first-century global economy," I believe, and the teachers featured in this book believe, that there are other important aims of education:

- ♦ To create a better world
- ♦ To cultivate a critical and thriving democracy
- ♦ To develop caring human beings
- ♦ To experience the joy of learning and reading
- ♦ To nurture people who think
- ♦ To inspire creativity and imagination
- ♦ To foster intellectual curiosity and questioning habits of mind

What Is Social Responsibility?

Sheldon Berman offers this definition of social responsibility: "The personal investment in the well-being of others and the planet" (1997, 12). I like this sentence; there's a lot packed into it. That "personal investment" part is explicit that the responsibility is on all of us to help improve the world, from the local to the global. It does not mean that we dictate the answers; rather, we create classrooms full of dialogue and multiple perspectives. Engage a class of seventh graders in a debate about gun control and some will argue heatedly that removing all gun control laws will make a better and safer society, whereas others will say that it will lead to more violence and we should ban all guns. This is the exciting give-and-take, the talk that should permeate our classrooms. Books and their related texts offer endless paths into spirited and soul-enhancing dialogue, turning our classrooms into living workshops of democracy.

If we were to crack open social responsibility, what would we find inside? Social responsibility does include factual knowledge and some vital skills, but it is equally about *habits of mind* and *dispositions*:

- ♦ empathy and caring
- ♦ government systems
- ♦ the common good
- ♦ problem solving
- ♦ critical literacy and critical thinking
- ♦ collaboration
- ♦ current events and social problems
- ♦ decision making

- global awareness
- social justice
- creative and innovative thinking
- environmental literacy
- moral and ethical consciousness
- social imagination
- war, peace, and nonviolence
- media literacy
- multicultural community (antiracism)
- voting

Right about now you may be thinking, "I don't have time to teach empathy or problem solving! I need to teach verbs and comprehension. I need to get my students ready for testing. I have a boatload of standards to cover." Understood—I know your sentiments and responsibilities all too well. Yet, as educators and citizens, we also have a duty to create compassionate and empowered classrooms. These aims of school are not mutually exclusive. We must figure out how to address both.

Even considering my earlier criticism of the Common Core, if you peruse the standards you will see that they don't dictate what books students should read or how you should teach. The standards *do* dictate that students read a variety of literary and informational texts, as well as learn critical-thinking skills, understand diverse perspectives and cultures, and build strong content knowledge—all components central to social responsibility, teaching through inquiry, and literature-based teaching. As you will read in Chapter 12, the teachers featured in this book are using the Common Core to justify their inquiry- and literature-based teaching.

Teachers need to choose what aspects of social responsibility work best for their students. Keep in mind that we don't have to devote an entire unit to an idea to make it an important part of our classrooms. Take global awareness, for example. Imagine all the opportunities teachers have during the course of a school year to discuss different countries, point out a location on a world map, focus a mini-lesson, read a short story set in another nation, or share a newspaper article about an unfamiliar culture. All of those experiences really do add up. What defines our teaching is the collective experience of an entire school year.

The National Council of Teachers of English and the International Reading Association, the two main organizations for English/language arts instruction, have created a joint set of standards that include making explicit connections among social responsibility, citizenship, and reading and writing. Here are some of their recommendations:

- Students read a wide range of print and non-print texts to build an understanding of texts, of themselves, and of the cultures of the United States and the world; to acquire new information; to respond to the needs and demands of society and the workplace; and for personal fulfillment. Among these texts are fiction and nonfiction, classic and contemporary works.
- Students participate as knowledgeable, reflective, creative, and critical members of a variety of literacy communities. (NCTE 1996)

The often-quoted education organization, Partnership for 21st Century Skills, strongly advocates for schooling for democratic aims. Social responsibility is threaded throughout the organization's "Framework for 21st Century Learning," which includes educating for critical thinking and problem solving, global awareness, civic literacy, environmental literacy, creativity and innovation, media literacy, social and cross-cultural skills, and economic literacy (p21.org).

Teaching Caring

No one has written more about teaching for caring than Nel Noddings. For decades she has argued passionately that *caring* should be a foundation of our K–12 curriculum. It goes without saying that in our test-obsessed school systems the notion of teaching caring is not exactly at the top of the list of professional development goals. Teaching caring is one of the foundations of kindergarten, yet it usually comes to a screeching halt once those children step into first grade and have to focus on "serious learning." Noddings writes:

> It is obvious that our main purpose is not the moral one of producing caring people but, instead a relentless—and, as it turns out, hapless—drive for academic adequacy. I am certainly not going to argue for academic inadequacy, but I will try to persuade readers that a reordering of priorities is essential. All children must learn to care for other human beings, and all must find an ultimate concern in some center of care. (1992, xii)

Noddings advocates teaching caring for family and friends; ideas; beautiful and helpful objects; animals, plants, ecosystems, and the Earth; the philosophical questions of life; and "strangers and distant others." She also believes that schools must give children real opportunities to study the most important focus of caring: themselves. This is even truer as children get older. She writes, "For adolescents these are the most pressing questions: Who am I? What kind of person will I be? Who will love me? How do others see me? Yet, schools spend more time on the quadratic formula than on any of these existential questions" (1992, 20).

Given how destructive the twentieth century was, with wars and genocides and poverty and ecological damage, teaching caring may be the most important content children can learn. Yes, we all want students to learn essential skills, but we want them to *use* that knowledge to work for more compassionate communities, a more harmonious world, a stronger democracy, and a healthier planet, and to be happier people. In her book *Happiness and Education,* Noddings (2003) takes her bold thinking further, arguing that schools have an obligation to cultivate happiness. She writes, "A large part of our responsibility as educators is to help students understand the wonders and complexities of happiness, to raise questions about it, and to explore promising possibilities responsibly" (23). Reading good books can help make that happen too.

Decision Making, Moral Consciousness, and Democracy

Back in 1960 (when I was a mere five months old) Shirley Engle wrote his seminal article on teaching social studies titled "Decision Making: The Heart of Social Studies Instruction." Arguing against fact-based, textbook-, and lecture-driven teaching, Engle wrote, "The social studies are centrally concerned with the education of citizens. The mark of a good citizen is the quality of decisions which he reaches on public and private matters of social concern" (1960/2003, 7). To make social studies about decision making, Engle argues that we need to get kids out of textbooks and into authentic discussions and debates, challenging them to grapple with moral decision making. Simply put, students learn to make decisions about important and complex issues—and *value* caring about them—by making real decisions about important and complex issues.

Contrast that with a study by researchers who interviewed 300 elementary kids about their experiences in social studies. Their conclusion is summed up by this sentence: "More than 95 percent of the students did not think their social studies class was relevant to their personal life" (Zhao and Hoge 2005, 218). The researchers also interviewed their teachers. Nearly half a century after Shirley Engle's article, most of the teachers reported using textbooks as their main teaching resource.

What Engle describes, however, is one of the primary aims of *school*, not just social studies. For example, Corinne Mantle-Bromley and Ann M. Foster advocate for the vital role of language arts in cultivating a healthy and vibrant democracy:

> Language arts teachers are fundamental to the transmission of democracy from generation to generation and more immediately, from school to the larger surroundings in which our young people live. The knowledge and skills students gain or do not gain in their language arts classrooms contribute to the kind of society they and future generations will experience. (2005, 74)

The authors go on to add that these habits of mind must be *made transparent to students* (italics in original, 74), meaning we must not be shy about using the language of democracy and social responsibility with students; we need to be explicit in connecting books and reading to a caring, critical, and participatory democracy. Only by making this content a clear and essential part of classroom life will students truly understand the importance of their role as caretakers for our planet.

Central to the thinking of Nel Noddings and Shirley Engle is the role of school in shaping students' moral consciousness. This connects back to the notion of "ethical inquiry" that I wrote about in the previous chapters. It is impossible to engage in morally neutral decision making about any social concern. Much of life is situated in ethical quandaries, and many of the decisions we make have hidden or unseen moral positions, from how to spend our money to what to do with our recycling; from whom to vote for to what food to eat; from what media we consume to what car we drive. Children's daily lives are filled with ethical decisions too, from joining (or not joining) cliques to how to spend their money, from choosing what video games to play (or not play) to how they treat other children and nature.

Schools teach knowledge, and all knowledge is inherently value-laden. People *choose* what knowledge to teach and what novels to read. Elliot Eisner coined the term *null curriculum,* which is all of the knowledge that is *not* taught in school. The null curriculum is always *much* bigger than the official curriculum. By selecting what knowledge will be—and will not be—part of a child's education, we are making moral decisions and influencing children's moral development. By making social responsibility a clear part of classroom life, we are making that moral development an explicit part of a child's learning.

Social Responsibility in Books

Our purpose is not to tell students what is right and wrong or just and unjust, but to use books and other texts for them to take part in a community of inquiry and decide these questions for themselves. Teaching for social responsibility is not about telling students what to think; it is challenging them *to* think.

Consider the novel *Wonder* by R. J. Palacio (2012) that I briefly mentioned in Chapter 2. Auggie Pullman is ten years old and was born with very serious facial abnormalities. After being homeschooled, he and his parents decide it's time for him to go to a school for fifth grade. *Wonder* is an extraordinary story—told from the perspectives of multiple characters—that encompasses many core values of social responsibility: how we see and treat people who are different from us, caring and empathy, forgiveness, unconditional love, human goodness, friendship, and selflessness.

Or consider an entirely different book, *Never Fall Down*, Patricia McCormick's (2012) devastating novel—based on the life of Arn Chorn-Pond—about the Cambodian genocide by the Khmer Rouge in the 1970s. Again, we have a book filled with many themes of social responsibility: global awareness; historical empathy; war, violence, and peace; oppression; social justice; courage; activism; and moral consciousness. Good books like these have the power to jolt our perspectives.

Or take a popular author such as Andrew Clements. On the surface, his books are about the simple (and sometimes silly) conflicts and complications that arise in the everyday lives of kids. His books include *Extra Credit, The Report Card, No Talking, A Week in the Woods, Things Not Seen, The Jacket,* and *The Janitor's Boy* (and, of course, *Frindle*). But subtly packed inside his stories are issues of social responsibility, such as gender, economic class, empathy, prejudice, decision making, appreciation for nature, friendship, family, and personal responsibility.

Sometimes teaching for social responsibility can begin by rethinking books we already use in class, plucking out new topics to shape a unit. Suddenly, *A Week in the Woods* becomes a unit about our interactions with nature. *The Janitor's Son* forms the foundation for a unit exploring economic class or the complexities of families. *Things Not Seen*, the story of a boy who becomes invisible and later befriends a blind girl, can connect to a variety of short nonfiction texts about people rendered invisible throughout history.

Why Go to School? Why Read? Why Teach?

I want to reiterate that the majority of books students read in school should be for pleasure. We must fill our classroom libraries with books that will catch students' interests and passions and feed a love for reading. We must be the model readers and thinkers who sing the praises of literature and can't wait to share a new novel by Rick Riordan or Laurie Halse Anderson or Sharon Flake or John Green or Rita Williams-Garcia. Any passionate, book-loving teacher can tell you that there is nothing quite like walking into a classroom of avid readers with a pile of new books. Their enthusiasm is palpable.

But some of the books we teach—that is, the books we take the time and energy to use as the basis of thoughtful units—should dive fully into the empowering knowledge of social responsibility. And through those books we help students understand that going to school and reading have other aims besides passing a test or getting a grade or writing yet another essay. In this way, we help them see that education is a transformative experience that can shape the people they will become and inspire them to create a better world.

Chapter 5
Real-World Resources

Short texts allowed all of my students to come to the literature table—
where we dined not on fast food, but on the delicious buffet that represented
the smorgasbord of literature genres available to us as readers.
—Kimberly Hill Campbell (2007)

Imagine a mom and her eight-year-old son walking through a park. The mom points out the many flowers as they walk. She stops at a yellow tulip, and they get down on their knees to examine the flower up close. She points out the parts of the flower: the petals, pistil, stem, and stamens. She carefully points to the tiny granules of orange pollen on the tip of the stamens and explains how bees help it to travel, all in the pursuit of making sweet honey.

Now, compare that learning in an authentic life experience with students sitting in a classroom with their science textbooks open to "parts of a flower" as their teacher lectures on bees and pollen. Rather than bury kids in textbook diagrams of flowers, we need to surround them with real flowers. John Dewey certainly knew this. He famously argued that school should not be a preparation for life, but rather life itself. This is particularly important in middle school as young adolescents tune in to the bustling world around them. The older kids get, the more they know what amazing resources schools are *not* using.

Without realizing, it we reinforce the dichotomy between "school learning" and real-life learning. My graduate students interview adolescents about their in-school learning and their out-of-school learning. Most of the kids don't even consider their out-of-school learning to be *learning*. They quickly adapt to the adult notion that "official" learning occurs in school with desks and textbooks and tests. Let's not ignore the irony here. Out-of-school learning—from learning to play the drums and video games, to learning how to load a dishwasher and to babysit—is almost always more meaningful and long lasting.

So, although a book serves as the anchor text of an inquiry unit, we fill the unit with many other authentic resources, all as part of the exploration into the unit questions and topics. I divide resources into two categories: short texts and nonwritten resources. Each of the units we designed in Chapters 7–11 has a chart listing all the resources we used (available on the companion Web site, stenhouse.com/caringhearts), as well as additional resources teachers could use.

Short Texts

When brainstorming ideas for short texts for a unit, we want to consider more than the obvious choices of short stories, poetry, and essays. Think of all the writing in the world: that is your library! One of the best reasons to use short texts is that they are, well . . . short. We can usually read them in one sitting (sometimes in less than twenty minutes), and that leaves plenty of time for a discussion, a mini-lesson, journal writing, or another related activity on the same day. Short texts engender *intimacy* and *immediacy*. They also provide a refreshing break for students whose school reading is often dominated by heavy textbooks and long novels. Short texts bring the astonishing world of writing to children.

Here are some of the short texts we can make part of a unit:

- newspaper editorials and op-eds
- Internet articles and blogs
- newspaper articles
- magazine articles
- editorial cartoons and comics
- published speeches
- published reports and research studies
- published letters
- essays
- survey results
- interviews and oral histories
- poetry
- short stories
- music lyrics
- book excerpts
- picture books
- graphic novels and graphic nonfiction
- published writing by youths
- published diaries and journals
- literary magazines and literary nonfiction

Of course, students must have copies of these short texts to read them. I'm well aware that schools often place limits on a teacher's photocopying or printing supplies. This is yet another hurdle to leap over if you want to make short texts an important part of your literacy instruction. One way around this is using laptops or tablet computers. Although not always ideal or available, technology can enable students to read some texts directly online. For printed texts that students can actually hold (which I prefer), here are suggestions if your photocopying is limited:

- Make a class set of copies but do not have students write on them, so you can collect them to reuse in subsequent years. They can write on sticky notes or graphic organizers instead of the paper copies.
- Make half as many copies as you have students and have them pair up for the reading.
- Ask your principal to pay for a class set of newspapers (many newspapers have classroom subscription programs that are less expensive).
- Buy class sets of short-story anthologies that can be used for years.
- Use copied texts with other teachers so you can share the expense.
- There is also the solution teachers know all too well: pay for the copies yourself.

Newspapers

When I taught elementary and middle school, I brought the *Chicago Tribune* and the *New York Times* to class each morning. Nearly every day we talked about something in the newspaper, often during our morning class meeting (Wolk 1998). A good newspaper may be the single best curriculum resource we have for teaching social responsibility, shaping knowledge of current events, and making relevant connections to content. Newspapers are inexpensive, interesting, and rich in vocabulary and ideas. They bridge school disciplines, and they can be recycled! (And they certainly qualify as the "complex texts" required by the Common Core State Standards.)

I suggest at the start of the year creating a series of mini-lessons on the different parts and purposes of a newspaper. We need to help middle schoolers learn the difference between a newspaper article, an editorial, a letter to the editor, an op-ed or commentary piece, and a regular column. We also need to teach that editorials are attached to a newspaper's political ideology. (Let's be brutally honest here. Most *adults* lack these newspaper-reading skills.) That's why I brought both newspapers to my classroom; the *Tribune* is conservative and the *New York Times* is liberal. Sometimes the newspapers have editorials on the same issue, arguing opposing opinions. Reading editorials on different sides lets students make informed decisions about which side to support, or perhaps articulate their own more nuanced positions. Because newspapers are written at a higher reading level than middle school, require specific background knowledge, and often have some difficult vocabulary, they may be best read as shared reading. (However, we also must find pieces that students can read independently.)

When looking for newspaper articles to use as part of a unit, I tend to focus on three nationally known papers: the *Washington Post,* the *Wall Street Journal,* and the *New York Times,* and one local paper, the *Chicago Tribune.* Flip through a newspaper on any given day and you can easily find articles that connect to the themes and issues in books. Here are five examples from the *New York Times* on the day I wrote this chapter:

- "March in Cairo Draws Women by Thousands"—an article about a women-led protest in Egypt over the military beating of female demonstrators. Historians called it "the biggest women's demonstration in modern Egyptian history."

- "For Illegal Resident, Line Is Drawn at Transplant"—an article about an illegal immigrant who needs a kidney transplant. The U.S. government will pay $75,000 a year for dialysis but will not pay $100,000 for the transplant so he won't need the dialysis.
- "How Do You Prove You're an Indian?"—an op-ed by an Ojibwe Indian about how some tribes make members prove their "Indian blood" to share in casino profits.
- "Egypt's Military Masters"—an editorial about how the military leaders of Egypt are undermining the recent Egyptian revolution.
- Two articles in the Sports section focus on head injuries in hockey and football, part of the debate about violence and the price of winning in American sports.

Let's take a look at the first article and notice some of the rich vocabulary in just the first five paragraphs: *humiliation, Cairo, colonialism, inaugurated, suppressing, discontent, feminists, patriarchal, harassment,* and *activism.* Such potent and challenging vocabulary is not a good reason to avoid these texts. On the contrary, it's another reason we should use them. We may need to scaffold our instruction with a prereading mini-lesson on a few key words or on needed background knowledge, and then perhaps read the article or column as shared reading. Students don't need to know every word to understand the big ideas in an article, especially if we're doing the reading. (Of course, there are limits for shared reading too, and if the vocabulary is simply too hard, then we need to find a more appropriate article.)

I would not limit myself to those three national newspapers, however. Searching for articles and editorials online gives teachers access to thousands of newspapers from every nation in the world. If you want articles showing how Egyptian newspapers are reporting their own revolution, you can hop over to the Internet Public Library (ipl.org), click on newspapers, click Africa, and click Egypt, and there you will find links to five English-language Egyptian newspapers. *The Egyptian Gazette* has the article "Women Stage Protest March in Cairo." Another, *Al-Ahram,* has an opinion piece titled "The Revolution Must Evolve."

Magazines

We all know magazines such as *Time* and *Newsweek,* and school magazines such as *Junior Scholastic* and *Upfront.* All of these can have terrific articles to delve into with middle schoolers, and (depending on your students) can be written at their independent reading level, making these texts more accessible for students to read on their own. But we need to cast our net wider to harvest interesting and relevant magazine articles for our diverse student populations. Because we can read a text as shared reading, we can also choose articles above students' independent reading levels. Magazines that we can use include:

- *Orion*
- *Rolling Stone*
- *Discover*
- *Sports Illustrated*
- *Harper's*
- *The New York Times Magazine*
- *Good*
- *U.S. News & World Report* (online)
- *Smithsonian*
- *The Utne Reader*

- *The New Yorker*
- *Mother Jones*
- *National Geographic*

- *The Atlantic*
- *Extra!*
- *Wired*

There are also magazines written for children, including *Muse, Ask,* and *New Moon Girls. Stone Soup, Teen Ink,* and *Teen Reads* are not just written *for* kids, they're written *by* kids.

Although some of these articles can be long, many are short and can be read in twenty to thirty minutes or spread over a few days. Imagine how refreshing it would be for a middle school boy to be encouraged to read a *Sports Illustrated* article such as "In My Tribe" (McDonell 2011), about the role of sports in American life, and then connect that piece to a sports novel by Carl Deuker, Chris Crutcher, Mike Lupica, or Paul Volponi. Or we might connect a similar article to the novel *Dairy Queen* (Murdock 2006) about a girl who wants to try out for her high school football team.

In addition to being part of a literature inquiry unit, many short texts can serve double duty as models of good writing—known as *mentor texts*. Students can use these writing samples in writing workshop and across the curriculum (Dorfman and Cappelli 2009; Gallagher 2011). Let's face it: one of the very best ways to help kids become better writers is to have them read lots of great writing.

As teachers we know all too well how many students truly struggle with reading informational texts. On this crisis in content-area reading, Harvey Daniels and Steve Zemelman write, "Students consume a drastically unbalanced and unhealthful reading diet, with negative side effects like low test scores, ignorance of vital information, and negative attitudes towards reading. They read too many textbooks and not enough 'real' books and articles" (2004, 14).

You remember all of those textbooks you dreaded and fake-read when you were in school? Well, today's kids still dread them. When I had to read them, I did the most sensible thing: I turned my brain off. If we want students to develop the skills needed to read and appreciate informational texts, they must have regular opportunities to read interesting and purposeful informational texts.

Essays, Reports, Short Stories, Poetry, and Picture Books

Anthologies of essays about science and the social sciences can offer wonderful contextual or supplementary reading for inquiry units. Although many of these nonfiction books were written for adults, we can use them with young adolescents with appropriate scaffolding.

The Internet is overflowing with research studies and reports that we can use with middle-grades students. For two inquiry units that I cotaught with Ron and Mary based on two different anchor books, Walter Dean Myers's *Monster* and Paul Volponi's *Black and White*, we also used the report "One in One Hundred: Behind Bars in America," published by the Pew Center on the States (2008). This was a perfect resource with which to explore the U.S. criminal justice system. Sometimes the executive summary of a report will suffice. Concise, accessible text can be a springboard for discussions and contextual analysis that middle school students are quite capable of comprehending.

Other short texts can come from books. Anthologies of short stories written for adolescents are an invaluable resource. (A list of short story anthologies can be found in Appendix C, also included on the companion Web site, stenhouse.com/caringhearts.) Few of us have the time to read every story, so I suggest tracking down a few book reviews online where they'll mention the better stories.

I also recommend collections of poetry for young adults, such as the anthologies edited by Naomi Shihab Nye and Betsy Franco. Some of their books of poems, such as Franco's *You Hear Me?* and *Things I Have to Tell You* were written by teenagers. Nye's book *What Have You Lost?* features poems about many different kinds of loss, such as friends and identity and death. (See Appendix D, also included on the companion Web site, stenhouse.com/caringhearts, for books of poetry.)

I not only use picture books with middle schoolers but also read them with my college students. Many picture books have sophisticated ideas and important content knowledge. Some of my favorites are *The Other Side, Home, Zen Shorts, Voices in the Park, Piggybook, A River Ran Wild, Hey, Little Ant, Families, If the World Were a Village, Zoom, Planting the Trees of Kenya, Madlenka,* and anything by Eve Bunting, Patricia Polacco, and Jon J. Muth. If you designed a unit about war, you could include a "text set" of picture books with war themes, including *Why?, The Librarian of Basra, The Cello of Mr. O, Patrol, The Seed, Baseball Saved Us, Hiroshima No Pika,* and *Faithful Elephants.* By "picture books," I don't mean just storybooks. We should also widen our search to include publications with extensive and explanatory illustrations and graphics, including nonfiction resources. (See Appendix E, also included on the companion Web site, stenhouse.com/caringhearts, for an annotated list of terrific picture books.)

Nonwritten Resources

If we limited the resources students use to written texts, we would eliminate about *half* the resources on the planet! Given the tremendous value adolescents place on media and music, using these resources will almost certainly increase student engagement and learning. Think about your own years as a middle schooler; how cool would it have been to listen to popular music connected to a novel? In addition, some information cannot be communicated well through writing. A photograph can tell a story or show a truth that a written text cannot. The great photographer Lewis Hine, whose early-twentieth-century images exposed the horrors of child labor, wrote, "If I could tell the story in words, I wouldn't need to lug a camera" (Stott 1986, 30). (There are two terrific middle-grades books about Hine: Russell Freedman's biography, *Kids at Work: Lewis Hine and the Crusade Against Child Labor,* and Elizabeth Winthrop's novel *Counting on Grace.*)

If variety is the spice of life, then it is also the spice of school. Why not embrace these diverse, thoughtful, imaginative, and intellectual resources and make them an important part of our teaching? Here are some of the nonwritten resources we can use:

- ◆ photographs
- ◆ artwork
- ◆ music
- ◆ Web sites
- ◆ podcasts
- ◆ timelines
- ◆ videos, movies, and documentaries
- ◆ radio news reports and interviews
- ◆ infographics
- ◆ video games
- ◆ television shows
- ◆ data and graphs

Some of these resources, like videos, include a variety of subcategories, such as videos of poetry slams, news reports, interviews, music, and speeches. Remember that we don't always need to read an entire article or show an entire movie or video to make a point or a connection.

Another resource is the TED.org Web site, which is a gold mine for teachers. *TED* stands for "Technology, Entertainment, Design." Each year innovative and creative thinkers from around the world give remarkable talks that are put up on the TED Web site. Almost all of the talks are fewer than twenty minutes. There are also independently organized TEDx events around the world, and many of these talks are also available on the Web. The creators of TED also have an interactive Web site, TEDEducation (ed.ted.com), with talks and lessons developed by educators. The Web site shows videos, lesson ideas, open-ended questions, discussion topics, and other resources linked by thematic topics.

Using the Internet

Chances are that much of your resource hunting will be online. If you should come across a good newspaper article when you're reading the print version, you can simply hop online and print copies rather than cutting it out and photocopying. It's a breeze getting an article online that you already know about. But looking for resources online, especially on topics or in media with which you may be unfamiliar, can be challenging. We need to become Web-savvy to save time and frustration as well as find great stuff. Although the range of content on the Internet is remarkable, perhaps 95 percent of it is junk or unusable for kids. We need to find that fabulous 5 percent.

For our inquiry unit on social problems (which is not in this book), one of the novels Ron and I used was *Make Lemonade* (Wolff 1993). In addition to having his students explore teenage pregnancy, we wanted to include some music about the absence of teenage fathers in their children's lives. I already knew one great song about this, "He Say, She Say" by Lupe Fiasco (and we used it). After a short Google search ("songs about teenage pregnancy") and some viewing on YouTube, I found two other songs by Tupac Shakur and a duet by Ludacris and Mary J. Blige. I went to another Web site and printed the lyrics.

Internet search engines are very literal. If I were designing a unit based on Gloria Whelan's book *Homeless Bird*, about a thirteen-year-old girl in India forced into an arranged marriage, I'd want my students to read some poems about women's and girls' rights. But first I would need to find that poetry. My Internet search might start with "women's rights poetry," yet that would produce 12 million hits! Because search engines work like natural selection, with results being listed according to their popularity with those specific search terms, chances are good that I'll find what I'm looking for in the first three pages of results. I also may not find anything I like with that specific search phrase, so I'll try a different idea, "girls poems empowerment." I might not like those results, so next I would try "poems written about being a girl." That will lead me to some terrific poetry.

Finding the best sources requires detective work. Many of the Web sites we can use to find resources are obvious, from *Time* and *Junior Scholastic,* to using Google Images to find great pictures, to YouTube, Vimeo, and Hulu to search for videos. But the Internet is a mighty big place with many terrific, fascinating, mind-blowing Web sites and blogs.

Here are some Web sites that can bring exciting real-world resources into our classrooms:

- **Pewresearch.org.** The Pew Research Center conducts polling and studies on endless topics and issues of the day. An outstanding resource.
- **nytimes.com.** Besides the outstanding coverage and originality of the *New York Times* newspaper, the Web site has great blogs such as "Student Opinion," which posts a question based on a news article for students to submit (and read) comments; each weekday, "Room for Debate" has multiple experts write short opinions on a current issue; and the "Lens" blog has exceptional photojournalism.
- **Good.is.** This is the Web site for *Good* magazine. Click on their infographics (or just type "infographics" and a specific topic into Google and click for images).
- **NPR.org** has wonderful resources from their many programs, especially their main news programs *Morning Edition* and *All Things Considered*.
- **PBS.org.** The Public Broadcasting Service Web site gives instant access to outstanding documentaries, investigative reports, news reports, and nature videos (and Elmo).
- **darylcagle.com** and **cartoonmovement.com** include political cartoons on every topic you can imagine. You can also seek out specific comics, such as Doonesbury.
- **Loc.org** is the Web site for the immense collection of primary sources in the Library of Congress. Another is the National Archives at **archives.gov** and **digitalvaults.org**.
- **Worldwatch.org** is one of the premier organizations studying and reporting on changes in the global environment. **Nationalgeographic.com** is another one.

Putting the Pieces Together

The resources that I've mentioned in this chapter will provide key pieces for the unit you're designing. Does it take time to find them? Absolutely. But once you locate a great resource, you can keep it in either a real file or a digital file and use it for years. To emphasize a point I made in earlier chapters, we don't need to teach large inquiry units for all books. Sometimes the best way to teach a book is to do it fast. Skip the extra texts and just read the novel, or limit the connected resources to a handful. Connecting a good book to just two or three real-world resources can make a dynamic difference in students' learning.

The more authentic resources we add to our literature studies, however, the more students will benefit. Just think about all the connections students can make from the novel *Red Glass*: a *New York Times* op-ed about the Killing Fields of Cambodia; the song "Miss Sarajevo" by the rock band U2; photojournalism of Central American children riding freight trains to get into the United States illegally; an article in *Harper's* magazine about the civil war in Guatemala; and even "six-word memoirs" published by teenagers. Connecting resources like this in a single unit—which is exactly what Karen and I did for the unit featured in Chapter 10—creates *synergy*, which my iMac dictionary widget defines as "the interaction or cooperation of two or more organizations, substances, or other agents to produce a combined effect greater than the sum of their separate effects." Inquiry-based teaching is like that: a synergistic experience that becomes so much more than the sum of its parts.

Chapter 6

Designing an Inquiry Unit

When curriculum, instruction, and assessment shift out of the covers of a textbook and into the real-world context of projects, everything changes. Instead of superficially "covering the curriculum" as chapters in a textbook, students and teachers need to uncover the more complex issues revealed through the structured inquiry of projects.

—Milton Chen (2010)

Have you ever built one of those giant jigsaw puzzles? Growing up I remember my mom during her puzzle phase, sitting for hours each week at our dining room table as she assembled a mind-numbing, 1,000-piece puzzle of a forest or bucolic farm. Creating an inquiry unit is like building a big puzzle, although you don't get the pieces in a box. Instead, you find those pieces and then fit them together, carefully crafting a learning experience that works as a whole. I find this process creative and thrilling, yet challenging.

Elliot Eisner has been a champion of progressive education reform since the 1970s. He wrote, "The aim of education ought to be conceived of as the preparation of artists." Eisner was not referring specifically to creating painters or poets. He characterizes artists as follows:

Individuals who have developed ideas, the sensibilities, the skills, and the imagination to create work that is well proportioned, skillfully executed, and imaginative, regardless of the domain in which the individual works. The highest accolade we can confer upon someone is to say that he or she is an artist, whether as a carpenter or a surgeon, a cook or an engineer, a physicist or a teacher. (2002, 8)

Eisner's notion of cultivating artists applies not only to our students, but to our work as educators. As an artist, the creator of original units of study, a teacher becomes a curriculum *designer*. I use the word *designer* purposefully, because like Eisner's artists, designers bring care, creativity, excellence, originality, and thoughtfulness to their work. They take pride in shaping something unique. Yes, it is more work than teaching out of a textbook or a prepackaged "novel unit," but it is infinitely more interesting and meaningful.

The Anatomy of an Inquiry Unit

Tear apart an inquiry unit and inside we would discover the different parts that teachers need to fit together to create that dynamic experience. In this chapter, we'll first take a look at the different parts of a literature-based inquiry unit, and then we'll put those puzzle pieces together as we shift into full-fledged unit design. In the end, I'll show an outline (or what I like to call a flowchart) of an entire unit designed around the dystopian novel *Rash* by Pete Hautman (2006). Here's a list of those unit parts, and then we'll take a look at each one more closely:

- ♦ Inquiry questions and unit themes
- ♦ Before reading
- ♦ Journal writing and discussion questions
- ♦ Writing prompts
- ♦ Mini-lessons
- ♦ Small activities
- ♦ Projects

Inquiry Questions and Themes

Seventh graders walk into their language arts or reading classroom on the first day of a new literature unit. Typically, they might hear something like this from the teacher: "We're starting a new unit on the novel *Elsewhere*." Okay, that's generic enough. But let's change that first day and give it some pop. *Elsewhere* is a fantastic young adult fantasy novel about a girl who is accidentally killed by a hit-and-run driver and wakes up on a cruise ship on her way to Elsewhere, where people slowly age backward to infancy and then return to Earth. Imagine the difference when students walk into the classroom and see the following question written on the board in large letters:

How should I live my life?

That question could frame the unit. It could be the title of the unit. *Elsewhere* is the anchor text that students will read, but their teacher might not mention it on the first day or even the second day. The purpose of a unit is not to tell students the answer to the main question, which doesn't have a correct answer. That is the beauty of inquiry-based literature teaching. Students must grapple with the questions and the possibilities, learning to think for themselves.

We don't need to limit ourselves to one question. We should brainstorm more questions to give the unit shape and substance—some factual, some opinion, some existential. In inquiry-based teaching, these are typically called *guiding questions* or *essential questions*. As Jeff Wilhelm (2007) writes,

"Guiding questions create a clearly focused problem orientation that connects kids to socially significant material and learning" (8).

Guiding questions bring what Selma Wasserman (2007) calls "big ideas" to a unit. Wasserman writes, "A curriculum experience that is rooted in big ideas not only identifies the direction of the study, but also illuminates its relevance for serious work" (292). Curriculum today is so sanitized, fact-based, and skill-centered that it numbs the mind. No wonder middle schoolers are so often intellectually disengaged; they are not studying ideas that matter to them or to society.

Consider, instead, how they might respond to the following unit examples and main inquiry questions designed by my college students:

♦ "What is a girl worth?" based on *Sold*, Patricia McCormick's novel about a girl in Nepal who is sold into prostitution.

♦ For a unit based on Laurie Halse Anderson's novel *Speak*: How do you speak out when you are silenced?

♦ For their unit on *The Hunger Games*: In our society, what do you feel has control over your life?

Some guiding questions for *The Hunger Games* might include: What is propaganda? What are historical examples of propaganda? Who has more power in the United States, the people or the government? How much power should government have? In what ways do governments control their citizens? In what ways are you in (and not in) control of your own life? Do we control media or do media control us? Are "reality" TV shows truly based on reality? Why are humans so violent?

Before Reading

Before beginning to read the book in a unit, we will want to do some activities and perhaps a few mini-lessons. It's typical to begin reading the book a week or more into the unit. Remember, the unit is not strictly about the book but about the main inquiry question or topic, so we want to take some time upfront to set up the focus of the unit, pique the kids' curiosity, and help them *care* about what we'll be exploring. As teachers we know that students often need some front-loading lessons before jumping into a book. We also have to consider the background knowledge they might need to understand the text or unit topic. And we might want to connect the unit or the book to the students' lives or the world today. Here are some examples of setting the scene:

♦ Before reading *The Loud Silence of Francine Greene*, we could create a series of mini-lessons on communism, the Red Scare of McCarthyism, and the Cold War.

♦ Paul Fleischman's novel *Whirligig* has an unusual structure, going back and forth in time and introducing new characters throughout the book. We might show excerpts of contemporary movies or television shows where the directors used a similar technique of shifting time and stories, giving students visual references for the format they'll have to follow through the book.

♦ Before reading *Crossing Jordan*, we could connect it to kids' lives by asking them to write in their journals about their own experiences with people of different races.

Journal Writing and Discussion Questions

Teachers ask a lot of questions every day. Perhaps the simplest way we can move from traditional teaching to critical and inquiry teaching is to *change the questions we ask*. We want to take the time to think of questions that ask for students' opinions and require them to make meaning from the text through inferences, ethical decisions, and connections to social responsibility. Most of these questions do not have simple answers and are the kinds of questions that should dominate our teaching. Some examples:

- ◆ After reading Chapter 20 in *Milkweed*: We see the horrifying inhumanity of the Holocaust. Why did it happen? Where does this "evil" come from? Are people born evil? Do all people have this potential for evil? Can someone be both good and evil?
- ◆ On page 74 of *Elsewhere:* Aldous tells Liz that a job is about "prestige and money" but an avocation is "something a person does to make his or her soul complete." What does he mean? Think of a future job or career you're thinking about. Is it more about prestige and money or fulfilling your soul?

Writing Prompts

As teachers, our goals should always be to create meaningful assignments that involve kids doing the same kinds of authentic writing we see in the real world: poetry, letters, short stories, articles, memoirs, plays, blogs, and speeches. And just as we advocate in writing workshop, we want this work to go through a more "formal" writing process, from drafting to revising to editing to completing a beautiful final copy. Yet, because these are units with a focus on social responsibility, sometimes we also want to choose writing prompts that ask students to delve more deeply into these issues. In a six- or seven-week unit, I would typically have just one or two of these assignments. Consider these ideas:

- ◆ After reading *Homeless Bird*, about the girl being forced into an arranged marriage in India: Write a three-minute speech to be delivered to the United Nations about the state of being female today.
- ◆ After reading Paul Volponi's *Black and White*: Working in pairs, write a skit that takes place five years after the story ends. Marcus is out of prison and bumps into Eddie on the street corner. Perform your skit.

Mini-Lessons

Mini-lessons are five- to fifteen-minute teacher lectures or demonstrations and among the best ways to integrate literacy skills and the specific content of social responsibility. Like the writing prompts, some mini-lessons should target the unit topic, whereas others should relate specifically to the book. The books you choose for your inquiry units will contain the roots of many mini-lessons, from genre studies to writing conventions. Mini-lessons have revolutionized teaching, so students spend the vast amount of time in school actively engaged in learning activities and discussions rather than sitting passively while their teachers do most of the talking. I divide mini-lessons into two categories, those focusing on skills (how to write a letter, for example) and those focusing on content (what is communism?). Here are some examples:

♦   While reading *Daniel Half Human* by David Chotjewitz, which takes place in Germany during the beginnings of the Holocaust, a few mini-lessons should explain the history and scope of propaganda, Nazi propaganda, and propaganda in our own country.

♦   Before students write the skit based on the book *Black and White*, do a mini-lesson on proper playwriting format.

Small Activities

You certainly don't need me to explain what an activity is, but I will highlight how teaching through inquiry makes activities more meaningful. Activities usually engage students in reading the short texts or using other real-world resources, and often the activities result in discussion. On the surface, inquiry-based activities may appear to focus on facts and skills, yet their primary purpose is helping students grapple with the big ideas behind the unit. For example, students learn skills, such as reading informational texts or critical thinking, within the context of reading a newspaper editorial about American immigration policies. Here are some examples:

♦   When reading *Bronx Masquerade,* Mary, another former student of mine, had her eighth graders work with partners to list stereotypes in the book and then list gender stereotypes they see in life.

♦   While reading *The Breadwinner,* Ben showed his sixth graders a video of a child laborer in Afghanistan. He then asked his students to compare the girl's experiences with their lives in Chicago. His students interviewed one another about what "jobs" they do in school and at home.

Projects

As stated in Milton Chen's (2010) quote at the beginning of this chapter, project-based teaching is a very close sibling to inquiry-based teaching. Small projects take about two weeks. Big projects are more labor intensive and require more time. I've had students work on big projects for as long as seven weeks. In literature units, projects are usually done after the book is completed. The scale of the project has to do with how much time we have and the complexity of the work we ask students to do. Most, if not all, of that work should be done in the classroom, where we can help students. Some ideas:

♦   Have students individually create a symbolic painting or mixed-media artwork based on a book's theme (Rief 1997).

♦   After reading *Deadline*, Chris Crutcher's thought-provoking novel about a boy who learns that he has a year to live, each student could interview a teenager and senior citizen about the joys, regrets, and meaning of their lives. Students could videotape the interviews and create a digital movie, write and illustrate the interview using the computer program Comic Life, or write them as narratives and publish a class magazine.

We can also think about field trips to reinforce lessons and outside experts to bring into our classrooms. Our communities are filled with people who are just waiting for an invitation to visit and share their expertise with kids. One of the most profound experiences I ever had in a school was when two teachers invited a panel of five people affected by AIDS to their eighth-grade classroom. Four of the visitors were HIV-positive, and the fifth was a woman who had lost her son to AIDS. It was extraordinary to hear their courageous stories and to witness the compassion and maturity of students whose worlds were enlarged that day.

Getting Started

When I design a unit, I start with a blank pad of paper. Actually, I use something else too: my head. Before I begin the nuts and bolts work of designing a unit, I've usually been thinking about it for some time, bouncing ideas around my head. Where do the ideas come from? Usually books. I believe in teaching through inquiry and projects for math and science and social studies too, but the process of designing a unit for those disciplines would differ. For a literature unit, my ideas usually come from books that I connect to an important and interesting question or topic. Sometimes an idea starts with a question or a topic and then shifts to seeking out related literature.

Once I have the book and have decided on a main inquiry question or topic, I pull out my pad of paper. For me, designing a unit is very low tech. No computers or tablets; I like to scribble my ideas on paper with words, lists, doodles, and arrows. I can see using my iPad for this process one day because there are apps that would work like a charm for designing a unit, such as Corkulous, Bords, Index Card, and Grafio. But right now I like the pen and paper. It feeds my creativity.

Designing the Unit

Let's use the dystopian novel *Rash,* by Pete Hautman (2006), and design a unit for seventh grad-ers. The story takes place in the year 2076 in the United Safer States of America (the USSA), where anything potentially dangerous (football, large dogs, tattoos) has been outlawed and a quarter of the country is in prison. The temper of sixteen-year-old Bo lands him in a jail-factory for teenagers in the Canadian tundra (owned by McDonald's), where the inmates make frozen pizzas all day. *Rash* has many of the qualities adolescents love in a book: action, the future, sci-fi, sports, a bit of romance, an artificial intelligence named Bork, and bad guys, including a ruthless prison warden. It also has good writing and an imperfect protagonist you care about.

Rash also has plenty of themes that connect to social responsibility, including how much control government should have over our lives, American manufacturing and labor practices, and whether we should be allowed to eat french fries!

Before I started designing the unit on paper, I had already assembled two essential pieces of the inquiry puzzle. First, I brainstormed teaching ideas *as I read the book*. When I think of a great question I can ask students while we are reading page 112 during the unit, I must write it down. Otherwise, it's highly unlikely I'll remember it when the class actually gets to page 112. And reading the book acts as an *idea generator*; as I make my way through the story, ideas for activities, connected resources, mini-lessons, writing prompts, and projects are flying through my head.

To help with this process I made a double-sided brainstorming sheet that I use as a bookmark. It has sections for all the categories I listed earlier in this chapter. As I read, I scribble down my ideas for the entire unit, not just on the book. Once I finish the book I add more ideas. Figure 6.1 shows the completed front side of the sheet for *Rash*. (See Appendix H, also included on the companion Web site stenhouse .com/caringhearts, for a blank brainstorming sheet.) The back of this sheet, found on the Web site, includes possible questions for journal writing and discussions, along with writing assignment ideas. Of course, I would never use all of these ideas. Instead, they will be potential pieces for my unit puzzle.

The second thing I do as I read is *mark up the book*. As I teach my way through a book, I don't want to have to search for all of the good stuff I saw when I first read it. When my students and I get to page 112 in the book, I want a quick reference so I can easily find that fantastic question I thought of during my prereading. Figure 6.2 shows Laura's marked-up copy of *The Hunger Games*.

BEFORE READING	TOPICS, THEMES & INQUIRY QUESTIONS	SMALL ACTIVITIES
• Mini-lesson on dystopian fiction, including classic novels like *Brave New World* • Mini-lesson on science fiction elements in dystopian fiction • What the registered symbol means • Mini-lesson on artificial intelligence	• Where is the line between freedom and security? • When should government limit our personal responsibility? • How much freedom should people have to act in ways that are dangerous to themselves? • How do governments use fear to control their people? • What are some examples in the past? • Are humans rational? • Is American society rational? • Do we have free will? • What are the human and economic effects of industrial work?	• Groups read a different dystopian short story and draw a small symbolic mural of life in the story and present it to the class. • Maintain an ongoing timeline of the history of the USSA as we read. • Work in groups and list the pros and cons of living in the USSA (after p. 77). • Silent graffiti. • In groups, brainstorm examples of how modern American society is and is not rational (after p. 217). • Create a Venn diagram comparing life in the USSA with our lives in the USA (toward the end of the book).

RASH by Pete Hautman

PROJECTS	MINI-LESSONS	
• Small groups choose one controversial issue involving freedom vs. security, become an expert, and create part of a class Web site to inform the public about what they learned. • The class writes a survey on a wide variety of "freedom vs. security" issues, gives the surveys, analyzes the data, and creates graphs. • Student pairs interview people and create an iMovie. • Students write and perform a play about freedom vs. security. • Each student creates a symbolic piece of art.	• McCarthyism and the Red Scare • Japanese American internment camps • The U.S. 3-strikes "Rockefeller Laws" • History of U.S. labor and manufacturing. • Descartes: "I think, therefore I am" p. 61 • Alan Turing and the Turing Test • Classic and contemporary dystopian novels • Quality writing on specific pages • Industrial Revolution and mass production	• The Patriot Act • The Fourth Amendment • The First Amendment • Propaganda • Free will • Artificial intelligence

Additional items under SMALL ACTIVITIES:
• Have a series of formal debates on issues of freedom vs. security: 1) the food we eat; 2) school searches; 3) surveillance cameras in Chicago; 4) mandatory drug testing in middle schools.
• *Rash* is a vision of a future America. Students work in pairs and create their own future society.

CONNECTED TEXTS	OTHER RESOURCES
• Editorials on surveillance cameras in Chicago • ACLU report on surveillance cameras in Chicago • Article on different beliefs of capitalism • American Library Association list of most-banned books • Classic dystopian short stories: "Harrison Bergeron," "The Lottery," and others • Bill of Rights • Articles on school searches, mandatory drug tests, and cell phone searches • Summary of the Patriot Act "Do We Still Need the Patriot Act?" on *New York Times Room for Debate* blog • Article on the debate of U.S. torture • Search-and-seizure policy of Chicago Public Schools • *New York Times* article about U.S. prison rate • Article about California law for age limits on sale of violent video games • Banned picture books • Article about Turing Test • Article about outsourcing American labor to China	• Data and graphs on incarceration in America compared with other democracies • Video or documentary on the U.S. for-profit prison-industrial complex • Photographs and video interviews on the Japanese American internment camps at densho.org • Online podcast of a panel debate on "freedom vs. security" on WBEZ hosted by the Illinois Humanities Council • Video of HUAC hearings with Joe McCarthy and the Red Scare • Video of Edward R. Murrow condemning McCarthyism • "10 Companies That Control Your Consumption" chart showing the enormous number of products 10 American companies own • Artificial intelligence computer-animated video Clips of Charlie Chaplin on the assembly line in Modern Times • The movie *AI: Artificial Intelligence* • Chicago Police Department Web site on Police Observation Devices (PODs) • Video of Urban Institute forum on the use of surveillance cameras • Map of surveillance cameras in Chicago – there are more than 10,000

Figure 6.1 The front of my brainstorming sheet with ideas for teaching *Rash*.

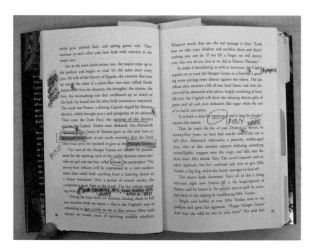

Figure 6.2 Laura Meili marked up her copy of *The Hunger Games* to help plan an inquiry unit.

As I read the book, I also consider themes of social responsibility that I could use to design a unit. With *Rash,* one good inquiry question kept buzzing around my brain:

Where is the line between freedom and security?

I knew the question would be interesting to middle school students who are pushing the boundaries for their own independence, as well as their own political awakenings. I knew the book would be relevant for our post-9/11 world, with our heated national debates on government power and people's rights. *Rash* is an example of a popular novel we can teach as a unit rather than just put in our class library for students to read on their own. Trust me: your students will thank you for choosing a book they don't want to put down.

Rash is 249 pages, but it's a rather quick read, with forty-nine very short chapters. Shared reading would work for most of the text, although I'll also want students to read selected parts on their own (after we get into the first sixty pages or so). Two considerations guide my decisions: I don't want to race through a book and zip past great learning opportunities, but I also don't want to drag out the reading, because that kills a good book. I like *momentum* when we read. Of course, how long a book takes to read depends on a host of variables: how it will be read, how often it will be read, how much time each day we have to read, where my students are as readers, and the complexity and length of the book.

If we have one hour a day, we should be able to read at least fifteen pages each class, with time left over for other work. Needless to say, our reading is not just reading, but also stopping at selected points to ask questions and talk about the book. That's roughly 200 pages read in thirteen school days. The students could read the other fifty pages on their own in school and at home. So, I'll plan a little more than two weeks to finish the book and build in some wiggle room if we need more time, which seems to often be the case.

I need to decide how long I have for the unit. Let's say I have six weeks or so. Two-and-a-half weeks of that will be spent reading the book. If I reserve the last two weeks for a culminating project, that leaves me with about eight days for short texts and activities related to them. I would plan to use at least the first full week for background-building activities before I start the book. I'd also use class time for activities on some of the days while we'd also be reading the book. I would plug this whole time frame onto my computer calendar. As I make unit decisions, such as when I'll insert certain activities and mini-lessons, I'll add them to the calendar. Designing and laying out a schedule for a unit on my computer or iPad would enable me to save everything for the next time I teach the unit.

The process of designing a unit is not neat and linear. I don't first design this part and then design that part; rather I'm thinking about all the parts simultaneously. As I'm reading the book with the question "Where is the line between freedom and security?" zipping through my brain, I'm also jotting down guiding questions:

- Where is the line between our individual responsibility to be safe and healthy and the government's responsibility to keep us safe and healthy?
- Is the Patriot Act more about giving us security from terrorists or taking away constitutional freedoms?
- What are some examples from history of our nation's struggles between freedom and security?
- How much freedom should parents give their teenage children?
- What role does fear play in our nation's focus on security?
- How big should our military be? How much money should our country spend to keep us safe? What does it mean to be safe?
- What is the purpose of prison? Is it to keep us safe? Punish criminals? Reform criminals? Educate criminals? What *should* their purpose be?
- What are we willing to give up to live longer?

We can certainly brainstorm guiding questions like these with students. My partner teachers and I didn't do that with the units featured in this book, and that omission is one of my biggest regrets. Students will think of questions that we don't, and many of theirs will be more relevant to their adolescent lives. Deciding which questions to ponder also gives students ownership of their learning. However, if we ask students to brainstorm questions, then we need to somehow integrate some of their questions into the unit or else that entire process becomes disingenuous, and middle-grades students have disingenuous radar.

This doesn't mean we set them loose to study baseless questions, such as, "How can we overthrow our tyrannical school administrators?" It means we honor their voices and ideas, have them pose questions, and then work together (along with using the teacher's questions) to collaboratively create a set of guiding questions. Adding our questions is vital, because most students will not ask critical inquiry questions, so it's our job to help them refine the process and include these perspectives.

I don't actually need to finish designing the unit before I start teaching it. As teachers, we don't always have this luxury. If I have a main question, the unit has a definitive focus and direction, and I have some opening activities and resources, I may jump right in and design it as I go. That's exactly how the units in Chapters 7–11 were designed.

Searching for Short Texts

I like to open a unit with a bang. I want those first few days to suck the kids into our inquiry like a black hole engulfs solar particles. I want to pique their interests and tap their emotions. I might have them read or watch something interesting and even provocative, engage in some vigorous debate, or connect the main question to their lives. I want to get them *thinking* from day one; to do that for the *Rash* unit, I need to situate the broad issue of freedom versus security in a more intimate or contemporary context that breathes with relevance. That's where I'm going to begin my search, primarily with informational texts such as news articles. I'll look for other kinds of texts later.

My first thought is this: searches on school property. This is a very controversial and constitutional issue. Do schools have the right to search students' lockers without a warrant? How about their desks? Their backpacks and purses? How about reading students' cell phone text messages or e-mails? School officials argue that they can engage in these searches to ensure safety and security, but based on what cause? And who decides when these searches are justified? Can a student refuse?

In *Rash*, the government has become the ultimate "nanny state," outlawing anything even remotely dangerous, including alcohol and french fries. Well, our own country has plenty of laws to protect us from food, car accidents, drug use, television content, and video games, as well as laws that have put 2 million Americans in prison. Should we have these laws? My task as the teacher is to find some good articles on these issues, ideally involving real people, especially middle and high school students.

The legwork for an inquiry unit keeps me in perpetual motion. My discoveries feed on themselves, helping me find more resources, which in turn help me design more activities and, equally important, *educate me* on the issues. On my initial search for resources for the unit on freedom versus security, I turned up these articles during an Internet search:

- ♦ "The 9/11 Dilemma: Freedom vs. Security" is an article published in *Upfront*, the *New York Times* magazine for middle and high school students (Smith 2011).
- ♦ "AG Cuccinelli's Go-Ahead to Search Student Cell Phones Raises Fourth Amendment Questions" is a two-page article from the Student Press Law Center Web site. The article discusses a ruling by the Virginia attorney general that school officials have the right to seize and search a student's cell phone (LoMonte 2010).
- ♦ "Why Is the N.Y.P.D. After Me?" is a terrific *New York Times* op-ed by Nicolas K. Peart (2011), an African-American college student. He's been stopped and searched by the New York Police Department *five times* for just walking down the sidewalk.
- ♦ "Freedom vs. Security" is a one-page opinion article in *Teen Ink* (no date) written by an unknown teenager arguing that the American people must "modify our rights to privacy" to allow the government to protect us against terrorists.
- ♦ "San Francisco Bans Most Happy Meals" is a *Chicago Tribune* article on different opinions about San Francisco banning McDonald's Happy Meals as a health risk to children (Bernstein 2010). (My brain instantly tells me this would be a great article to begin the unit with—middle schoolers would have a *lot* to say about banning Happy Meals!)
- ♦ "Albanese: Supreme Court Got It Wrong on Violent Video Games" (Albanese 2011) and "Ruling On Violent Video Games: Score One for 1st Amendment" (*Los Angeles Times* 2011) are opposing pieces on the Supreme Court ruling that a law banning the sale of violent video games is unconstitutional since video games are free speech.
- ♦ "NJ Middle School Implements Drug Testing Program" is a news article about a middle school that instituted random drug testing (CBS New York 2011).
- ♦ "Strip-Search of Girl Tests Limit of School Policy" is about a school that strip-searched an eighth grader (Liptak 2009).
- ♦ The search and seizure policy of the Chicago Public Schools.

- "As It Turns 10, the Patriot Act Remains Controversial" is an NPR story on different opinions of the Patriot Act (Johnson 2011).
- "Caught Spying on Student, FBI Demands GPS Tracker Back" is from *Wired* magazine and the story of twenty-year-old Yasir Afifi, a half-Egyptian, U.S.-born citizen who found an FBI GPS tracking device on his car (Zetter 2010).
- "Politics Over Principle" is a *New York Times* (2011) editorial arguing against a bill signed by President Obama giving the government the authority to detain suspected terrorists, including American citizens, indefinitely without a trial.
- "U.S. Prison Population Dwarfs That of Other Nations" is a *New York Times* article about the huge American prison population (Liptak 2008).

Now, again, the chance that I'll use all of these texts in the unit is *zero*. It's too much! Besides, I'll be using other texts (perhaps some poems, a speech, and the Bill of Rights) and other nonwritten resources. So how do I decide which texts to use? Good unit designers are good editors; they must decide not only what resources to use but also what resources to cut and skip. These are holistic decisions. When considering each resource, I need to see how it might fit in the unit as a whole and use these resources to guide me in creating a well-focused, thought-provoking, and relevant unit. I need to ask myself which resources hold the most interest, would connect to the students, and be the best use of our time.

The First Two Days

As I think about the unit further, I consider that reading about the legality of school searches should occur on day two. On day one we should do an anticipation guide activity, which is a great way to open a unit before reading a book. Using statements, some contentious and provocative, students could rate their opinions based on a 1–10 scale, from Strongly Agree to Strongly Disagree. Figure 6.3 shows an anticipation guide I created based on the format from Kelly Gallagher (2004).

After they had completed the anticipation guide, I could choose three statements and have the students choose one to write about in their journals, explaining their reasoning. Next would come journal-sharing time. We'd sit on the rug in a large circle with our journals, and volunteers would read what they wrote. (If I had picked a prompt and written about it in my journal, then I would bring my work too.) At first, we would just read what we wrote, so there would be no editorializing. If I allowed them to just start talking and paraphrasing what they wrote, they would soon learn that they don't really need to write—they can just talk. But *writing is thinking*, so we would begin with some students reading what they wrote. Then I would open it up for discussion, where everyone would be free to comment on what people read. I want the students to do most of the talking, but I also have no problem redirecting the conversation, clarifying a point, or asking a direct question to make our talk purposeful.

Then it would be time for Take-a-Stand. For this activity, we would push the desks and tables out of the way to open the entire classroom. I would spread signs across the floor that read STRONGLY AGREE, AGREE, NEUTRAL, DISAGREE, and STRONGLY DISAGREE. I would take a statement from the anticipation guide for our discussion, and say it to the class. For example, I might say number four from the guide: "The school principal should be allowed to search our lockers at any

Anticipation Guide

Name _____

Before You Read		After You Read
1—2—3—4—5—6—7—8—9—10	1. The principal should be allowed to search your locker without your permission or a search warrant.	1—2—3—4—5—6—7—8—9—10
1—2—3—4—5—6—7—8—9—10	2. A student tells the principal that someone in our school has sent bullying text messages to another student. The principal should be allowed to read every text message on the student's cell phone without permission.	1—2—3—4—5—6—7—8—9—10
1—2—3—4—5—6—7—8—9—10	3. If a country is at war with us, we should arrest American citizens with that country's ancestry until the war ends.	1—2—3—4—5—6—7—8—9—10
1—2—3—4—5—6—7—8—9—10	4. A Friday and Saturday night curfew of 9 p.m. is appropriate for seventh graders.	1—2—3—4—5—6—7—8—9—10
1—2—3—4—5—6—7—8—9—10	5. Having police surveillance cameras in your neighborhood is a good idea.	1—2—3—4—5—6—7—8—9—10
1—2—3—4—5—6—7—8—9—10	6. It is more important to be safe than it is to be free.	1—2—3—4—5—6—7—8—9—10
1—2—3—4—5—6—7—8—9—10	7. Anyone should be allowed to buy violent video games.	1—2—3—4—5—6—7—8—9—10
1—2—3—4—5—6—7—8—9—10	8. Police should be allowed to stop, question, and frisk anyone who looks suspicious.	1—2—3—4—5—6—7—8—9—10
1—2—3—4—5—6—7—8—9—10	9. Our government should pass laws to encourage people to eat healthfully.	1—2—3—4—5—6—7—8—9—10
1—2—3—4—5—6—7—8—9—10	10. It's possible to make a machine think and feel like a human.	1—2—3—4—5—6—7—8—9—10
1—2—3—4—5—6—7—8—9—10	11. Humans by nature are rational beings.	1—2—3—4—5—6—7—8—9—10
1—2—3—4—5—6—7—8—9—10	12. Human beings have free will.	1—2—3—4—5—6—7—8—9—10

Scale: Left to right, Strongly Disagree, Somewhat Disagree, Neutral, Somewhat Agree, Strongly Agree

Figure 6.3 My anticipation guide for *Rash*.

time." I would reiterate to the class that these are not my opinions, just statements for the purpose of debate. The kids would stand at the sign they agree with, and then sit on the floor. I would ask for a volunteer to stand, face the other side, and explain the position. Then someone from the other side would stand and rebut that argument. Those students would continue debating and then others could join in. As the debate progresses, I may also tweak my statements. For example, I may say this:

> *Okay, so most of you think the principal should not be allowed to search your lockers, especially without a search warrant. But let's say a girl is found taking pills in the bathroom. The principal is told there are other students with pills, so he has the right to search everyone's locker. How do you respond to that?*

What I'm doing here is raising the complexity to the scenario, adding nuance, which requires kids to weigh different options, rethink their previous decisions, and question their stances. These are central to creating what Arthur Costa (2008) calls a "thought-filled curriculum" that not only gets kids to *think* but also *teaches* them how to think *skillfully*.

In this process, I wouldn't hesitate to call on students because I want many voices heard, and as teachers know, a handful of students often dominate discussions. A key part of Take-a-Stand is that at any time students are free to move to another place if they change their minds. Their explanations can get heated, and sometimes *very* heated, which is very good. Of course, I need to make sure the discourse remains respectful and does not devolve into screaming chaos. I've used this activity with many middle schoolers, and I can tell you that when it's time to stop, they don't want to leave the classroom. They want to keep debating—especially because they're not discussing the next book report, but ideas and questions that really matter in life.

My Resource Search Continues

Over the following weeks, I continued my search for more resources to explore the question of freedom versus security. If you look at the unit flowchart, you will see these other resources I found, including video oral histories of the Japanese American internment camps, a CBS news report video, footage of the Army-McCarthy hearings during the "Red Scare" of McCarthyism of the 1950s (and related video of famed journalist Edward R. Murrow), short videos on artificial intelligence, the Chicago Police Web site on the city's network of 10,000 surveillance cameras, and YouTube clips of Charlie Chaplin's silent film masterpiece *Modern Times*. All of these connect to issues in *Rash* and the larger unit questions.

As my unit inquiry progressed—and that's what this was, my own inquiry to design an inquiry unit—I came up with more ideas for activities and resources. I decided to have the students take a break from the book for just a day to read dystopian short stories in small groups (and chose five terrific stories by celebrated writers such as Ray Bradbury, Shirley Jackson, and Harlan Ellison), look at graphed data of the American prison population, and read five very short opposing opinions on the Patriot Act from the *New York Times* "Room for Debate" blog. Most of these texts and videos would not require a great deal of time to read or watch.

Reading *Rash*

When reading with students, I like to pull everyone together. I like to imagine the classroom as a group of friends or family sitting around a family room. We might gather on a large rug in the classroom or, if we're lucky, find some sofas and comfortable chairs. I want to remove the desks as barriers and bring intimacy to our reading and discussion. And being physically close gets more students involved in discussions. It also helps with classroom management.

Once we start a book as part of an inquiry unit, I like to read it every day. Reading a good book daily propels us forward and brings a valuable routine to the classroom and the unit. Assuming most of the students enjoy the book, they will look forward to reading time and won't hesitate to complain (publicly) if we skip a day.

Remember those "before-reading" ideas I brainstormed earlier? I may need to use some of those ideas before starting the book. These would include mini-lessons the students may need to frontload their reading so they can better comprehend the text.

After these mini-lessons, we would begin the book as shared reading. I would read as the students followed along in their own copies. Why use shared reading? First, it helps students get over the hump of beginning a book. If I had a dollar for every independent reading book my students abandoned before they started Chapter 2, I would be a wealthy man. Kelly Gallagher writes, "The first chapter of a book is usually the most confusing for students, and it's the place where an immature reader is most likely to lose focus" (2004, 58).

The second reason is that shared reading helps students become better readers. They don't need to worry about decoding or fluency or vocabulary. They can focus on comprehension, enjoying the story, appreciating the writing, and their own meaning making. It also enables us—the teachers—to be model readers, and not just for fluent reading, but for *passionate* reading. Janet Allen believes shared reading should be the "heart of reading instruction." She writes, "In a survey of over six hundred middle and high school students that I recently conducted, the area they cited as responsible for their greatest gains in reading achievement was shared reading" (2000, 58).

The advantage here is obvious. As I read, students are not just hearing the words; they're *seeing* the words, and matching them to my reading. And many students are not just "following" my reading; they're reading the words in their minds, but with a good fluent reader setting the pace, so their own reading is faster. Allen mentions another important value of shared reading. One of the reasons ninth graders told Allen that her shared reading was so valuable was this: "When I read alone, I have a hard time reading *and* thinking about the book" (59). When I do the reading, it frees up their minds to *think*. In fact, if you read the opening of *Rash,* you'll see that it practically begs you to think.

The third reason is simple. Shared reading is *shared*. It helps cultivate a community of readers and thinkers. Reading a novel (or a short text) as part of an inquiry unit is really about using books (and especially fiction) to help us explore problems. Shared reading emphasizes that much of the best problem solving is done *together*. Now, would I share-read every text? No way. Again, variety is the spice of life. I also want to *use* shared reading—along with some modeling such as think-alouds—to help students become stronger independent readers. So I'll certainly choose texts for students to read on their own.

Finally, reading a book as part of a unit that teaches social responsibility does not mean we can't also have students engage in more traditional literature assignments. Teachers can do both. We just need to choose very wisely what is truly purposeful and meaningful. We must ensure that we don't turn the unit into an endless stream of skill-building exercises.

The Final Project

A final project can focus on the overall unit or specific themes from the book. I loosely put projects into two categories. Some projects require research, such as interviewing someone or studying a historical example of freedom versus security in our country. Other projects don't require any research and seek more creative input from students, such as designing and creating a metaphorical mural on a theme of a book. For *Rash*, I came up with five different possible culminating projects:

♦ Working in small groups, students could create surveys measuring attitudes about U.S. civil liberties that should or should not be constrained based on issues of freedom versus security. They would conduct the survey, analyze and graph the results, and then post them on a unit Web site.

- Working in pairs, students could interview a variety of people (young and old) about their opinions on the same topic. They could videotape and edit the interviews to create an iMovie.
- Students could choose one issue—such as mandatory drug tests in schools or the Patriot Act—and work in small groups to become the class "experts." I'd allow them to choose what to create to show what they learned, such as a Web site, a podcast, or a graphic nonfiction publication.
- In small groups, students could write and perform an original play about a freedom versus security issue. In addition to the performance, the final project would require a beautifully written and edited copy of the play.
- Each student could create a symbolic or metaphorical art piece in response to a theme in *Rash*. Each creation must go through a drafting process as in writing workshop, and all the art would be displayed as a class exhibition.

Sometimes it's helpful and refreshing to give students choices. For example, you could let students choose one of the projects I just mentioned, or you could follow my third example and assign a similar topic but allow students to choose what project to create. By offering projects in different mediums—writing, technology, art, math, and drama—we give students an opportunity to demonstrate their knowledge through one of their preferred methods of learning. (You do need to be sure the projects require the same amount of time and intellectual rigor.) These projects also show exciting interdisciplinary possibilities. A literacy teacher can collaborate with a math teacher on the first project, a social studies teacher on the third project, and an art teacher on the fifth project.

So, which project would I choose? It depends on the specific students, on what other projects they had done recently, on available materials and resources, how much time I have, if another teacher would work with me, what projects I think we'll be doing in upcoming units, and, quite frankly, what I feel like teaching. For the final unit flowchart I decided to have them do two projects: the group survey project and an individual multigenre research paper (Romano 2000).

The *Rash* Inquiry Unit

Figure 6.4 is the final flowchart for the unit with *Rash*. To simplify the flowchart, I didn't include most of the mini-lessons. Keep in mind this is a proposed unit for an imaginary class (it is much easier to teach imaginary students!). Needless to say, any unit we create would be for a very real class in a very real school, requiring us to design a unit for that specific context. (See Appendix I, also included on the companion Web site, stenhouse.com/caringhearts, for a blank flowchart.)

Let's unpack some of the parts of the flowchart. The fifteen boxes in Figure 6.4 represent a six-week unit, but every box does *not* represent one day. (This also applies to the unit flowcharts in Chapters 7–11.) The first five boxes before reading *Rash* each represent one day. That's the first five days—what many teachers refer to as the "before-reading" part of a literature unit. But once we begin the book, most of our time will be spent focusing on the book, with occasional side trips to other resources. The middle of the unit—what teachers refer to as the "during-reading" portion of a unit—would actually last at least two weeks for this novel.

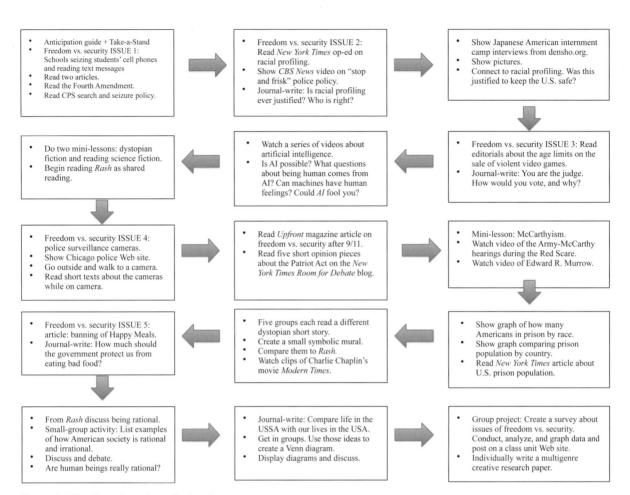

Figure 6.4 The flowchart of my *Rash* unit.

Some parts of the unit, such as a few during-reading activities, most of the journal writing, and our very important class discussions, are not included in the flowchart. The questions I wrote that are listed on the unit brainstorming page will give you an idea of the rich and thoughtful journal writing and discussions we would have. After we finished *Rash*, we would enter the "after-reading" part of the unit. My plan is that the unit would consist of about one week of before-reading activities, two weeks of during-reading activities, and three weeks of after-reading work (with that important wiggle room built in).

So, how did I put all of these ideas and resources together to create the final unit in Figure 6.4? I sat down with a blank flowchart and started filling in ideas. As I worked through this process, I would get more ideas and see how best to fit them together. I would scratch stuff out, move this resource here and that activity there, cut that article, add this video, and realize what specific resources I may still need to find. I would also look for potential problems in the unit and try to mix up the type of resources used, so students would not read short texts three or four days in a row but intersperse reading activities with nonwritten resources, such as videos or photographs. Other than reading the book, figuring out how to fit all of these pieces together is my favorite part of the unit design process. You will notice on the flowchart that, as I finalized the unit design, parts of my earlier thinking changed, including the first two days.

Teaching That Matters

It is June and the school year is ending, and you are probably torn with the conflicted emotions about your students leaving and your exhaustion from having endured ten months of school. You're eager for the year to end, but you are also letting go of another group of adolescents, many of whom have formed distinctive bonds with you. Some of these students (let's be honest) can't leave soon enough. But they have all been part of your classroom community, and breaking up a community is hard.

Let me refer to a point I made back in Chapter 1. As those students walk out of your classroom on the last day of school, how do you want them to be *different* from when they walked in on the first day of school? Beyond the typical school content, what are your hopes for how your students will have changed from your time together during the past 180 school days? Not just what do you want them to *know*, but how do you want them to *be*? How you answer that question should play a vital role in how and what you teach. It is stating your purposes and hopes for what school *could be*. For some teachers that will involve varying degrees of . . . shall we say . . . subversive teaching. We work in systems of schooling and paradigms of curriculum that are not kind to creative and critical teaching. It is our job as professional educators to figure out—even with all those hindrances and roadblocks and frustrations—how to make this magic happen with students.

Back in 1938 John Dewey wrote, "What avail is it to win prescribed amounts of information about geography and history, to win the ability to read and write, if in the process the individual loses his own soul?" (49). The same is true for teachers. Using literature and inquiry to teach for social responsibility is essential to cultivating the kind of thinkers and citizens and caring communities we need. But it is also a way for teachers to bring greater purpose and creativity to their work, own vital elements of their teaching, and allow them to hold on to their souls.

Chapter 7

Does Technology Always Make Life Better?

"How much is me?" Her lips tremble. Her eyes pool. Lily intervenes. "Ten percent. Ten percent of your brain. That's all they could save. They should have let you die."

—*The Adoration of Jenna Fox*

Have you surfed the Web today? Tweeted? Watched TV? Played Angry Birds?

American children spend more time with media than they do in school. The typical eight- to eighteen-year-old interacts with media more than seven and a half hours a day. If we account for media *multitasking*—combining activities such as surfing the Internet while listening to music—that number jumps to a staggering *eleven hours* of media content per day. Nearly half of our teens send text messages every day, an average of 118 texts—more than 40,000 a year, according to the Kaiser Family Foundation (Rideout, Foehr, and Roberts 2010). Seven and a half hours a day with media equals about *one-third of their lives*. As a teenage girl said in an interview on National Public Radio, "Technology is *everything*. What do you do in life that doesn't involve technology?"

According to the Kaiser report, every type of media usage by eight- to eighteen-year-olds increased between 1999 and 2009—except one. Which one? Reading. The well-known study by the National Endowment for the Arts, *To Read or Not to Read,* shows that reading for pleasure has declined as time online has increased (2007). Among the findings: less than one-third of thirteen-year-olds are daily readers.

Given the powerful role—both good and bad—that electronic media and technology play in our daily lives, media literacy is one of the greatest voids in our school curricula. The skills and habits of mind to *critique* media and technology are essential to living a socially responsible life, yet the typical student spends about zero time analyzing these influences.

How have these media changed us? How have they changed society? Is it all for the better? How would we spend our time if we did not have or if we reduced our use of this technology? It is questions like these that teachers and students must explore in school. Where else will young adults get this knowledge, the ability to question media and their own media use and to think critically about the roles and consequences of media and technology in their lives?

On one hand, media and technology have caused kids to spend more of their free time indoors. As one study succinctly puts it, "Fewer and fewer youth are heading outdoors each year. In recent decades—amidst changing technological and social landscapes—the American childhood has rapidly moved indoors, leading to epidemic levels of childhood obesity and inactivity" (Outdoor Foundation 2010). Richard Louv (2005) coined the phrase "nature-deficit disorder" to describe the lack of time children spend with nature, like hiking in the woods and canoeing. Louv quotes a fourth-grade boy who said, "I like to play indoors better, 'cause that's where all the electrical outlets are" (2005, 10).

On the other hand, digital technology has the power to propagate active citizenship and promote democracy in our own daily lives and around the world. It has made mountains of information, ideas, and differing opinions readily available at our fingertips. And we are witnesses to the power of this technology. The remarkable Arab Spring uprisings across the Middle East, starting in 2010, were largely fueled by social media. The peaceful revolution in Egypt, which resulted in the resignation of President Hosni Mubarak, began on Facebook. This was the world's first *Facebook revolution.* The political protests in Tunisia, Libya, Yemen, and Syria were in part planned and promoted through Twitter, Facebook, and text messaging, and YouTube helped spread the amazing images of the protests around the world. At the same time, those governments, quickly learning the power of social media, were blocking Web sites, shutting down the Internet, and using media to spread propaganda. This is the remarkable power—for both good and bad—that technology plays in our daily lives.

Examining Our Technological Lives

Helping children learn this media knowledge and these critical habits of mind gives them some of the new literacies they need to thrive in the twenty-first century. Rather than being passive consumers of media and technology and allowing it to overwhelm their lives, they become more critical and thoughtful and, we hope, live a healthier and more balanced life. These were the ideas that motivated Ron and I to engage his Chicago seventh graders in an exploration of technology, with an emphasis on media.

This particular unit was not intended to study the *content* of media, but to focus more on raising his students' consciousness about their own media use. We wanted them to consider how they spend their time, understand technology's influence, from the cell phones in our pockets to the nuclear missiles in our silos, and examine the ethical questions raised by this modern technology.

I suggested to Ron that we use the novel *The Adoration of Jenna Fox* by Mary Pearson (2008) for our unit. *Jenna Fox* examines the use and abuse of technology, the limits of science, and, more specifically, issues of bioethics. Themes of identity, moral decision making, parental love, and what makes us human are central to the story. We saw this book as a powerful opportunity (and a great read) to engage Ron's students in examining some profound ideas. Like *Rash,* this novel is an example of a "popular" book that we need to teach more often. Nearly all of Ron's kids *loved* this book. Figure 7.1 shows the flowchart for the unit. The citations for all the unit resources in Chapters 7–11 are included on this book's companion Web site, stenhouse.com/caringhearts, along with some of the activities from each chapter's flowchart that don't appear in the book.

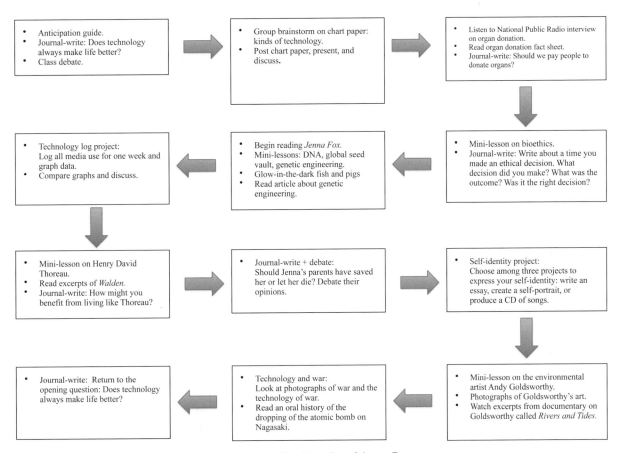

Figure 7.1 Our flowchart for the inquiry unit based on *The Adoration of Jenna Fox.*

The Adoration of Jenna Fox by Mary E. Pearson

Jenna Fox is science fiction and set in the future. Jenna is seventeen years old and wakes from a year-long coma, the result of a car accident. Much of her memory is gone. She does not recognize her parents or remember the accident. She says she does not "feel right" or know the meaning of simple words like *apple*. Her parents have given her a series of DVDs of her life so she can watch them to relearn her memories.

Whereas Jenna, her mom, and her grandmother have just moved and are living in a new house in California, Jenna's dad, a famous and rich physician, is living back home in Boston because of his work. We sense mystery and intrigue as Jenna slowly uncovers her past and unravels her present. We discover that after her car accident, Jenna was going to die. Her father had been working on a new technology, which was against the law to use, to save people by turning them into near robots. By replacing her bones and tissue with artificial materials and her blood with blue "Bio Gel," and literally backing up the undamaged 10 percent of her brain onto a computer, Jenna's dad saved her life. But did he? Is that person still Jenna? Or did he create a new Jenna? What makes us who we are?

A few other characters are key to the story. Jenna's grandmother, Lily, has an odd disdain for her granddaughter. (That's Lily talking to Jenna in the quote at the start of this chapter.) Lily was a doctor too, but she quit practicing because of her concerns about the lack of limits on science and technology. Lily believes society, doctors, and the government have allowed science to go too far, and the survival of her own granddaughter is a symbol of that excess. Another important character is Jenna's neighbor, Mr. Bender, an environmental artist.

OPENING ACTIVITY: Anticipation Guide

We began with the students' opinions. We asked the class to complete an anticipation guide that focused on technology, media, and bioethics, and connected specifically to *Jenna Fox*. Anticipation guides are useful because they give teachers a snapshot of their students' opinions, which in turn lead to good topics for discussions and journal writing.

Teaching Tip

Here are some tips for creating and using anticipation guides:

- To create an anticipation guide, brainstorm the related issues, topics, and questions of your unit and turn them into statements—sometimes *provocative* statements.
- Try to connect some of those issues to your students' lives today, helping to make some of your statements more relevant.
- Have students complete the guides at the start of the unit (or before you begin reading a book) so you get their "baseline" opinions.
- You can also ask students to complete the guide again at the end of the unit (or after they read the book) so they (and you) can see if their opinions have changed.
- Be sure to tell the students that these are not your opinions but are just statements for the purpose of discussion and reflection.
- Read through all the statements with the class first to make sure they understand them (but be careful not to bias their thinking).
- Use the completed guides to engage students in discussion and debate—exactly the habits of mind we want to cultivate for active citizenship.

JOURNAL-WRITE: Does Technology Always Make Life Better?

We wrote a question on the board: Does technology always make life better? This question would shape the entire unit, so we wanted to get the students' thoughts about it right from the start. What does technology mean to them? What role does technology play in their lives? Do they view any technology critically? Do they acknowledge that technology has negative, even deadly, consequences? By opening the unit with these inquiries, we were not only beginning with their ideas and opinions but also using the ensuing discussion to build background knowledge and engage the students in debate.

Most of the class believed that, yes, technology does always make life better. Some volunteers read their writing aloud. Here is part of what Vanessa shared:

Yes, technology always makes life better, because without it, it's like throwing half of your life away. That is because without technology we wouldn't have anything like machines that make the technology. And the food we eat is made from technology. Our phones, computers, televisions, and even hospitals, because they need machines to tell their heart rate, and without that the people would be dying.

Very few of the students wrote more nuanced and critical responses on the complexity of technology's role in our lives. But Crystal did:

It depends. Because of technology we are able to have medicine and able to take care of sick people. Technology also has entertainment, such as TV. It also helps us work on stuff & helps us communicate with the world. But technology also throws us off important things we need to do. Such as the Internet. There is so much that you can do that you forget something else that you really need to do. Technology is like an obsession. We concentrate on it more than we do other things that need to get done. This is a debate. It's not an obvious question. There are electronics that are useful to us, but it can also throw us off.

Teaching Tip

Teachers know the divergent thinkers in their classroom. As soon as I heard Crystal read her writing on our first day, I knew she was going to be someone who would bring unique and critical perspectives to the unit. I don't think we should hesitate to take advantage of such thinking. Of course, we don't want to overemphasize one student's opinions or suggest that her ideas are more important than anyone else's thoughts. But if we want to make multiple perspectives, idiosyncratic opinions, and critical ideas an important part of the classroom, we should openly encourage this divergent thinking. It has the added benefit of honoring those students and their often minority and "unusual" perspectives. As teachers we should also recognize that students have important and valuable ideas that we may not have considered. No longer are just the teacher and the textbook the authority on knowledge; we are all thinkers and contributors.

Our Discussion Continues

When Jaime read his writing to the class, he opened the door to a lively discussion: "No, I don't think it does make your life better. . . . It does not make your life better if you just sit there all day using the computer instead of playing in the park or outside in your front yard." We used this insight to offer a different perspective, that although technology entertains us and commands our attention, it also distracts us from other things. Jaime considered it vital that we get outside and be active and social, and technology can keep us from doing that.

Vanessa took issue with this view. Her concern had to do with safety. She said that in the previous week forty-one people in Chicago had been shot (four of them died) in a fifty-hour period. Ron affirmed her point, saying they had discussed the shootings in class. Vanessa said that her mother wouldn't let her go outside, which is common in urban America. If the choice is between going outside and possibly getting killed or staying in and playing video games or texting your friends, she said, technology will win.

While acknowledging the reality of the violence, we asked the students if their only alternative to going outside was staying inside and texting or using any media. Crystal shook her head emphatically. "No, it's not the only option." But Vanessa replied, "What else is there to do but text message?" Elizabeth saw the violence as an excuse. She added, "You don't need to go to the park. You can go out on your porch. You can still get outside."

I asked the class if they had ever heard of the phrase *spiritual death.*

No one said anything.

"I don't mean 'spiritual' in a religious sense," I said.

"You mean *inside* you?" a boy asked.

"Well . . . that maybe we're not getting physically hurt by staying inside so much and 'obsessing with media,' as Crystal wrote, but that we're suffering a spiritual death, yes, inside us. We spend so much time with all of this technology and media, but is it really making us happy? Is it fulfilling our lives?"

The room was silent. The kids were clearly thinking.

Nathan brought our talk to a close by connecting this insight to his life. "My mom was just told she has cancer," he said. "She has to have an operation. We do need to get outside. We can't stay inside all the time." Seeing his mom so ill made him consider how we spend our time and what's really important in life.

ACTIVITY: Group Brainstorming: Kinds of Technology

Ron and I wanted to know how his students defined *technology* so we could incorporate those ideas into our discussions. Although most of the unit was going to focus on electronic media, we wanted the students to understand that technology does not necessarily require electricity. As my friend Chuck Cole (a former science teacher) reminded me, a pencil is a form of technology. Simple machines, such as ramps and levers, are technology. So are submarines and fighter jets. Working in groups of four, the students brainstormed types of technology and listed them on chart paper. Altogether they compiled more than sixty examples, including guns, nuclear bombs, toilets, hairspray, and solar panels.

We posted all their chart papers, let each group talk, and then discussed examples of technology that were not on their list, such as ramps and wheels that helped build early civilizations. This activity also enabled us to discuss *many* forms of technology—from toilets to bombs to iPods—and further build students' background knowledge. And it situated all of this technology back in the journal prompt they had just written about and discussed. Does everything on these lists always make life better?

RADIO REPORT: National Public Radio Interview
SHORT INTERNET TEXT: Organ Donation Fact Sheet
QUICK-WRITE: Should We Pay People to Donate Organs?

We wrote two words on the board: *biology* and *ethics*. What do they mean? The kids offered a few ideas, and then we added a plus sign between them: BIOLOGY + ETHICS = ? We settled on this: "Making decisions about what is right and wrong about living things." That's how we introduced *bioethics*. Not surprisingly, this was entirely new information to Ron's students, as was the term *ethics*. I'm certain most of them had considered ethical issues in their lives but not in an explicit and conscious way.

One of the statements on the anticipation guide was, "People should get paid to donate organs." United States law does not allow people to be paid for organ donation. We used this as an example of bioethics. We passed out and read an organ donation "fact sheet" from the "Donate Life America" Web site (donatelife.net). We read some of the facts, including that every eleven minutes a person is added to the organ transplant waiting list and that each day an average of eighteen people die from the lack of available organs. So, we asked the class, "What should we do? People are dying. What's the ethical decision?"

After some discussion, we played an interview from the NPR news program *All Things Considered* on the lack of transplant organs in the United States. The program interviewed a doctor on ways to increase organ donation, including paying people to donate. He disagreed with this approach, saying it would result in "rich people living off the bodies of poor people." We discussed organ donation to build a bit of background knowledge and see if any of the students had a personal connection to it. We had the class do a quick-write on their opinions regarding paying people to donate organs and then had a lively debate. Interestingly, a few students who argued that it was right to pay people for organs used poverty to *support* their position. Whereas the doctor saw this as exploitation, they saw it as *economic opportunity*.

MINI-LESSONS: DNA, Genetic Engineering, and the Global Seed Vault
INTERNET VIDEO AND PHOTOGRAPHS: Glow-in-the-Dark Fish and
Glow-in-the-Dark Pigs
MAGAZINE ARTICLE: "Techno Food"

We started reading *The Adoration of Jenna Fox* as shared reading. Ron and I switched off reading aloud as the kids followed along. (Later in the unit, once we got into the story, they took the book home some days to read assigned pages.) Lily, Jenna's grandmother, says this sentence to Jenna early in the book: "Sometimes we just don't know when we've gone too far." Pages 36–38 in the book are vital to framing the bioethical themes of the story. These topics are specifically raised or alluded to in these pages:

- DNA
- government regulation of science
- genetic engineering
- cross-pollination
- epidemics
- overuse of antibiotics
- seed preservation
- limits on science and technology

We also learn (in part through inference, which requires more background knowledge) that Lily has serious ethical problems with what science has been doing in the name of "progress." Lily thinks there should be limits—including laws and government regulation—on the development of technology. This was a key idea we wanted the kids to explore. Technology has made our lives easier and brings us endless enjoyment, but we also pay a price for that—individually, socially, psychologically, and environmentally.

By taking the time to frame these issues and why they're controversial, we used the book to encourage students to question and critique media and technology in their own lives. We were also using the novel to build their science background knowledge. Helping the kids understand these ideas was no easy task. (In an ideal school world, I would teach this as an interdisciplinary unit with a science teacher.) We used a series of short readings and mini-lessons, including showing the class a diagram of DNA with a double helix molecule and then a diagram showing how scientists genetically engineer plants. (All of these are easy to find online. Search the phrase and click on images.)

Then we showed a video about zebra fish, a common pet in tropical aquariums (glofish.com). These fish had been genetically engineered to glow in the dark as a "product" to sell. The students were enthralled as they watched the small fish in iridescent orange, red, and green swim back and forth with the sounds of ethereal music playing through the classroom. We explained that these fish do not exist in nature, that people *created* them by injecting genes from sea coral into the eggs of zebra fish. The kids thought these fish were very cool.

Next up were glow-in-the-dark pigs. We projected a news article with pictures of iridescent green pigs genetically engineered by scientists in Taiwan (Hogg 2006). The classroom filled with sounds of disbelief and awe, and some hoots and hollers. The students asked rapid-fire questions: Why did they do this? How did they do this? Can they actually see a glow-in-the-dark pig somewhere? We read portions of the article right off the screen. Scientists said that the genetic engineering would help with their stem cell research. If they inject the pig's stem cells into another animal, they can easily track their development because a protein in their cells will glow green. We explained that the scientists had added genetic material from jellyfish to pig embryos and then implanted the embryos into sows. When the pigs were born, they were green—and when those pigs mated, their offspring were green too!

Ron and I posed a question to the class: "We have glow-in-the-dark fish and pigs. What if parents could choose to have a glow-in-the-dark child? Should they be allowed to have that option?" The room erupted! Nearly everyone thought parents should *not* have that option. Destiny said, "No, they shouldn't be allowed to do that because it's too freaky!" But Anthony disagreed: "If they want that, why not?"

We asked, "What about glow-in-the-dark dogs? Should that be allowed?" Whereas the previous question had caused an uproar, this query resulted in near pandemonium. The students loved the idea! Soco said that she would no longer step on her dog during the night. We asked how many would want a glow-in-the-dark dog, and half the class raised their hands. Genetically engineering dogs to glow in the dark was okay, but creating glowing people crossed the line. Without knowing it, the students were engaging in a bioethical debate. They were taking ethical stances, exploring real social and moral dilemmas, looking beyond prurient and entertainment interests to consider the value and consequences of scientific advancements. Suddenly the futuristic fiction of *Jenna Fox* leaped off the pages of a novel and into this Chicago classroom.

PROJECT: Technology Logs
MINI-LESSONS: Analyzing and Graphing Data

Imagine if you had to log all of the electronic media you used in one week. What would your media log look like? How much time would you have for watching TV? Bouncing around online? Listening to music? Talking on the phone? E-mailing? Texting? Tweeting? What would it all add up to? What if you multiplied the weekly log results by fifty-two to get your total for a year?

For one week, Ron's students tracked all of their electronic media use. We created technology logs to make their data collection easier. The following week, after their technology logs had been completed, students graphed their data. We went low-tech and had the students draw their graphs by hand. (Sometimes it's best to skip the computer and have students create work with their own hands. It teaches them craftsmanship.) We wanted accurate graphs, drawn well, so we did a few math mini-lessons and passed out custom-designed tally sheets, showing the students how to convert their data into total minutes for each type of media. We also passed out calculators. Ron was able to devote three class periods to this process (more than an hour for each class) so we could walk around and help students, ensuring their math was accurate and their work was high quality. I loved that Ron's kids were doing math in reading class, showing the true integrative nature of inquiry-based teaching. Figure 7.2 shows Heidi's graph.

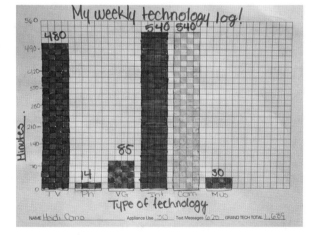

Figure 7.2 Heidi's graph of her week with electronic media.

Overall the graphs certainly showed us the media-saturated lives of seventh graders, yet the results also broke some adolescent stereotypes. Benjamin showed that he's not much of a television watcher, but he loves music and remains plugged in to tunes for hours a day. I loved that he included photography, a media category that no one else in the class had considered. Ben told me he loved to take pictures, so he included that in his data collection and on his graph. Some students, like Ben, didn't have a cell phone and didn't seem to care. Heidi, on the other hand, isn't much into music, but spends her media time watching TV, on the Internet, and using a computer. On her data sheet Heidi also reported sending 625 text messages, which supports the research showing that one-third of American teens send more than 100 text messages a day.

Teaching Tip

Educator Ron Berger, who taught fifth grade for many years, is a nationally known advocate of project-based teaching and having students create what he likes to call "work of excellence." We need to cultivate and *teach* this culture of craftsmanship in our classrooms. Berger writes:

When my class begins a new project, a new venture, we begin with a taste of excellence. I pull out models of work by former students, a videotape of former students presenting their work, models of work from other schools, and models of work from the professional world. We sit and we admire. We critique and discuss what makes the work powerful: what makes a piece of creative writing compelling and exciting, what makes a scientific or historical research project significant and stirring; what makes a novel mathematical solution so breath-taking. (2003, 31)

New Resources

In Chapter 3, I wrote about the fantastic Web site TED.org, which includes short lectures on a wide array of topics. TED talks are deeply intellectual and absolutely fascinating. For example, Dr. Dimitri Christakis, a pediatrician who does research on young children and media, describes how the *kind* of media children interact with from birth to three years old has lasting effects on their brain development, especially on their ability to focus and pay attention. Slow-paced and more realistic media, such as *Mr. Rogers*, is beneficial, whereas fast-paced and less realistic media, such as the *Powerpuff Girls*, literally builds a brain that expects that unreal, fast-paced world. By watching this presentation, middle schoolers could see that their interactions with media can have very real consequences. (See the video at tedxtalks.ted.com/video/TEDxRainier-Dimitri-Christakis.)

For another perspective, we could show a TED video by celebrated online game designer Jane McGonigal. She says that 3 billion hours of online video games people play each week is not nearly enough. That's right. *Not enough*! Why? McGonigal argues that online gaming has the power to create a better world by encouraging people to work together to solve problems. You can read about this in her book, *Reality Is Broken* (2011). Her video is here: ted.com/talks/jane_mcgonigal_gaming_can_make_a_better_world.html.

MINI-LESSON: Henry David Thoreau and *Walden*
BOOK EXCERPT: *Walden*
JOURNAL-WRITE: Living Like Thoreau

On page 65 of the novel, Jenna persuades her parents to let her attend a very small high school with an environmental curriculum. When Jenna joins the class, the students are reading Henry David Thoreau's classic, *Walden*. When Thoreau went to live at Walden Pond for two years in 1853, he was (in part) removing himself from "modern" life and immersing himself in a simple life filled with the natural world. As he famously wrote:

> I went to the woods because I wished to live deliberately, to front only the essential facts of life, and see if I could not learn what it had to teach, and not, when I came to die, discover that I had not lived. I did not wish to live what was not life, living is so dear; nor did I wish to practise [*sic*] resignation, unless it was quite necessary. I wanted to live deep and suck out all the marrow of life, to live so sturdily and Spartan-like as to put to rout all that was not life, to cut a broad swath and shave close, to drive life into a corner, and reduce it to its lowest terms, and, if it proved to be mean, why then to get the whole and genuine meanness of it, and publish its meanness to the world; or if it were sublime, to know it by experience, and be able to give a true account of it in my next excursion. (85)

Giving the school an environmental focus with Jenna and her classmates reading *Walden* was certainly no frivolous decision on the part of the author, Mary Pearson. This is good writing; it is a thematic contrast to the technology that saved Jenna.

We made *Walden* packets for the class with a portrait of Thoreau on the cover, photos of Walden Pond taken around 1900, a picture of a replica of Thoreau's cabin (just 10 feet by 12 feet), and five excerpts from the book, including the text above. I did a mini-lesson about Thoreau and the writing of *Walden*, showing students a copy of the book. To deepen their understanding of the historical and technological contexts, I drew a timeline on the board, with the American Revolution on the left end. As a class, we added some major historical events (the Civil War, World War II and the Holocaust, the Vietnam War, and so on), and then added the dates of some major technological breakthroughs the kids could relate to (the lightbulb, the telephone, the TV). Then I added *Walden* at 1853 so the students could understand that the "modern" society Thoreau was attempting to get away from was not modern at all by today's standards. We wanted to make sure the class understood that when Thoreau went to Walden Pond, he could not watch cable TV or play video games. After reading the quote above, we read this excerpt:

> This is a delicious evening, when the whole body is one sense, and imbibes delight through every pore. I go and come with a strange liberty in Nature, a part of herself. As I walk along the stony shore of the pond in my shirt sleeves, though it is cool as well as cloudy and windy, and I see nothing special to attract me, all the elements are unusually congenial to me. The bullfrogs trump to usher in the night, and the note of the whippoorwill is borne on the rippling wind from over the water. Sympathy with the fluttering alder and poplar leaves almost takes away my breath; yet, like the lake, my serenity is rippled but not ruffled. (122)

I chose this passage for three reasons: it's beautifully written, shows Thoreau's tender love for nature, and represents the opposite of how so many people, especially in urban settings, fail to appreciate the quiet natural world around them. This excerpt—which comes from his chapter titled "Solitude"—stands as a great contrast to our loud, flashy, media-saturated lives. We read aloud a few more similar excerpts, briefly discussing each one.

I wish I could share that reading *Walden* transformed these kids into Thoreau-maniacs, got them singing the wonders of nature, and redefined for them what truly matters most in life. The truth is they didn't have much to say in response. I think reading Thoreau was not much different from reading a text in Chinese. But rather than a different language, it was a different *reality*.

Just because the kids did not have much to say verbally, we did not assume they would have little to say in writing. We asked Ron's students to write in their journals about the ideas in *Walden*, connecting them to their lives that are so entwined with modern technology. Here was the prompt we gave them:

Imagine, like Henry David Thoreau, that you decided to live in the woods, near a large pond for a year. You would not have any electronic technology, such as TV, video games, phones, music, or computers. How might you benefit from this experience?

Destiny's response to the entire class was immediate and loud: "I would *die*!" Chatter ran through the room like a tidal wave. We expected this response. Most of the kids understandably felt this was an impossible situation, something they could not imagine. Ron and I explained that we understood that they would miss the technology. I said, "I'd miss some of it myself. But that doesn't mean we wouldn't *benefit* from the experience." That was their challenge: to step outside life today and consider how they might benefit from living in the woods without modern electronic technology.

Much of their writing was rather insightful, going beyond Ron's expectations. While they were writing, and some kids were reading each other's papers, Ron whispered to me, "They're sharing their writing. That's great. They usually don't do that."

Jimmy, who did little work in school, was often in trouble, and had a behavior modification sheet that traveled with him from class to class, took his thinking to previously unseen places. We lavished Jimmy with some well-deserved praise, urging him to read his writing to the class:

Some ways this will benefit me are that I could experience new things. The stuff that I could benefit from are exploring the woods, fishing, hunting, swimming. Also, I would see how life could feel being away from technology and friends. I could also learn how to survive on my own. Because there's not always going to be someone there in life to help you out. Another way I will benefit from living in the forest is to see animals that I haven't seen in person before. Also, I could probably start a journal so I could show and tell people how it feels to live in the woods with no stress or technology. Another thing is that since I don't have nothing to do I could make something to do. I could walk around and get some fresh air. I could see how the environment is like. I could get away from the drama and dumbness that people are doing these days. I could focus on new art instead of just graffiti, and maybe I could put the two kinds of art together. Also, it could change the way I act when I return home.

ACTIVITY AND PROJECT: Who Am I?
ART: Self-Portraits
ESSAY: "Tiffany" from *Sugar in the Raw*

Self-identity is a major theme in the lives of adolescents and young adults. Pulled in multiple directions to shape who they are—friends, family, media, and school—adolescents can seemingly change their identities from moment to moment. They are on a quest to answer the question, Who am I? On page 29 of the novel, Jenna also implores, "Tell me who I am." Ron and I knew *Jenna Fox* could be a powerful lens through which his students could explore how they see themselves. Admittedly, this was an entirely separate exploration from using the book to inquire into media and technology. But after weeks of reading, writing, and discussing media, we saw it as a welcome tangent.

We had planted a seed about self-identity in our earlier reading of the book. Throughout the novel, there are definitions of words vital to Jenna's life: *hate*, *empty*, *human*, and *identity*. The meaning of these simple words has been lost to Jenna because of her accident. On page 212, she offers a definition of herself:

Jenna *n.* 1. Coward. 2. Possible human. 3. Maybe not. 4. Definitely illegal.

To examine this passage in more depth, we had Ron's students write definitions of themselves. Here are some they shared:

Christian *pn.* 1. Angry: short temper; quiet about anger. 2. Lazy: won't work hard; don't like challenges. 3. Funny: humorous; loves laughing.

Crystal *pn.* 1. Quick temper: stressed; can't control anger. 2. Anti-social: doesn't like to talk much; likes to be alone at times; doesn't connect with family much. 3. Creative: imagines weird things; creative ideas; draws out emotions. 4. Understanding: knows what it's like; understanding of life; knows how people feel.

Toward the end of the unit, we wanted the students to create something to express their self-identity. We gave students some choice in what they created, including options for art and music. Almost all of the kids chose to use the art option. Figure 7.3 is the assignment sheet we gave to the class. I am a very big believer in giving students—and going over with students—project assignment

Who am I?

The Adoration of Jenna Fox

Who are you? Jenna Fox repeatedly asks herself who she is. On p. 29 she says, "Tell me who I am." We want you to tell us who you are. None of us are simple people; we are complex human beings with identities made up of many ideas, interests, joys, tragedies, images, quotes, people, experiences, good habits, bad habits, cultures, and, of course, our own unique DNA. Others—friends and family and teachers—try to define us, and sometimes they understand us, they get to know who we really are, and they honor our unique being. But other times, they don't understand who we are and what makes us tick and what we think about and feel and worry over, our dreams, and how we see the world and the questions that fill our minds and the passions that pack our hearts. Consider what it took for Jenna to know herself. Use this project as a way for you to inquire about—or ask questions and explore—who you are.

So, tell us who you are.

Create something that explains your complex identity.

You have three ways to do this. Choose the one that will allow you to communicate the best:

1. Create a self-portrait drawing, collage, and/or photography with words, images, pictures, and symbols. You can use a simple silhouette or draw a more detailed picture or use a digital camera. But your self-portrait must also contain essential words, images, quotes, and so on that show what defines you. How you do this is up to you.

2. Create a song list of songs that define your unique identity. Then burn a CD of the songs. Give your CD a title—something that further explains who you are. Include a song list with a sentence or two about why you chose each song. And design a cover for your CD that fits in your CD's plastic case.

3. Tell us who you are in writing. Make it interesting writing. Make it exciting. Make the words leap off the page. Be inventive and creative and highly thoughtful.

Whichever of these three options you choose, take this seriously, be courageous enough to look at yourself honestly, be bold enough to create something exciting, and care enough to produce work that is high quality. *This is due Friday, June 4.*

Figure 7.3 "Who am I?" project assignment sheet.

sheets. These can motivate the kids, explicitly state the requirements and expectations, and include due dates.

To help students create more interesting, detailed, and thoughtful self-portraits—again, to help them produce those "works of excellence" that Ron Berger (2003) writes about—we created a slide show of self-portraits we collected from the Internet to use as models of quality and diverse imagery. Our sampling included dozens of examples by children, teens, adults, and famous artists such as Frida Kahlo, Vincent van Gogh, and Pablo Picasso. We told students to "fill the page" using a variety of media—painting, drawing, photography, collage, mixed media—and to integrate images and text.

Crystal, who loves to "draw out emotions," as she explained in the definition she wrote for herself, used manga (Japanese stylistic comics) to create her self-portrait. We could see in her self-portrait the "stressed" and "angry" and very thoughtful parts of her written definition. Her self-portrait reads (in part), "Laughter can be a mash of sadness" and "Sometimes my choices come by so fast I can't keep up" and "Madness can take its toll & sometimes it's hard to contain." (See Figure 7.4.)

For the music option, students were to cut a CD of songs that defined their identity and then write brief liner notes that explained what each song says said about who they are.

Figure 7.4 Crystal's self-portrait for *The Adoration of Jenna Fox* unit.

MINI-LESSON AND ART: Environmental Artist Andy Goldsworthy
DOCUMENTARY FILM: Rivers and Tides

Mr. Bender, Jenna Fox's neighbor, is an environmental artist, creating art from (and in) nature. He serves as a modern-day Thoreau in the story. He even has a pond in his backyard! (Remember, Jenna was reading *Walden* in school.) When we pointed this out to the class, they were amazed at how all of the pieces of the story came together thematically.

I did a mini-lesson on Andy Goldsworthy, perhaps the world's most famous environmental artist. I collected dozens of photos of his breathtaking art from online and showed them to the class. Next we played a YouTube segment from a documentary about Goldsworthy called *Rivers and Tides*

(Riedelsheimer 2004). This segment showed him making his art using only natural materials, discussing his relationship with nature, and talking about what drives his passion. All of this was new to Ron's students. They had never imagined anyone could do this. Our hope was to extend this into a project where each student would take a week to plan and create his or her own piece of environmental art on the school grounds, but unfortunately we ran out of time. Of all the units I worked on in this book, this was my biggest disappointment, but I take solace in knowing that these kids have discovered environmental art and heard a bit of wisdom from Andy Goldsworthy.

PHOTOGRAPHS: Technology and War
ORAL HISTORY: "A Survivor's Tale"

We projected a big picture on the screen: an American fighter jet in flight, armed with missiles and bombs, coming straight at the class. It seemed about to fly through the screen. (I found the picture on the Internet.) We did not want to end the unit without having the students consider one more type of technology: war. We had just one day to wrap up the unit. Needless to say, we certainly could not do justice to the topic of war with a single class session, but one day was better than zero days.

We returned to the question we had asked on the first day of the unit: "Does technology always make life better?" We had spent so much time reflecting on issues of bioethics and media that we were fairly certain the students were not thinking about war and weapons as technology. Returning to the examples of technology the students had listed during our initial brainstorming session, we found only five references to war-related technology.

We wanted to show that the technology of war has consequences and requires responsibility, moral decision making, and active involvement in our daily democracy. The United States has the most powerful military on Earth. What are ethical ways to use that technology? As we push into the twenty-first century, technology is taking us down entirely new military paths. For example, there is a deep political and moral debate about the nation's use of pilotless drone military and surveillance aircraft. There are many short texts and videos online about this debate that we can use with middle schoolers. After the fighter jet we showed students more photos:

- The bombs dropped on Hiroshima and Nagasaki: Little Man and Fat Boy
- The destruction of Hiroshima and Nagasaki after the bombs were dropped
- Mushroom clouds of atomic bomb tests
- Destruction and missile launches from recent wars, including those in Iraq and Afghanistan
- Nuclear submarines

Next, we read and discussed a short oral history from a survivor of the atomic bomb on Nagasaki. The piece is in the young adult anthology *War Is . . . Soldiers, Survivors, and Storytellers Talk About War* (Aronson and Campbell 2008). "A Survivor's Tale" was written by Fumika Miura and included this:

August ninth approaches, and I am reminded again of the atomic bombing of Nagasaki fifty-seven years ago, when I was a sixteen-year-old schoolgirl. I'm seventy-three now, and even now I seem to hear screams for help. That one plutonium bomb killed 74,000 people and heavily injured 75,000. It had the explosive power of 21,000 tons of TNT, and the temperature of the ground at the hypocenter rose in a flash to 3,000 to 4,000 degrees. Almost everyone within four kilometers of the explosion was burned and killed, or received external injuries. (148)

We were able to discuss this text only briefly because that was all the time we had. Our unit had to end.

JOURNAL-WRITE: Does Technology Always Make Life Better?

Two weeks later, I came back to Ron's classroom to have his students revisit our original question. We gave them a writing prompt, but we called it a quick-write because it was the last day of school. Here was the prompt:

Look back over our entire unit on technology, media, and science and The Adoration of Jenna Fox. *Think about the topics and questions we've explored and debated. Now, go back and look at the original question: Does technology always make life better? How would you answer this question now?*

None of the students showed vast transformations in their thinking about technology, but we were not expecting that. We wanted the unit to open their minds a bit to consider technology from more critical perspectives. Clearly, the kids saw a new *complexity* to technology. And they realized that for all of the good technology does, it has negative consequences too. At the start of the unit, Heidi had rated the anticipation-guide statement "Technology always makes life better," with a nine; she "strongly agreed" with that statement. In her journal response to this question on the first day of the unit, she wrote just four sentences:

Yes, it does. For example, when you have a project you could research information on the computer. Also, phones let you communicate with people in case of an emergency. They make life way easier.

On the last day of the unit, she lowered her anticipation-guide rating to a seven and wrote this:

Technology doesn't always make life better. Sometimes technology is really bad and has a lot of consequences. Technology is not always good. For example, in war it could cause death. In The Adoration of Jenna Fox *technology ruined her life. It made her less human. Technology can ruin lives and families. Too much technology can become dangerous, just like the atomic bomb. There has to be a limit on technology. There can't be too many deaths, injuries, and families getting apart because of new things they build with technology. That's why technology is not always good. It doesn't always make life better.*

Technology, Media, and Democracy

Historians say that a turning point in the 1960 presidential election came during a debate between Richard Nixon and John F. Kennedy. During the debate, Nixon looked unkempt and sick. His beard stubble, or "five o'clock shadow," made him look even worse. In the past, this would not have made any difference at all. But this debate was different; it was our country's first televised presidential debate (and, remember, on black-and-white TV). Before this, people had listened to the debates on the radio. They couldn't see anything. Now they did. Compared with Nixon, Kennedy looked pristine. Most people who watched the debate on TV said Kennedy had won; most people who listened on the radio gave the win to Nixon. (You can watch the debates on YouTube, yet another great real-world resource we could have used with Ron's students as an example of how technology and media influence society and politics.)

Let's compare that incident with the 2008 and 2012 presidential elections. During the 2007 primary elections, both the Democrats and the Republicans participated in CNN-YouTube Debates, taking questions from people via YouTube. Many believe the Obama campaign's social media savvy helped him win the election. After he was elected, he was called the "YouTube President" (Vargas 2008). In 2012, President Obama conducted a Google+ "Hangout" where he answered questions from among 130,000 submitted electronically. Consider this remarkable contrast to Richard Nixon's 1960 black-and-white stubble: according to a 2011 study, "94 percent of social media users of voting age engaged by a political message watched the entire message, and 39 percent of these people went on to share it with an average of 130 friends online" (Samit 2011).

Technology and media have not just shaped a new American society but also created a new American democracy. For students to be critically engaged participants in that democracy, they must be far more than expert users of digital media. They must have the skills to critique that media and understand how media can control and shape information. They also need the wisdom to know that sometimes the best thing to do is to take a respite and turn off their devices. Twenty-first-century democracy does not just need media-smart citizens; it also needs well-balanced people who unplug themselves, spend time outside with nature, take the time to read a good book, and engage in conversations with real people.

Why Should I Care About the Environment?

People in Ember rarely threw anything away.
They made the best possible use of what they had.

—*The City of Ember*

David Carroll, a nature writer and artist, grew up fascinated by the natural world and by turtles in particular. His memoir of living amid the wetlands of rural Pennsylvania is called *Self-Portrait with Turtles*. Carroll writes of his regular sojourns as a child into the wild, wading through swamps and streams, to observe the astonishing life around him:

> The sheer joy of being there, of simply bearing witness, continued to be paramount. I went out neither to heal my heartbreak nor to celebrate my happiness, but to be in nature and outside myself. Turtles, spotted turtles most significantly, were a living text moving upon an endless turning of the pages of the natural world. (2004, 27)

Carroll's writing breathes with the beauty and vitality of life on Earth. Reading his book, I'm reminded of the inherent wonder and curiosity children have about the world around them, and the fascination that people—including adults—have with nature. I live across the street from a park with a small lagoon, and every day in the spring and summer, adults stand and sit near the water, watching the ducks, geese, fish, and turtles. People are especially excited when our neighborhood blue heron pays us a visit, and it seems that the adults are more captivated than their kids. I like to sit on a bench at the lagoon and read. When that lovely heron is there, standing stone still in the water, looking for a fish to gulp, I find it difficult to focus on the words in my book.

Thomas Friedman, *New York Times* columnist and Nobel Laureate in economics, has argued passionately for the United States to embark on a "green revolution." He wants our nation to *lead the world* in living green. It is fair to say that Friedman's argument has more to do with ending our country's reliance on foreign oil and growing a world-leading economy than with saving the planet. However, in his book *Hot, Flat, and Crowded,* he writes:

> But at some point we also need to get beyond these economic and even practical arguments and get back in touch with the deepest truth of all: Green is a value that needs to be preserved in and of itself, not because it is going to make your bank account richer but because it makes life richer and always has. An ethic of conservation . . . declares that maintaining our natural world is a value that is impossible to quantify but also impossible to ignore, because of the sheer beauty, wonder, joy and magic that nature brings to being alive. (2008, 314)

That's how I feel when I watch the blue heron. Like David Carroll and Thomas Friedman, I'm in awe of this planet, and I believe that school must play a vital role in cultivating Americans to be caretakers of Earth and all its living things.

With global warming, the destruction of rain forests, human-caused extinction of plants and animals, "dead zones" in the oceans, and industrialized farming, we're seeing the everyday consequences of perpetuating environmental ignorance and apathy. Our country has just 5 percent of the world population, but we use a third of the global resources and cause a third of our planet's pollution. Edward O. Wilson, the famed Harvard biologist, writes, "For every person in the world to reach present U.S. levels of consumption with existing technology, would require four more planet Earths" (2002, 27).

How long can this continue? Until our schools make environmental literacy an official priority, it's up to teachers to make this knowledge and these ecological habits of mind a vital part of their students' education. And let's face it, as adults we're behind the game. Many of our students are far more environmentally conscious than we are. That awareness may not translate into turning off their bedroom lights or the bathroom faucet when they brush their teeth or even reducing the amount of stuff they buy, but they were born into a world infinitely more conscious of caring for the planet than we were. Adolescents are ready, willing, and interested in exploring the environment in school.

With this thinking in mind, I suggested to Leslie Rector that we design an inquiry unit for her sixth graders focusing on environmental literacy. I had known Leslie for about six years, ever since she was one of my graduate students. Leslie teaches in a Chicago public school where most of her students come from lower-income Mexican American families. We decided to use *The City of Ember,* a dystopian novel by Jeanne DuPrau. Because Leslie had a self-contained classroom and the freedom to schedule her day, we were able to teach the unit during a liberating one- and even two-hour block of time. Figure 8.1 shows the flowchart for our unit.

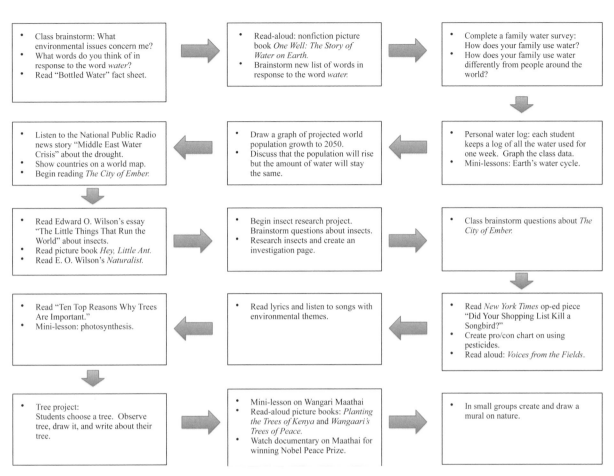

Figure 8.1 Flowchart for the unit with *The City of Ember*.

The City of Ember by Jeanne DuPrau

Set in the future, *The City of Ember* takes place in an underground civilization. Two hundred and forty years before, people were sent underground with instructions for when and how to reemerge. Through the generations of life in Ember, those instructions, and all past history, has been lost. The people of Ember have no idea a world exists above ground.

Ember is dying. The city, with about 400 people, is powered by a giant generator that continually breaks down, thrusting the entire city into blackness. The generator is powered by the rush of an underground river that flows into a dark void. Without flashlights, fire, or a boat, few people have dared to follow the river to see where it leads.

Two young adolescents, Lina and Doon, believe there is a way out of Ember and that they must escape Ember to survive. Lina and Doon are different people who complement each other. Lina is the artist and Doon the scientist, yet both of them are also explorers.

The City of Ember is a powerful allegory for life on Earth. Just as the generator is breaking down, parts of Earth and its ecosystems are suffering and damaged. And just like our own planet, Ember has limited resources.

Embracing the Natural World

If I were the king of school, I would make sure that some of the learning for environmental literacy was done outdoors. There are schools around the country that are making this authentic experiential learning an important part of their curriculum (Broda 2011; Sobel 2008; Stone 2009). According to the National Wildlife Federation, a typical American child spends just *four to seven minutes a day* in unstructured outdoor play (2011). With recess becoming extinct, neighborhood parks often empty, and with kids indoors with electronic media or with their friends at the mall, schools have an urgent responsibility to get students outside to experience the natural world. Many children go through life never paddling a kayak or climbing a giant sand dune or swimming in a lake.

As a teacher, my best field trip was to see the sunrise. A hundred of us arrived at school at six o'clock on a chilly morning and walked twenty minutes to a Lake Michigan beach. It was exhilarating to be there when the excited screams of children seemingly lifted the sun over the horizon.

Unfortunately, the environmental unit based on *The City of Ember* started in the middle of a Chicago winter, and Leslie's administration was not too keen on letting us outdoors. We wanted to be realistic, so we decided to use the seven-week unit primarily to raise her students' awareness of the natural world around them. Living in Chicago we see far more cars and concrete than turtles and blue herons. It's easy for people in urban America—kids and adults—to take the natural world for granted and miss the more hidden, yet very vibrant, nature around them.

Any child who has turned over a big rock on top of some dirt knows the remarkable ecosystems that lie just beneath our feet but often out of sight. We hoped this unit could encourage Leslie's students to consider what they can do, even in small ways, to care for the natural world. We framed the unit with three very common elements of nature that every kid sees nearly every day: water, trees, and insects. Through that lens, we would explore the question, Why should I care about the environment?

Opening Discussion

We began with a question: What environmental issues and problems concern me? We were gathered on the large rug and Leslie sat next to her chart paper easel with the question written on top. As the students called out their concerns, she jotted them down:

- ♦ Oceans would dry out
- ♦ We'd have no water
- ♦ Pollution
- ♦ Pollution would kill the plants = no plants = no humans
- ♦ Black Earth with no electricity
- ♦ Floods
- ♦ Earthquakes and other natural disasters = loss of life and property damage
- ♦ No food
- ♦ Economy = no money
- ♦ No animals
- ♦ Earth's atmosphere
- ♦ People not caring
- ♦ Overpopulation = running out of resources

This list showed us that many of the students most certainly had concerns about the environment. This revelation also enabled us to start building—on day one, but as a natural part of our discussion—students' environmental background knowledge and vocabulary. We discussed their concerns and then flipped the sheet over and wrote WATER in the middle. What words came to their minds in response to *water*? Again, Leslie wrote their ideas down:

drink	swimming	animals
ocean	dolphins	blue
agua	flood	tsunami
liquid	waves	people
lake	recycle	death
shower	sea	seaweed
fish	life	drowning

We put a plastic bottle of water in the middle of the rug and asked the kids how many had bottles of water like it at home. Most of their hands shot up. A few of them talked about the bottled water their parents buy. We passed out a one-page fact sheet titled "Bottled Water and Energy" that we had found on the Web site for the environmental organization Pacific Institute (pacinst.org). Through shared reading, we studied and discussed some statistics:

- ♦ Americans buy about 31.2 billion liters of bottled water a year. Manufacturing them requires 900,000 tons of plastic and 17 million barrels of oil and produces about 2.5 million tons of carbon dioxide.
- ♦ It takes two liters of water to produce one liter of bottled water.
- ♦ The total energy required to produce one bottle of water is equivalent to about one quarter of a bottle filled with oil. (Pacific Institute, n.d.)

The last two items astounded the class. To understand this process, students needed more background knowledge—which is really another way of saying we were teaching Leslie's students new knowledge. How would it require *oil* to create a bottle of *water*? Here's how: energy is needed to create the bottle, to run the manufacturing plant, to transport the empty bottles to the plant, to transport the bottled water from the factory to the store, and so on. All of that energy requires oil or coal or something to power it all. Suddenly, Leslie's students were not just looking at one bottle of water. They were seeing the chain of resources required to get that bottle of water into our classroom.

We asked the students to think of alternatives to buying bottled water. Some suggested that we could simply drink tap water. Leslie and I pointed out that some bottled water *is* tap water. (Again, more new knowledge and vocabulary: What does "purified water" mean?) Some of the students said that buying bottled water makes life easier, and we agreed; however, that does not make it the wisest or the best choice. Leslie placed her aluminum water bottle next to the plastic bottle, and we discussed the benefits of using refillable containers. Then our discussion veered in another direction: Why should we even care about water? After all, the world is full of water. Right?

NONFICTION PICTURE BOOK: *One Well: The Story of Water on Earth*

Yes, our planet is full of water. Unfortunately, just 2 percent of the resource is freshwater, and most of that is frozen in glaciers and the polar ice caps. Other sources are underground. How much freshwater do we have easy access to? About .036 percent of all the water on Earth is in lakes and rivers. Seven billion people need that to drink, cook, bathe, wash clothes and dishes, water crops, and have an occasional water balloon fight. And we cannot make more water. The water on Earth a billion years ago is the same amount of water on Earth today. Our population keeps expanding, but the amount of water stays the same. We already have a *billion* people without easy access to drinkable water. The story of water is an essential story for all of us to hear.

Much of this information is in *One Well: The Story of Water on Earth* (Strauss 2007). The book also explains the science of water, the water cycle, water pollution, and how people, plants, and animals use water around the world. For example, the average person in North America uses 143 gallons of water per day, the average Russian uses 72 gallons, and the typical Haitian uses just 4 gallons. *One Well* ends with a plea to care for water resources:

> Water has the power to change everything. A single splash can sprout a seed, quench a thirst, provide a habitat, generate energy, and sustain life. It also has the power to unite—or divide—the world. Water is the most basic and most important need of all life on Earth.
>
> But Earth's *One Well* is in trouble. There is simply not enough clean water to go around. (nonpaginated)

We started reading the book aloud on that first day and continued to read it aloud for twenty–thirty minutes each day for the next week. After just the first day of reading, we asked the class to list words again in response to the word *water*. Here's the second list:

thirst	oil	whales
bottle	plastic	molecules
rain forest	condensation	evaporate
H_{2O}	fog	stream
atmosphere	soil	carbon dioxide
well	vapor	boat
snow	clouds	filtration
salty	pretzel	Dead Sea
container	dirt	

After just ninety minutes, the students were seeing very different meanings in water (see Figure 8.2).

Figure 8.2 Leslie Rector's students compare their list of words about water, before and after reading *One Well*.

Teaching Tip

We should have asked each student to jot down a few questions at the end of the activity. That would have created "bookends" for the day, starting with their questions and ending with their questions. One way to do this is by collecting "exit slips," which students quickly fill out at the end of an activity or a class. Another option is to post a sheet of chart paper on the open door with a title such as "Some questions we have from today are . . ." As kids leave, they can attach their questions, written on sticky notes.

PROJECT: Family Water Questionnaire
PROJECT: Water Journal

Reading how much water Americans use in a day is a rather abstract concept for eleven- and twelve-year-olds. We wanted them to get an idea of how much water *they* use. We created a questionnaire for the students to complete with their families. This activity also helped to connect the students' families to school and our curriculum. The survey included these questions:

- How does your household use water?
- What are your family's top seven uses of water?
- Do you think people around the world without running water use water differently than your family?
- If your family did not have running water and had to walk two miles each day to get water from a well, what would your plan be to get the water and what would your family do differently knowing you had to make trips to get your water?

From their responses, it was evident that reading and discussing *One Well* had an effect on most of the students. It especially gave them a *global perspective*, helping to put their lives in Chicago in context. We discussed that the most important job for millions of girls and women is to walk miles away to get water and bring it back to their families. (And we showed them pictures on the Internet of girls and women in Africa doing exactly that.) On her family questionnaire, Yazmin wrote:

Yes, we think that it's so different because people in other countries don't have this technology and have to walk long, long miles just to get water. And they have really different ways of getting everything done, and for them it's really hard because they don't have cars or transportation. I think for us living without [easy access to] water we would not survive, or we would probably survive, but it would be really hard and it would take up a whole day!

Yazmin's writing showed us that she was beginning to think globally and understand that people around the world live a very different (and much harder) life than she lives in Chicago. Moises came up with a powerful simile to show how precious water is:

I think people in different countries use water differently. People probably use water so carefully that they make it seem like medicine. In some countries when a child takes a bath and another one has to take a bath, he or she uses the same bathing water.

All of the students made folded Water Journals they could fit into their pockets. For one week, they had to keep track of all the water they used. We did a mini-lesson focusing on establishing averages for the water required for typical household activities, such as bathing, flushing a toilet, washing dishes, cooking and drinking, and washing clothes. (We pointed out that their totals would not include one of our biggest uses of water: the water required to manufacture and grow everything we buy—such as bottles of water.) There were some large variations in the survey data, in part because some students were not as accurate or diligent as others, but many students were not that far apart. Alejandro collected this data:

Thursday: 64 gallons
Friday: 65 gallons
Saturday: 64 gallons
Sunday: 57 gallons
Monday: 58 gallons
Tuesday: 52 gallons
Wednesday: 54 gallons
TOTAL: 468 gallons

Although the students' totals were considerably lower than the actual amount of water each American really uses (more than 700 gallons a week), the numbers shocked them. They never imagined they were consuming so much water; they never even *thought about* water. Picturing a gallon of milk—something kids know—and then multiplying that by 468 plastic gallon milk jugs can help them understand (and actually see in their mind) just how much water they routinely use. Extending that consumption for an entire year means Alejandro alone uses at least 25,000 gallons of water. Multiply that for the entire class and we get almost 700,000 gallons for just one classroom. Multiply that by 300 million Americans and the amount of water we use is astounding. And that's just our country, a mere 5 percent of the world.

ACTIVITY: World Population

To help the students understand two of the key issues from *One Well*—that there is a finite amount of water on Earth, and we cannot manufacture more water—we had them graph world population projection data. This was a short activity to emphasize one vitally important point: The population of Earth will continue to rise, but the amount of water on Earth will remain the same—and we already have water shortages. From their graphs, the students saw that the Earth's population is expected to rise to more than 9 billion people by 2050. This helped them understand that we cannot take water for granted.

NEWS STORY AND PHOTOGRAPHY: "Mideast Water Crisis Brings Misery, Uncertainty" on National Public Radio

To continue with the global perspective on water, the class listened to the news report "Mideast Water Crisis Brings Misery, Uncertainty" (Amos 2010) on National Public Radio about terrible droughts in the Middle East. We wanted the students to hear the stories of people who do not have enough water to drink. Students also had printed copies of the story so they could read along as we streamed the audio from the NPR Web site and projected the accompanying pictures of bone-dry earth onto the classroom screen. To integrate some geography, we pulled down the classroom map and passed out laminated world maps to each student. We did a quick mini-lesson to help them locate the countries and cities being discussed in the news report.

ESSAY: "The Little Things That Run the World"
AUTOBIOGRAPHY: *Naturalist*
PICTURE BOOK: *Hey, Little Ant*

Figure 8.3 Students follow along as Leslie Rector reads from *The City of Ember*.

By this time we had started reading *The City of Ember* (see Figure 8.3). Because of the significant blocks of time Leslie had reserved for the unit, we could read the book together for about thirty minutes and then devote another thirty to sixty minutes to activities with short texts or other real-world resources. (Later in the unit, when we were engaged in the unit projects, the class worked on them for the entire ninety minutes.) From the novel the class learned that one of the main characters, Doon, is interested in insects:

> Doon had always been fascinated by bugs. He wrote down his observations about them in a book he had titled *Crawling and Flying Things*. Each page of the book was divided lengthwise down the center. On the left he drew his pictures, with a pencil sharpened on a needle-like point: moth wings with their branching patterns of veins; spider legs, which had minute hairs and tiny feet like claws; beetles, with their feelers and their glossy armor. On the right, he wrote what he observed about each creature. He noted what it ate, where it slept, where it laid its eggs, and—if he knew—how long it lived. (52)

Whereas Lina is the story's artist, Doon is the story's budding naturalist with an insatiable curiosity about his world of Ember. We used Doon's interest in nature to connect to the creatures that inhabit our environment. We began by reading the essay "The Little Things That Run the World," by biologist Edward O. Wilson (1997). Sitting on the rug, with everyone holding a copy of Wilson's short essay, we began by defining some key vocabulary in his essay (*vertebrate*, *invertebrate*, and *ecosystem*). Here is the main thesis of Wilson's essay:

> The truth is that we need invertebrates but they don't need us. If human beings were to disappear tomorrow, the world would go on with little change. Gaia, the totality of life on Earth, would set about healing itself and return to the rich environmental states of 100,000 years ago. But if invertebrates were to disappear, it is unlikely that the human species could last more than a few months. (144)

When Wilson writes that "little things run the world," he's saying that bugs do not need us to survive; in fact, they would do better without us. But humans need bugs; without them, our species would become extinct, like dinosaurs. We emphasized this point because we wanted the students to understand the significance of Wilson's analysis. If all those little bugs we see crawling and flying every day were to disappear, *so would we*! As humans we must have insects to survive. After we finished reading, there was a silent pause, and then George, with his curly mop of hair and infectious smile, said to the class, "Who would have ever thought that an ant could be so important?" Exactly. And before we read this essay and had this discussion, I doubt George did.

Edward O. Wilson is one of the world's leading ant experts. I read aloud an excerpt to the class from his wonderful autobiography, *Naturalist* (1994). We wanted to hold Wilson up as a model of someone who is a passionate caretaker of the Earth and who looks at the natural world with everyday wonder and fascination—just as Doon does in *The City of Ember*. Leslie and I hoped to cultivate similar habits of mind in her students. Wilson's book begins with a story from when he was seven years old, in 1936:

> I stand in the shallows off Paradise Beach, staring down at a huge jellyfish in water so still and clear that its every detail is revealed as though it were trapped in glass. The creature is astonishing. It existed outside my previous imagination. I study it from every angle I can manage from above the water's surface. Its opalescent pink bell is divided by thin red lines that radiate from center to circular edge. A wall of tentacles falls from the rim to surround and partially veil a feeding tube and other organs, which fold in and out like the fabric of a drawn curtain. I can only see a little way into this lower tissue mass. I want to know more but am afraid to wade deeper and look more closely into the heart of the creature. (5–6)

New Resources

The world is certainly filled with remarkable resources teachers can use to have students explore the environment. Here are three: Annie Leonard's animated videos on consumption and the environment at storyofstuff.org; the PBS video *Silence of the Bees* on colony collapse disorder, which is what scientists call the very large decline in the number of honeybees; and the Great Backyard Bird Count (birdsource.org/gbbc/), a national event that empowers all Americans, young and old, to count birds and record their data on the Web site. Though the official bird count happens each February, teachers can have students do it anytime.

Next, we read the picture book *Hey, Little Ant* (Hoose and Hoose 1999). The book is written in script format as a conversation between a boy with a raised shoe and an ant beneath his shoe. The boy is considering squishing the ant, while the ant is pleading for his life. In one key part, the two characters suddenly switch sizes, with the boy being as tiny as an ant and the ant as big as the boy, towering above him. The ant says, "If you were me and I were you, what would you want me to do?"

More than merely a story about caring for living things, *Hey, Little Ant* is an allegory about the abuse of power. We discussed this with the class, explaining the meaning of *allegory*. Before reading the book, we passed out a sheet for the students to jot down some ideas. They had to draw an image of "power" and find an example of "ants" and "shoes" in their own lives. For *power*, Angel drew a superhero; Luisa drew a king and a president; Cristal drew her parents and wrote, "Parents have the power to ground us." Flor drew a picture of the Earth with cracks in it and wrote, "Power = to destroy."

To the question "Who are the ants in your life?" many of the students mentioned their siblings. Dulce exemplified this, writing, "The ant in my life is my 13-year-old sister. She gets on my nerves and I feel like squishing her with my shoe." Alejandro wrote that little kids are ants "because they don't get power to make decisions."

Teaching Tip

This activity is a good example of connecting the focus of our inquiry unit to the students' lives. This point helps to show the struggle between more progressive, child-centered teaching and teaching for social responsibility. The more you move into teaching for social responsibility, which requires a curriculum with specific knowledge to be taught, the more we tend to move out of child-centered teaching. It takes work to find the right balance and to remember that we want to continually strive for students to make these connections.

Because we wanted the students to go further than merely seeing the power of their siblings and parents, we discussed some of the different "shoes" and "ants" in the world and in life, from bullies at school to gangs in Chicago, from how cultural and gender groups use power, to the military actions of powerful countries. This story of one little ant is a microcosm of the endless stories of the use and abuse of power, past and present. And although the Earth can be a powerful force, with natural disasters destroying homes and communities and many lives, in the end we all have the power over life on Earth. We can make decisions to help the planet and its ecosystems thrive, or we can make decisions perpetuating its damage. We had the students list some of the big ideas they identified from our discussion of *Hey, Little Ant*:

- Having the courage to make the right (and sometime less popular) decisions
- Using power responsibly
- Not being judgmental

♦ The value of putting yourself in others' shoes
♦ Controlling our anger
♦ Not bullying others

PROJECT: Insect Inquiry

Using Doon in *The City of Ember* as a model, Leslie and I wanted each student to study an insect. We were hoping they would get a better understanding of how every insect—no matter how small and seemingly insignificant—has an important place in our food chain and Earth's ecosystem. I love connecting the reading of a novel to nonfiction inquiry; it can help students make powerful connections and understand how reading fiction can help us make sense of real life.

The students brainstormed a list of what they knew and what they *thought* they knew about insects. It's important to help kids critique these assumptions so they can correct misconceptions. Exploring questions is the heart of inquiry-based teaching, so working together we used their list to create *guiding questions* for their insect research:

♦ What do they eat?
♦ What are their predators?
♦ What are their habitats?
♦ Where are their habitats?
♦ How do they mate?
♦ What is their life cycle?
♦ How do they learn?
♦ How do they know their "job"?
♦ How do they communicate?
♦ How do they help humans?
♦ Do they have wars?
♦ Why do some insects live underground?
♦ How do they protect themselves?
♦ Do insects have territorial boundaries?
♦ How do they go to the bathroom?

These questions were pared down to a list of eleven *essential questions* the class was required to investigate. (They could research additional questions if they wanted.) Based on these questions, we passed out a graphic organizer for the students to record their research notes. Leslie also made an example investigation page of her own about ladybugs (also known as *Coccinella septempunctata*) to show the class. This is important because that served as the *high-quality model* for her kids to see before they began their own work. She displayed a collection of nonfiction library books about insects, which students could look through to help them decide which insect to research.

> ## Teaching Tip
>
> It was important to create the initial list of research topics with the students. We wanted their questions to come first. Not only does this give them ownership of the inquiry process, but it also lets them pose questions we (the "all-knowing" teachers) may not have considered. The inquiry process does not stop there, of course. We want to take their ideas and expand them, make connections, integrate some critical thinking and perspectives, cut redundant questions, and (very important) build some purposeful boundaries so they don't end up investigating everything under the sun. In the end, it becomes a *collaborative* list of essential questions.

Figure 8.4 Adonis and Moises work on their insect project.

We asked the students to create an "investigation page" about their insect, which included a large sheet with pictures, diagrams, and text. In interdisciplinary spirit, the students did the insect work during the science part of the day, and we continued reading the novel during the reading part of the day (see Figure 8.4).

They had about an hour each day to work on their insect projects. We began with a few mini-lessons about research and note-taking skills. Students had three days to do their research on laptops and another four or five days to turn that research into their investigation pages. All of this was done right in the classroom so Leslie and I could be there to help them and continue teaching research skills.

READING: *The City of Ember*

After reading the first few chapters, we had the students work together to generate a list of questions about the text. This was a form of Gallagher's (2004) "20 Questions" activity done to reinforce the ideas that good readers ask questions of a text as they read, and that as we're getting into a book, there is a *lot* we don't know. By having students explicitly take questions from their heads and put them on paper, we make that "unknown" dimension of reading very visible and help them understand that as readers they need to *work through* the early parts of a text until more pieces of the story emerge.

Beyond helping with comprehension skills, student-generated questions also enable teachers to connect student curiosities to the bigger ideas of the unit. Literature helps us examine these questions within the context of a story—and then expand and connect those issues to our lives and the world.

As the students made their way through the novel, they wrote in their journals. Most of Leslie's students were not strong writers, and we wanted them to write more.

NEWSPAPER OP-ED: "Did Your Shopping List Kill a Songbird?" from the *New York Times*

ACTIVITY: Pesticides: Pros and Cons

BOOK EXCERPT: *Voices from the Fields: Children of Migrant Farmworkers Tell Their Stories*

I pulled the *New York Times* op-ed piece "Did Your Shopping List Kill a Songbird?" from my files. It's written by biologist Bridget Stutchbury (2008). Her essay explains how our nation's grocery shopping is killing songbirds. She writes, "Bobolink numbers have plummeted almost 50 percent in the last four decades." Why? Because farmers in Central and South America are using pesticides to grow fruits and vegetables for consumers in North America and Europe to buy during the winter—when much of that produce is out of season. She wants readers to consider buying fruits and vegetables when they are in season and more of them are grown in the United States.

Helping students see *connections* is one of the most valuable aspects of teaching social responsibility. These connections remind us that our actions have consequences, and that solving problems can be a complex endeavor. Leslie's students had no idea that fruits and vegetables *have* seasons, or that there are consequences—like tipping over a row of dominoes—from what we choose to eat.

After we read and discussed Stutchbury's article, we passed out a chart from the Nutrition and Food Web Archive (nafwa.org) showing the North American growing seasons for fruits and vegetables. We shared what fruits and vegetables we all love (and hate) to eat. We also discussed that it requires sacrifice to commit to different buying habits. We were honest with the class that these kinds of decisions are not easy, but they are an option.

Simply saying pesticides are all bad is too pat. What would traditional farmers say about that? Chemical manufacturers? We worked as a class to create a pro/con chart for using pesticides to grow food. Here's what they came up with:

Pros	Cons
Keep bugs and rodents off the fruit.	It's poison and can kill wildlife.
Lowers the cost.	Unhealthy for farmers.
We can eat off-season fruits all year.	People eat the pesticides in the fruit.
It's easier to grow.	It's unnecessary.
It's healthy for us to eat fruit year-round.	We keep fair-trade farmers employed.
We create more jobs.	

As we were creating this list and discussing the issue of the farmers' health, Leslie and I immediately thought of the same book, *Voices from the Fields* (Atkin 2000). This short nonfiction book is full of the voices and pictures of children of migrant farmworkers in the United States. It tells their stories, including what it's like to work in the fields. Not surprisingly, Leslie—who is a passionate advocate for immersing a classroom in children's literature—had the book in her classroom. We grabbed it and took some time to share an excerpt and pictures with her students. The connection was now visible: All of those wonderfully luscious piles of fruits and vegetables we see in stores require *people* to pick and distribute them. (They also require those pollinating bees we discussed earlier.)

Having students create pro/con lists is an important strategy for teaching social responsibility and critical thinking. It challenges them to consider multiple views of an issue—and, in particular, perspectives they disagree with—and understand complexity and nuance. They can learn that they may agree with certain elements of an opposing view and that the decisions that we believe to be ethically right also have trade-offs. We may choose to forgo certain fruits and vegetables in the winter—and it would be better for the Earth and the farmworkers' health if we did—but there are consequences from those decisions as well. Sometimes our decisions are not simply a choice between good and bad; some decisions require us to choose between "the lesser of two evils."

Teaching Tip

Here are two strategies teachers can use to help their students better understand informational texts, such as a newspaper article. As Harvey Daniels and Stephanie Harvey put it, we can have kids "read with a question in mind" (2009, 123). Giving kids a question *before* they read can pique their curiosity and help them read with greater purpose—to answer the question. For this article, we could have given them the question, "Why are so many birds dying?" Cris Tovani (2011) suggests having students sometimes annotate a text. Copy the article with plenty of white space all around and have students write questions and thoughts as they read. Not only does this empower kids to ask their own questions, but Tovani uses this as assessment because their annotations are a visual representation of their reading, thinking, and comprehension. It's important that she does a mini-lesson to model how to annotate a text so her students can see it being done.

SHORT INTERNET TEXT: "Top Reasons Trees Are Valuable"
MINI-LESSON: Photosynthesis

David Suzuki and Wayne Grady wrote a short biography of a single tree, a Douglas fir, called *Tree: A Life Story* (2004). They wrote, "Trees are remarkable beings. Yet they stand like extras in life's dramas, always there as backdrops to the ever-changing action around them, so familiar and omnipresent that we barely take notice of them" (2). Leslie and I wanted her students to notice trees. We wanted to do for trees what we had done for insects: help the students *see* trees, understand why trees are so essential to our lives, and raise their appreciation for the beauty and majesty of trees. Okay, I admit it. I'm an unabashed tree lover, with a tree identification app on my iPhone. In the park across from my home, I even have a favorite tree: a bald cypress.

Gathered on the rug we passed out "Top Reasons Trees Are Valuable," an essay by Steve Nix, a professional forester (Nix 2009). We read and discussed Nix's list, which includes the importance of trees to produce oxygen, clean the air and soil, and fight soil erosion.

To help the class understand some of the science of trees, we conducted a mini-lesson about photosynthesis. We wanted to emphasize that without trees, humans cannot survive, and without the sun, there would be no trees. Again, this was an opportunity to help the students consider something we typically take for granted (trees, the sun, and the air we breathe) from a different perspective. And it also helped to reinforce the connectivity (or systems thinking) of nature and life on Earth. If we remove or kill or damage one piece, we affect the entire system.

Leslie and I wanted to take the class on a walk around the immediate neighborhood of the school so we could look at different trees. Unfortunately, the school administrators would not give us permission to do so. They said something about standardized testing being three weeks away. (Funny, I've never seen any research showing a correlation between looking at trees and lower test scores.)

So we went outside to the playground and were limited to the trees inside the fence. There were few trees, and there was not much variety. We told the students to examine a tree: get up close, look at the branches, feel the bark, observe the details. Although it was February and there were no leaves to see, the kids saw more than they expected, such as markings and patterns on the bark. There were a few pine trees along a fence, and Adonis came excitedly over to Leslie and me with a single pine needle between his fingers. He said, "Look! If you break the needle in half, you can *smell the pine*!" Neither Leslie nor I had ever thought about doing that. Adonis held the needle to our noses, and sure enough, we did smell the pine. Soon, other kids joined in, and many of them smelled the pine too. It was one of my most exciting moments in our unit (see Figure 8.5).

With few trees to look at, our time outdoors was sadly short. On the way back inside the school, Alejandro said to Leslie, "You know, Ms. Rector, I've been going to this school for years, and I never stopped to look at the trees."

Figure 8.5 Adonis shows us all how to smell the pine!

PICTURE BOOKS: *Planting the Trees of Kenya: The Story of Wangari Maathai* and *Wangari's Trees of Peace*
DOCUMENTARY FILM: The Nobel Peace Prize: Wangari Maathai

Trees are not just about science and nature. There are political, economic, and cultural dimensions to trees. Wangari Maathai, the late founder of the Green Belt Movement (greenbeltmovement.org), grew up in a small village in Kenya and won the 2004 Nobel Peace Prize for her environmental efforts and activism. She empowered (and actually employed) thousands of women in Kenya to plant trees. Her movement has spread to nine African countries and has resulted in the planting of 30 million trees and the creation of 6,000 tree nurseries. Maathai turned women into wage earners, renewed Africa's natural habitats, provided people with easier access to firewood, and brought the beauty of trees to millions of people. All of this has created a more peaceful planet.

By sharing Wangari Maathai's story with Leslie's students, we brought together multiple ideas: the benefits of trees far beyond their science and beauty, people working to improve the environment, global awareness, the plight of women and girls in developing countries, and the power of one person to make a remarkable difference in the world. As we had done with Edward O. Wilson and his passion for insects, we presented Wangari Maathai to the students as a model of someone working to make a better world through trees. We read aloud two picture books about Maathai to the class, *Planting the Trees of Kenya* (Nivola 2008) and *Wangari's Trees of Peace* (Winter 2008). These books showed the students how different writers and illustrators tell the story of the same person.

Next, we showed the class a short documentary film about Maathai (Nobel Committee 2004). This helped the students make a connection between the environment and politics, which explicitly shows how the health of the environment is deeply rooted in the actions of a democracy. When Maathai began her work, the president of Kenya was Daniel arap Moi, who considered her a political threat. As the Green Belt Movement grew, Maathai took part in many pro-democracy activities, resulting in clashes with Moi and the Kenyan government. At one point, she was arrested, and in 1992, she participated in a hunger strike to free political prisoners. In 2002, she was elected to parliament and became assistant minister in the Ministry for Environment and Natural Resources. (Sadly, Maathai died in 2011.) Maathai's story reminds us all that the environment and politics are inextricably linked and that by creating a greener planet we are creating a more peaceful planet. The Nobel Committee wrote:

> Maathai stood up courageously against the former oppressive regime in Kenya. Her unique forms of action have contributed to drawing attention to political oppression—nationally and internationally. She has served as inspiration for many in the fight for democratic rights and has especially encouraged women to better their situation.

ACTIVITY: Nature Murals

To complete the unit, the students put themselves in groups and chose a topic from nature to create a mural. They had to celebrate an "everyday" aspect of nature, such as rain, wind, flowers, or the sky, and include some factual information. There were three reasons for doing this project. First, we wanted to celebrate the end of the unit with a large piece of artwork that would require no additional research; second, we wanted to emphasize the focus of the unit, which was our appreciation of elements in everyday nature, like flowers and trees; and finally, we wanted a project that would require the kids to use some of what they had learned throughout the unit.

Becoming Caretakers of the Planet

In his book *Earth in Mind,* environmental educator David Orr (1994) writes of the "dangers of education." Orr's concern is not that our schools will fail, but rather that they will *succeed*. Let's face some facts here. Other than teaching about Earth Day and recycling, most schools do very little to engage students in an honest, deep, and critical exploration of our environment and how humans are affecting the natural world. By focusing so much on the economic and test score aims of education while ignoring the ecological consequences of our daily lives, educators are directly and indirectly perpetuating our environmental ignorance and apathy. They fail by succeeding.

Orr takes this point further. He argues that a typical sanitized textbook-based curriculum is divorced from our "lived experiences" and denies children the truly relevant learning they crave, ignoring their inherent curiosity and amazement about the natural world and keeping them from developing personal passions and values for their lives:

> What are the dangers of education? There are three that are particularly consequential for the way we live on the earth: (1) that formal education will cause students to worry about how to make a living before they know who they are, (2) that it will render students narrow technicians who are morally sterile, and (3) that it will deaden their sense of wonder for the created world. (24)

Teachers can work against these dangers of education and create vibrant and authentic classroom experiences that encourage young adolescents to confront difficult and complex questions about life, our personal choices and decisions, and our environmental policies and priorities. One of the best ways to do that is through good books. When we choose books with environmental themes and issues, we can pull these issues out for students to explore. The unit resources are included on the companion Web site, www.stenhouse.com/caringhearts.

Chapter 9

What Is Empathy?

Rob had a way of not-caring about things. He imagined himself as a suitcase that was too full, like the one they had packed when they left Jacksonville after the funeral. He made all his feelings go inside the suitcase; he stuffed them tight and then sat on the suitcase and locked it shut.
— *The Tiger Rising*

As I wrote in Chapter 2, no one has written more, and written more eloquently, about the vital need to teach *caring* in our schools than Nel Noddings (1992). In contrast to most schools today that teach a narrow definition of caring in the primary grades, Noddings writes that caring should be a foundation of curriculum and an essential aim of school:

> Many otherwise reasonable people seem to believe that our educational problems consist largely of low scores on achievement tests. My contention is, first, that we should want more from our educational efforts than adequate academic achievement and, second, that we will not achieve even that meager success unless our children believe that they themselves are cared for and learn to care for others. (1995, 675)

Related to caring is *empathy*, defined by Merriam-Webster as "The action of understanding, being aware of, being sensitive to, and vicariously experiencing the feelings, thoughts, and experience of another of either the past or present without having the feelings, thoughts, and experience fully communicated in an objectively explicit manner."

There is a growing list of advocates for empathy being essential knowledge for life in the twenty-first century. (As if we did not need empathy in the twentieth century?) Daniel Pink, author of the best-selling book *A Whole New Mind*, devotes an entire chapter to empathy. Pink argues that schools and society must dramatically shift their aims and curriculum to better prepare children for twenty-first-century jobs and life. Pink writes, "We are moving from an economy and a society built on the logical, linear, computerlike capabilities of the Information Age to an economy and society built on the inventive, empathic, big-picture capabilities of what's rising in its place, the Conceptual Age" (2006, 1–2).

In other words, why make kids memorize textbooks full of endless facts when they carry that information in their pockets on a smartphone? Or when the work involving that knowledge is now done by robots and computers or outsourced to India? What we need, Pink argues, are students with the skills of innovation, imagination, human connection, and emotion to create and design and cultivate the new world.

Pink argues that empathy is far more vital than merely the ability to feel and understand what someone else is feeling. Empathy connects to the abilities to think critically, shape our self, and develop our ethical consciousness. He writes, "Empathy allows us to see the other side of the argument, comfort someone in distress, and bite our lip instead of muttering something snide. Empathy builds self-awareness, bonds parent to child, allows us to work together, and provides the scaffolding for our morality" (160).

Empathy and caring are also central to social responsibility, citizenship, and democracy. Many of our daily actions and decisions are rooted in empathy, and an active citizenry with conscious caring helps us cultivate democracy and embrace diversity. In his book *Emotional Intelligence*, Daniel Goleman (1995) writes:

> Empathy, as we have seen, leads to caring, altruism, and compassion. Seeing things from another's perspective breaks down biased stereotypes, and so breeds tolerance and acceptance of differences. These capacities are ever more called on in our increasingly pluralistic society, allowing people to live together in mutual respect and creating the possibility of productive public discourse. These are the basic arts of democracy. (285)

Given our society's rhetoric about how much we want our children to "be good," it is tragic that we continue to feed them never-ending curricula and standardized testing on comma usage and comprehension and geometry, yet explore virtually nothing about their capacity for empathy and caring. If we believe these are important for our students and our society, then we have an obligation to figure out how to make them an important part of our classrooms. Once again, books and stories of all kinds can help us make that happen. As the eminent philosopher Martha Nussbaum writes, "As we tell stories about the lives of others, we learn how to imagine what another creature might feel in response to various events. At the same time, we identify with the other creature and learn something about ourselves" (Harmon 2002, 177).

Caring in the Classroom

Natalie Tyrell teaches sixth grade in a suburb of Chicago. The population at her school is 88 percent Latino. The year I visited to coteach a unit on caring and empathy, Natalie's class had a similar cultural makeup, with two African Americans, two whites, and one Asian American among her twenty-nine students. Her classroom is small, and the students' bulky chairs were attached to their desks, making it difficult to rearrange them and open up more room. In short, this was not an ideal space for inquiry teaching, but then again, many teachers are in classrooms just like Natalie's, so we made it work.

Most of the students behaved wonderfully, but four boys in the class presented a challenge. They often pushed the boundaries with inappropriate comments or too much talking. As any teacher can tell you, one kid with chronic behavior issues can pull down an entire classroom and make your work infinitely more demanding. Multiply that by four and you get the idea of what Natalie confronted each day.

Natalie thought a unit on empathy and caring would be perfect for her kids, especially these boys. It could challenge their thinking and encourage them to consider new perspectives, as well as how their actions affected others. We did not expect radical transformations. Our hope was to open their minds and hearts a bit and, in turn, nurture a more peaceful classroom.

Natalie and I decided to use two very short books, one fiction and one nonfiction. The first book was Kate DiCamillo's 2001 novel, *The Tiger Rising*, followed by Leon Walter Tillage's 1997 short autobiography, *Leon's Story*. Natalie's school did not own copies of *Leon's Story*, so she bought a class set of paperbacks. We saw both books as an opportunity for her students to empathize with characters going through very difficult times. These are very emotional books, and we wanted her kids to embrace that emotion.

I usually advocate for an inquiry-based literature unit to be five to seven weeks long so we have time to go deeply into the topics and questions. This also provides time for a more significant culminating project. We had only three weeks for this unit, however, so most of the activities would center on the two books and not as much on connected short texts and resources. That three-week limit was set in stone. Spring break started at the end of that period, after which Natalie needed to begin another unit, so there was no wiggle room. The short time span also eliminated any possibility of a large post-reading project. These are the kinds of difficult compromises teachers need to make sometimes to make their passions a reality in their classrooms.

Natalie did not feel pressured to include other curricular goals in the unit. This was good, given the tight squeeze on time. She had recently completed another unit for reading. The freedom to skip mini-lessons on comprehension and activities to build reading skills enabled us to devote nearly all of our time to the exploration of caring and empathy. Looking back, it's amazing how much we were able to accomplish in just fifteen school days. Figure 9.1 shows the unit flowchart.

The Tiger Rising by Kate DiCamillo

The Tiger Rising is a deeply sad book. Eleven-year-old Rob Horton is certainly going through very tough times. His mother has recently died and his father refuses to discuss her, mention her name, or even let Rob cry. He tells his son, "Crying ain't gonna bring her back." So Rob stuffs all of his feelings into a metaphorical "suitcase" that keeps pounding to burst open. To make matters worse, Rob is relentlessly bullied by the Threemonger brothers.

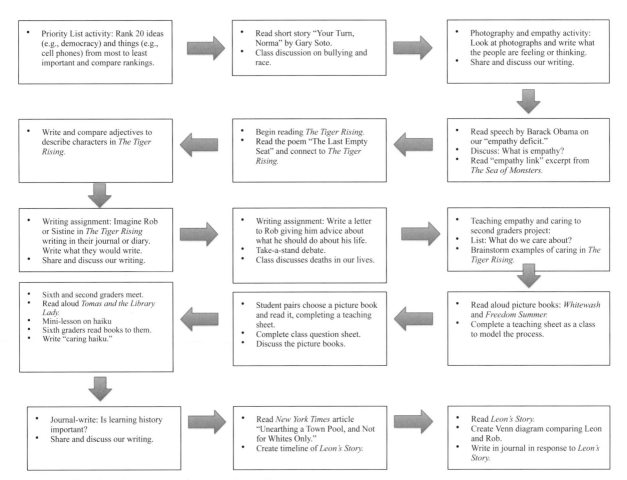

- Priority List activity: Rank 20 ideas (e.g., democracy) and things (e.g., cell phones) from most to least important and compare rankings.

- Read short story "Your Turn, Norma" by Gary Soto.
- Class discussion on bullying and race.

- Photography and empathy activity: Look at photographs and write what the people are feeling or thinking.
- Share and discuss our writing.

- Write and compare adjectives to describe characters in *The Tiger Rising*.

- Begin reading *The Tiger Rising*.
- Read the poem "The Last Empty Seat" and connect to *The Tiger Rising*.

- Read speech by Barack Obama on our "empathy deficit."
- Discuss: What is empathy?
- Read "empathy link" excerpt from *The Sea of Monsters*.

- Writing assignment: Imagine Rob or Sistine in *The Tiger Rising* writing in their journal or diary. Write what they would write.
- Share and discuss our writing.

- Writing assignment: Write a letter to Rob giving him advice about what he should do about his life.
- Take-a-stand debate.
- Class discusses deaths in our lives.

- Teaching empathy and caring to second graders project:
- List: What do we care about?
- Brainstorm examples of caring in *The Tiger Rising*.

- Sixth and second graders meet.
- Read aloud *Tomas and the Library Lady*.
- Mini-lesson on haiku
- Sixth graders read books to them.
- Write "caring haiku."

- Student pairs choose a picture book and read it, completing a teaching sheet.
- Complete class question sheet.
- Discuss the picture books.

- Read aloud picture books: *Whitewash* and *Freedom Summer*.
- Complete a teaching sheet as a class to model the process.

- Journal-write: Is learning history important?
- Share and discuss our writing.

- Read *New York Times* article "Unearthing a Town Pool, and Not for Whites Only."
- Create timeline of *Leon's Story*.

- Read *Leon's Story*.
- Create Venn diagram comparing Leon and Rob.
- Write in journal in response to *Leon's Story*.

Figure 9.1 Flowchart for our empathy and caring unit.

Two things send Rob on a transformative journey. First, he finds a very real tiger locked in a cage in the woods. The tiger is a metaphor for Rob's feelings: potent and confined. Second, he meets a girl, Sistine Bailey, who is also missing a parent: her father left her family for another woman. While Rob struggles with sorrow, Sistine struggles with anger. Sistine—a force to be reckoned with—demands that they free the tiger. When Rob tells her, "The tiger ain't ours to let go," Sistine barks back, "It's our tiger to save." This is a story of two children saving each other.

Leon's Story by Leon Walter Tillage

Leon Walter Tillage was an African American school custodian, born in 1936. The book, which is very short, is based on a series of interviews he did with Susan Roth about his life under the brutal and inhumane Jim Crow laws in North Carolina. (He passed away in 2011.) Growing up, Leon was immersed in the hatred and violence of racism. Although the book does not flinch in telling his personal story of tragedy, it also exudes his gentle charm and wisdom. In an afterword Roth says to Leon, "But Leon, you have no bitterness. How come?" Leon tells her, "What good would that do? I know there were bad times. But you know there were rejoicing times too" (106).

OPENING ACTIVITY: The Priority List

Natalie and I decided to start by identifying what her students valued. By consciously making the effort to connect with other people who are struggling or different from us, we develop humility and can then shift to another's perspective. This requires us to prioritize our values. For example, we might honor feelings over material possessions. We created an activity called the "priority list," which included twenty items, such as "cell phone," "trees," "TV," "being loved," and "democracy." We told the students to rank the list from least important to most important, emphasizing that they should not assign rankings to please their friends or us. As the kids completed the sheets, Natalie and I did as well.

I loved listening to the kids explain their reasoning (see Figure 9.2). Why, for example, had Jonathan ranked "having friends" third but "being loved" thirteenth? During our discussion, intriguing debates ensued. Jenny said she ranked "fashionable clothes and shoes" fifth and democracy nineteenth. Destiny took serious issue with this. She was the only one who ranked democracy first, arguing that without freedom we have nothing. But Stephanie supported Jenny, arguing that clothes are part of your identity and enable you to express yourself. Students wondered why Natalie and I both ranked trees number one. We explained that trees give us oxygen and without oxygen there is no life. Some students had ranked trees near the bottom. This list does dispel a stereotype. Contrary to what many adults and society say about young adolescents, they ranked TV, shopping malls, video games, and fast food at the bottom.

Figure 9.2 Stephanie shares her rankings with her classmates.

SHORT STORY: "Your Turn, Norma"

JOURNAL-WRITE AND CLASS DISCUSSION: Bullying, Meanness, and Race

In addition to the two anchor books chosen for the unit, we used a short story. Natalie and I did not want her students to leap into the topics of empathy and caring without some context. We had not mentioned the words *empathy* and *caring* yet and felt we could begin that conversation through a good short story.

We selected "Your Turn, Norma" by Gary Soto (1998) from his wonderful anthology *Petty Crimes.* The story focuses on Norma, an eighth grader who has zero self-esteem and is bullied and beaten by a girl gang in her school. She appeals to her mother, who, overcome with exhaustion from her grueling job at a dry cleaner, tells her daughter, "If you be nice, then they act nice back."

To discourage students from getting pregnant, Norma's school uses a common technique of requiring students to take turns caring for a doll that mimics a newborn's behaviors. The doll, which Norma names Amber, is ragged from years of going from kid to kid, but Norma loves her; Amber is her only friend.

We chose this story for three reasons. First, it explores bullying, emotions, and the responsibilities we may have to help others—all closely connected to empathy and caring. The story was also culturally relevant because the characters are Latino from low-income families, like many of Natalie's students. Finally, Gary Soto is a wonderful writer; he uses beautiful language and rich metaphors.

Through the first half of the reading, some students chuckled, especially when Norma was getting bullied or hit by Diana, the gang leader—not exactly the response we were hoping for. Later in the story, after she is attacked by Diana, we see the damage and hopelessness in Norma and the wreckage of her doll. We carefully reread a few sections and asked the students if they saw any similarities between Norma and the doll.

I asked, "What's wrong with the doll?"

Some kids responded, "She's messed up."

I said, "That's right. Broken doll . . ."

Alex chimed right in, completing my sentence: " . . . broken girl."

"Exactly," I said. "Broken doll. Broken girl."

Alex added, "She has no self-esteem."

We explained metaphor here: how the doll can be a metaphor for Norma, how Norma, in a sense, is trying to care for herself. She's trying to survive a desperate situation, looking for hope in a doll. And from that point forward, through to the end of the story, no one laughed. The room was silent.

Natalie's students did not regularly write in journals, but we wanted to use this unit to help them build that practice. Because journal writing tends to be quick, it's perfect for a smaller unit that's tight on time. We also wanted to use this journal writing as an opportunity to have the kids either consider their own responsibility to help others being bullied or to situate bullying in their own school. We gave the class two prompts. Students could choose which one to write about:

1. Imagine you go to Norma's school and you see what is happening to her. Do you have any responsibility to help her? Why or why not?

2. Give your school a grade (A through F) for bullying and explain your grade.

Students who read aloud their response to the first question did not think they had any responsibility to help Norma. But many of them defined "help" as joining in fighting Diana, the gang leader; they wrote that it was not their fight and they did not want to get into trouble. Natalie and I pointed out that there are other ways to help, such as finding an adult who will listen and take action. From their responses to the second question, it was clear that the students did not think bullying was a problem at their school. (Of course, this did not mean it *wasn't* a problem.)

The journal prompts did not result in much meaningful dialogue or debate, so I tweaked question two. I said, "Instead of 'bullying,' grade your school on how *mean* the kids treat each other." The reaction was instantaneous. Murmurs rippled through the classroom.

Destiny announced, "It's a Z. Not an F, a Z."

Most of the class agreed. Many students commented that kids were very mean to each other. Hailey, who is white, responded, "There is a lot of meanness. There is meanness by nationality."

A boy who is Latino disagreed. He said, "There isn't anything by nationality."

"Oh, yes there is," Hailey said. "I hear kids calling me 'white cracker' all the time."

Tension zipped through the classroom. Hailey stood and walked to the tissue dispenser. She started to tear up. The boy repeated his disagreement with her.

Natalie asked if our opinions might be based, in part, on our own cultures. In the context of this school and classroom, the boy was the majority culture and Hailey was the minority.

Shiondrell, who is African American, joined the discussion, speaking with the confidence of an adult. "Look. I used to go to an all-black school," she said. "Kids there called *me* 'white cracker' because I wouldn't talk like them or because I wanted to get good grades. So I understand what Hailey is saying. I have more in common with Hailey, who is white, than I did with any of those other kids who have the same skin color as me."

Natalie went to Hailey to talk to her. This conversation continued for another fifteen minutes, with students expressing their views about race and meanness and simply how kids treat each other. Michael told the class, "Sticks and stones will break my bones, but names will never hurt me."

We asked if that saying was true. Do names really not hurt? Shiondrell said that words of meanness directed at her made her stronger and gave her more self-confidence. But most of the class said that words hurt. We took this discussion back to Soto's story, focusing on the gang's tormenting of Norma. The kids agreed about the terrible verbal harm being done to Norma. We don't need to use fists to cause pain and inflict damage, they acknowledged. Words can be weapons too.

Teaching Tip

Good journal writing and the discussion that follows it open unknown avenues for exploration. Before we assigned those two writing prompts, Natalie and I had no idea it would lead to a discussion of race. This is what good inquiry does. It creates spaces for students and teachers to have conversations that flow naturally, and it enables teachers to choose—usually right in the moment—to take a conversation in an unexpected direction. Sometimes it is truly remarkable where a conversation can go if we enter that talk with the goal of cultivating authentic dialogue. And after twenty-four years in education, I am still learning how to facilitate a good discussion.

> ## New Resources
>
> There are some excellent texts we can use with kids to explore bullying. Two of the best are young adult short story anthologies. First is *Dear Bully: Seventy Authors Tell Their Stories* (Hall and Jones 2011). The authors' Web site, dearbully.com, posts a new short story about bullying every week. The second anthology is *Cornered: 14 Stories of Bullying and Defiance* (Belleza 2012). There is also the semiautobiographical young adult novel *Playground*, by the famed rapper 50 Cent (2011), who says he was a bully. The amazing Deborah Ellis (who wrote *The Breadwinner* trilogy) has written a nonfiction book called *We Want You to Know: Kids Talk About Bullying* of her interviews with kids and teens (2010). *Confessions of a Former Bully* by Trudy Ludwig (2010), written and illustrated like the *Wimpy Kid* books, is from the perspective of a ten-year-old girl who is a bully.

ACTIVITY: Photography and Empathy

Photographs can be a powerful way to explore empathy. We posted sixteen pictures around the classroom. The pictures (which I found online) were "emotional": a weary-looking teenage girl in an Asian country with a baby on her back and an army tank in the background; a girl with her face buried in her hands with a house behind her destroyed by fire; children in Pakistan carrying heavy loads of bricks; the famous picture of a young Polish boy with his hands in the air under the guns of Nazi soldiers. We also had some "happy" pictures of kids playing. We told the students to walk around the room in silence and write one sentence about what the main person in each picture was thinking or feeling.

The class struggled with this. Most of the students could not step out of their own perspective and into the minds of the people in the pictures. Most wrote about what they saw in the pictures ("Kids who are tired from carrying bricks") or the feelings of the person but from their own perspective ("I think the woman is sad about the earthquake"). This is actually to be expected, given that young adolescents are just beginning to move from concrete to abstract thinking. It is yet another reason to engage middle-grades students in these types of learning experiences. More than just teach empathy, such activities guide students toward more complex thinking and reasoning. This period of deep developmental changes applies equally to young adolescents' moral development, which is connected to their rising abilities to step outside their egocentric realities. As Mickey Caskey and Vince Anfara write in their *Research Summary for the Association for Middle Level Education*, "They transition from a self-centered perspective to having consideration for the rights and feelings of others" (2007). Middle school teachers can get their students intellectually excited and engaged by tapping into these new abilities to think and feel.

We stopped the activity and took some time to talk about what we wanted them to do. I said, "Remember, you need to write what the people *in the pictures* think and feel, not what *you* see or feel. Imagine you walk up to the person in the picture and ask them, 'What are you *thinking* about right now? What are you *feeling* right now?' You need to write exactly what they say to you. Try to see their situation through *their* eyes."

Although the activity started off slowly, it helped many students make the leap from the natural default of looking at the world through their eyes to consciously trying to see and feel through the eyes (and heart) of someone else. Natalie and I thought it was a great success.

Extended Ideas

We wanted the students to do some longer writing, but unfortunately, we didn't have the time. Here are three ways to use writing to help students look at the world through the eyes of another person:

♦ Pair students to write two different versions of a short story involving two adolescents. Each version would be written from the perspective of one of the characters.

♦ Take a historical event—such as the Montgomery bus boycott or the Vietnam War—and have students write multiple-voice poetry from the perspectives of the different people involved.

♦ Have students rewrite a fairy tale from the perspective of another character, as John Scieszka did in his picture book *The True Story of the Three Little Pigs!* in which he retells the classic story from the perspective of the wolf.

SPEECH: President Obama
MINI-LESSON: What Is Empathy?
BOOK EXCERPT: *The Sea of Monsters*

On day three of the unit, it was time to introduce the word *empathy*. We passed out copies of an excerpt of a speech delivered by President Barack Obama when he was a U.S. senator. This part of his speech focused on our country's lack of empathy. Here's a sample of the excerpt that we read aloud as shared reading:

> There's a lot of talk in this country about the federal deficit. But I think we should talk more about our empathy deficit—the ability to put ourselves in someone else's shoes; to see the world through those who are different from us—the child who's hungry, the laid-off steelworker, the immigrant woman cleaning your dorm room.
>
> As you go on in life, cultivating this quality of empathy will become harder, not easier. There's no community service requirement in the real world; no one forcing you to care. You'll be free to live in neighborhoods with people who are exactly like yourself, and send your kids to the same schools, and narrow your concerns to what's going in your own little circle.

Not only that—we live in a culture that discourages empathy. A culture that too often tells us our principal goal in life is to be rich, thin, young, famous, safe, and entertained. A culture where those in power too often encourage these selfish impulses. (Obama 2006)

Before we read the speech, we defined a few terms, such as *deficit* and *laid off,* because we knew the students would need this background knowledge for better comprehension. After we read the excerpt, I asked the class if they had ever heard of the word *empathy*. Not a single student knew what it meant. This didn't surprise us. In hindsight, we should have defined the word *before* we read the speech. That way the students would have had better understanding as we read.

During the ensuing discussion about empathy, connecting it back to Gary Soto's short story and the photography activity, a boy excitedly said to the class, "That's just like the empathy link in 'Percy Jackson!'" In an example of serendipitous teaching, Natalie was reading aloud the second Percy Jackson and the Olympians book, *The Sea of Monsters* (Riordan 2007), to the class; that's what the boy was referring to. We grabbed the book from Natalie's desk and reread the following excerpt, emphasizing that although the book is fantasy, empathy can create extremely powerful bonds in our very real lives.

"I'll come rescue you," I promised. "Where are you?"
"The Sea of Monsters, of course!"
"The sea of *what*?"
"I told you! I don't know exactly where! And look, Percy . . . um, I'm really sorry about this, but this empathy link . . . well, I had no choice. Our emotions are connected now. If I die . . ."
"Don't tell me, I'll die too." (74)

Natalie and I prized the idea of two people being so linked through empathy that it became a kind of *physical connection*. We used this to help the kids differentiate between sympathy and empathy. In the former, we feel sorry for someone or something; we have compassion for them or what they're going through. But when we empathize, we go further; we are *with* that person, consciously trying to stand in their shoes, to feel their emotions, to see the world from their perspective, to understand their situation.

This discussion is another example of the great *synergy* we want to build into our unit design. We were able to connect all of these pieces of our unit puzzle—Gary Soto's short story, our picture activity, President Obama's speech, and Rick Riordan's fantasy novel—with the common thread of empathy.

ACTIVITY: Beginning *The Tiger Rising*
POETRY: "The Last Empty Seat"

The Tiger Rising is a wisp of a book—only 116 quickly read pages, with very short chapters. Because we had to complete the unit in three weeks, we planned to read the entire book in just five days (ultimately we needed six days to finish). Because of this limited time, the connected readings and activities we did were all short and quick. This did not diminish their value; sometimes our best teaching and students' best learning happens from a fifteen-minute text or activity.

On that first day of reading, we learned a lot about Rob and Sistine (see Figure 9.3). Rob has a bad, itchy rash on his legs that everyone knows about. Soon after Sistine meets Rob, they argue and she tells him that she "hates him." On page 22, Sistine walks through the school bus and finds just one seat remaining, next to Rob. Sistine tells him, "There isn't any-place else to sit. This is the last empty seat." We asked the class why no one sat next to Rob. They came up with four good reasons:

Figure 9.3 Alejandra reads *The Tiger Rising.*

- They're afraid they might catch his rash.
- They don't like him.
- They fear someone would think they're Rob's friend.
- They fear getting bullied or hit by the Threemonger boys.

This scene, and that exact line, "This is the last empty seat," reminded me of a poem I had read years before titled "The Last Empty Seat" by Richard Goodkin. Although it is about a very similar idea—people not wanting to sit next to someone—it was written in a very different context. It's in an anthology of poems written by African American high school students during the civil rights move-ment (Larrick 1970). In the poem, a person is in some type of venue, perhaps a movie theater, and looking for a place to sit. You can infer that he is African American, and many of the people already seated are white. There are some seats open, but each time he approaches one, the person next to it quickly places something on it so he can't sit there.

We passed out copies and read the poem aloud. After the first reading, some of the kids said, "I don't get it." So a student read it again, and we went through the poem, taking the time for them to understand. We discussed the similarities and differences between the two scenes. Here are the same words—"the last empty seat"—written in very different contexts, but with related meanings. Our hope was that the students would try to see the world from the perspectives of two people: one an African American kid looking for a place to sit in a very racist world and one a bullied kid who is already sitting but whom no one will sit next to.

READING: *The Tiger Rising, Chapters 20 and 21*

Rob has already shown Sistine the tiger he found locked in the cage in the woods. He has discovered that the tiger belongs to Mr. Beauchamp, the wealthy man in town who also owns the run-down

Kentucky Star Motel where his father works and where they live. Beauchamp has hired Rob to feed the tiger, which means he has the keys to the cage.

Rob and Sistine are back in the woods, standing before the tiger, watching it pace back and forth in its cage. Sistine insists they must free the tiger. Rob doesn't know what to do. He can't help himself, and tells Sistine he has the keys. He can unlock the cage and let the tiger go free. She insists he unlock the cage. Rob refuses. Sistine grips the chain link of the cage and violently shakes it:

> "I'll get you out of here," she said to the pacing tiger. "I promise." She rattled the cage as if she were the one who was locked up. The tiger paced back and forth without stopping.
> "Don't," said Rob.
> But she didn't stop. She shook the cage and beat her head against the chainlink, and then he heard her gasp. He was afraid that maybe she was choking. He went and stood next to her. And he saw that she was crying. *Crying.* Sistine. (77)

"Why is Sistine so angry?" we asked the class. "Why is she gripping that cage with her fists and shaking and yelling and crying? Why is she so desperate to free that tiger?"

Leslie said, "Because she has a suitcase too."

This was a pivotal part of the story. I got excited. "Yes! I agree! She has her own suitcase. What's in it?"

Karla wanted to answer: "Her father."

"Yes. Her father is gone. He left them. Isn't it interesting? Rob and Sistine are different in so many ways, but they are also very similar. They are both grieving for a missing parent. But they are expressing it in entirely different ways." I reread a part of the chapter. Rob and Sistine are talking with the wise Willie May, the motel's housekeeper:

> "Ain't that just like God," she said, "throwing the two of you together?" She shook her head. "This boy full of sorrow, keeping it down low in his legs. And you"—she pointed her cigarette at Sistine—"you all full of anger, got it snapping out of you like lightning." (81)

We talked about this—how different people confronted with similar challenges in life, such as losing a parent, can react in such different ways. One person is paralyzed with grief and another is consumed with rage, but both are immersed in emotion.

Extended Ideas

With more time to devote to the unit, we would have explored these ideas and emotions in greater depth, having the kids relate them to their own lives. This would have been a perfect place to guide them through a personal narrative, following a complete writing process. Many advocates of using literature with adolescents emphasize the importance of students being able to identify with characters. We could take that idea further and help the students identify with the *emotions* in this story. Really, how often do students write honest personal narratives about the tragedy or anger or sadness or fear in their lives? Sharing these written emotional connections as a classroom community would reinforce how we are all bonded as humans and experience a sweeping range of emotions throughout our lives.

WRITING ASSIGNMENT: Letters to Rob
ACTIVITY: Take-a-Stand Debate

The students were to imagine they were Rob's friend; they had seen the endless bullying at school and knew everything that was going on in his life, from the tiger to Sistine to his sorrow for his mom's death. They had to write Rob a letter, advising him about what he should do with his life. This is what empathic people do; ideally, their empathy is followed by *action* to help those in need. Here are two letters:

Dear Rob,
So, hey buddy, how's it going? I heard about the Threemonger brothers. That must be rough, how they act. I think that's lame. How you taking it? And Sistine, you like her? Ok, ok, enough questions. So, I think I can help you with the big problems in your life. Well, you know how you told me about your suitcase, and I thought about it. You need to let it out. Just because your dad said not to cry, that don't mean nothin'. You best let it out because there ain't no reason in not letting it out! Now, your whole Sistine and tiger problem, I think you should just let Sistine know about your job and the keys to the cage. She might push them out of you just like she did with your mother's name. The tiger was yours first. You saw it, not her, and just because Mr. Beauchamp owns the tiger, that don't mean you don't have to tell Sistine. Now, you think. If you were the tiger in a cage and you were in there only to attract customers, how would you feel? Do you like this tiger? If you say yes, set it free, as you would want to be. I give you the best my friend. Hope and good luck with your choices. I hope I could've helped.
Sincerely,
Nicholas

Dear Rob,
I know it's hard for you with all these problems. I want to give you some advice. I think you should tell Sistine everything that's inside that suitcase, inside your heart. You can't leave your feelings inside forever. It was great that you told Sistine your mother's name. Your suitcase is opening, little by little. About the tiger. What are you going to do? Beauchamp let you feed the tiger and gave you the key to the tiger's cage. Are you going to tell Sistine that you have it? Let me tell you something. Remember that story Willie May told you, about her bird? I suggest you do the same thing. How do you feel when you see that poor tiger locked up in a cage? It feels the same way like your feelings, trapped. I hope my advice works for you. Please write back.
Sincerely,
Lucero

Perhaps more than anything these letters showed us that the students were taking the idea of helping others in need seriously. With middle schoolers there can be a fine line between an assignment such as this being taken seriously and becoming a joke. Granted, it was an assignment and Natalie graded it, but from reading their letters it is clear that most of these sixth graders took the assignment to heart. Nearly every student mentioned Rob's suitcase, and all of them told him to open it. As Jonathan wrote, "You should open the suitcase in your mind and let your emotions go."

This activity also allowed us (and the class) to see that we have different—and often contradictory—advice to offer Rob and Sistine. Both Nicholas and Lucero, just like nearly everyone in class, told Rob to set the tiger free. But not Eric. He wrote, "About the tiger, I think you should let the tiger stay behind the Kentucky Star in the cage. Do not let Sistine tell you what to do like she made you tell her your mom's name. It is your choice to let the tiger out not hers." And about those bullying Threemonger brothers, just about everyone echoed Alex's advice: "I also heard that some guys are picking on you. You should just fight them and get it over with." But Shiondrell, with her strong sense of independence, had a different perspective, writing, "I think you should let the Threemongers keep talking about you. Show them that you don't care."

These letters also gave Natalie's students an opportunity to identify directly with these characters. For example, Hailey wrote to Rob, "I know how you feel about your mom. I grew up without my dad and wishing he could be there. I do have my step-dad, but it's hard not knowing who your real dad was. He left me when I was two." Hailey's comments reinforced the importance of choosing books and stories that allow students to identify with characters. Connections like these are direct paths to empathy and caring.

We connected the students' letters to a Take-a-Stand activity to engage in a vigorous debate about the advice they extended to Rob. We also wanted them to hear other students' ideas and be open to changing their opinions (see Figure 9.4).

We began with this statement: "Rob's dad is right. Rob should fight the Threemonger boys." Something interesting happened then: Even though almost all of them had written that Rob should fight them, the class split evenly between boys and girls on that point in the debate. Many thought the bullies would never leave Rob alone until he fought back. Others argued that fighting would just make the problem worse. Some of the kids said Rob needed to stand up for himself; he was allowing himself to get bullied. Most of the students were eager to let their voices be heard, even Jose, who more often cracked jokes and pushed behavior boundaries. Natalie and I were thrilled that a student who spends so much time pushing her buttons and causing classroom conflict was thoroughly engaged in an intellectual debate about right and wrong.

We made another statement: "Rob should cry because of the death of his mom." The entire class went to the "agree" side—except for Alex. He was standing in neutral all by himself. This surprised me, because Alex was one of the most empathetic kids in the class, always eager to share his opinions about Rob's feelings or his own. But that is part of the beauty and power of inquiry-based teaching. Given the opportunity to openly explore important issues, you never really know what views and ideas students will express. Here was Alex, standing alone, bravely confronting his twenty-eight classmates. We asked him to explain his reasoning. He said that although Rob should have cried when his mom died, there comes a point when you need to stop crying and move on with your life.

Figure 9.4 Destiny and Alex debate in Take-a-Stand.

This led us into a discussion about death in our own lives. Some kids talked about the death of a family member, others about the pain of losing a pet. We shared our stories, and then the room was quiet. Many of the students had experienced death. Talking about it can help students make connections with their classmates as well as their teachers. I shared with the class some of the story of my mom's sudden death. Driving to the school earlier, I had no idea I was going to do that. Teaching with good literature, engaging with themes of social responsibility, cultivating a humane curriculum, you never know where it will lead. This is part of the *spontaneity* that Elliot Eisner (2002) says is vital in a classroom. Sometimes those turn out to be the best moments of all.

READING: *The Tiger Rising: The Death of a Tiger and the Tears of a Boy*

Finishing a good book with a classroom of middle schoolers is a bittersweet experience. You are excited to be finished, but you are also sorry to let go of the book. Reading *The Tiger Rising* went by in a flash. Although we did not have a great deal of time over those six days, we were able to discuss and debate ideas and experiences central to life, as well as explore our own empathy and feelings for Rob and Sistine. Natalie and I had no doubt that most of the kids—if not all of them—*loved* this book.

This was clearly evident as we read aloud, in slow and somber voices, the end of the story, when Rob and Sistine do free the tiger, and then Rob's dad shoots and kills the tiger in self-defense. Some of the kids spoke of their sadness over the death of the tiger. I think they also empathized with Rob's dad. They knew he did not want to kill the tiger. They said he had no choice. He had to protect Rob and Sistine. But that act by his dad triggers Rob's suitcase to burst open, and, finally, in his father's arms, he hears his father say how much he misses his wife and that it is okay to cry.

PROJECT: Teaching Caring and Empathy to Second Graders
PICTURE BOOKS: *Whitewash* and *Freedom Summer*

We had just three days to do a post-book project. We wanted the class to explicitly expand their thinking from *The Tiger Rising* to caring and empathy. After racking our brains to come up with an idea for a good project, it finally came to us: one of the best ways to really *learn* something is to *teach it*. A common example of that is connecting reading buddies. Middle school teachers who have paired their students with younger kids to read books together see the special power of this experience (Freidland and Truesdell 2004). Far beyond cultivating responsibility and maturity in the older kids, I've seen firsthand middle schoolers take their learning commitment to a higher level when it's done for the purpose of teaching younger students. (Some researchers have started calling this the Protégé Effect.)

Natalie talked to Gina, a second-grade teacher in her school, about joining the project. She loved the idea. Natalie's sixth graders would use picture books to teach Gina's second graders about caring and empathy. I've written in the past about the wonders of using picture books with middle school students to teach social responsibility (Wolk 2004). This was taking that one step further, empowering Natalie's students to use those books to teach younger kids.

The class was thrilled to work with younger students, especially as "teachers of caring." We explained how important it was for them to take this project seriously and the responsibility required when guiding young children. To make this work well, Natalie and I knew her students would need explicit help in planning their reading and teaching of the picture books. I created a two-page planning sheet for the students to complete as preparation for their readings and to broaden their understanding of empathy and caring (see Figures 9.5a and 9.5b and Appendix L for a blank sheet). We asked students to do the following:

- Identify specific examples of caring and/or empathy in the book.
- Ask themselves if they identified with any characters.
- Identify emotions in the story.
- Brainstorm questions that do not have one correct answer that they could ask second graders.
- Identify background knowledge second graders may need to understand the story.
- Identify potential vocabulary words second graders may need help with.
- Plan how they will explain to second graders what *caring* and *empathy* mean, and brainstorm examples from their own lives.

We modeled how to read a picture book aloud, pull out themes of caring, and complete the planning sheet. We used *Whitewash* by Ntozake Shange (1998), which features an African American girl, Helene-Angel, who is attacked by a white gang. They cruelly spray-paint her face white, and Helene-Angel hides in her bedroom for a week. When her grandmother persuades her to come out, Helene-Angel opens the door and sees her friends' smiling faces, expressing their concern, support, and friendship. After we read the book aloud, we modeled the process of completing a planning sheet by filling one out as a class, using the overhead projector.

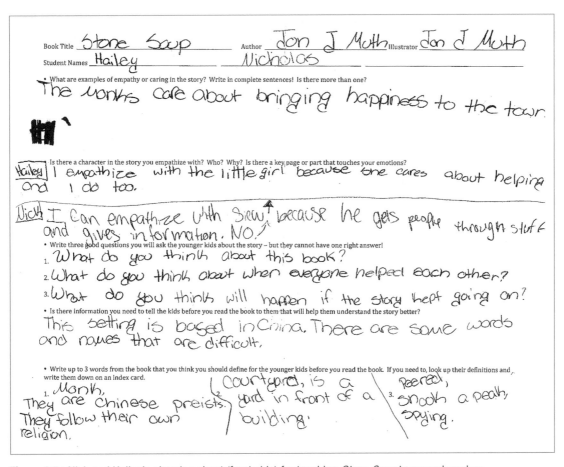

Book Title Stone Soup   Author Jon J Muth Illustrator Jon J Muth
Student Names Hailey   Nicholas

• What are examples of empathy or caring in the story? Write in complete sentences! Is there more than one?

The monks care about bringing happiness to the town.

Is there a character in the story you empathize with? Who? Why? Is there a key page or part that touches your emotions?

Hailey I empathize with the little girl because she cares about helping and I do too.

Nick I can empathize with Siew because he gets people through stuff and gives information. NO.

• Write three good questions you will ask the younger kids about the story – but they cannot have one right answer!

1. What do you think about this book?
2. What do you think about when everyone helped each other?
3. What do you think will happen if the story kept going on?

• Is there information you need to tell the kids before you read the book to them that will help them understand the story better?

This setting is based in China. There are some words and names that are difficult.

• Write up to 3 words from the book that you think you should define for the younger kids before you read the book. If you need to, look up their definitions and write them down on an index card.

1. Monk, They are Chinese preists. They follow their own religion.
2. Courtyard, is a yard in front of a building.
3. smooth a peach, spying.

Figure 9.5a Nick and Hailey's planning sheet (front side) for teaching *Stone Soup* to second graders.

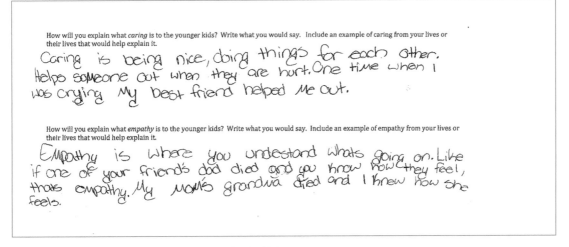

How will you explain what *caring* is to the younger kids? Write what you would say. Include an example of caring from your lives or their lives that would help explain it.

Caring is being nice, doing things for each other. Helps someone out when they are hurt. One time when I was crying my best friend helped me out.

How will you explain what *empathy* is to the younger kids? Write what you would say. Include an example of empathy from your lives or their lives that would help explain it.

Empathy is where you understand whats going on. Like if one of your friend's dad died and you know how they feel, thats empathy. My mom's grandma died and I knew how she feels.

Figure 9.5b Nick and Hailey's planning sheet (back side).

We modeled reading aloud one more picture book, *Freedom Summer* by Deborah Wiles (2005). We chose this book because we wanted a story that would connect to our upcoming reading of *Leon's Story*. *Freedom Summer* takes place in 1964, just when the Civil Rights Act was being enacted and ending the racist Jim Crow laws. One of those laws was the segregation of public swimming pools. But, as the story shows, rather than integrate their pools, many cities in the South simply closed them by filling them with tar or dirt.

We put together a text set of picture books with themes of caring or empathy (below). Natalie wanted students in boy-girl pairs, to break them out of the routine of grouping themselves with the same sex (with the added benefit of breaking up those four boys). After the kids paired up, Natalie made a few adjustments, and we passed out the books.

Zen Ties	*Librarian of Basra*
A River of Words	*Stone Soup*
The Cello of Mr. O	*Listen to the Wind*
A Day's Work	*Teammates*
Someday a Tree	*Wangari's Trees of Peace*
Nasreen's Secret School	*Wilfred Gordon McDonald Partridge*
The Summer My Father Was Ten	

The students spread out and began to read the books. Some struggled to pull the "caring" out of their books, which introduced some esoteric and entirely new ways for them to think about the theme. Wrestling with ambiguity is an important part of learning, of course, and we were pleased that the activity enabled students to see that we can care for an endless array of things and ideas, such as the nature and poetry of the great poet William Carlos Williams in the picture book *A River of Words*.

PROJECT: Teaching Empathy and Caring to Second Graders
PROJECT: Writing "Caring Haiku"
PICTURE BOOK: *Tomas and the Library Lady*
POETRY: Haiku by Matsuo Basho

Natalie's class met their second-grade picture book buddies in the cafeteria. We had an hour to complete the work. After that, hungry fifth graders would pour in to eat lunch. As the students sat on the floor together, sixth graders Vanessa and Ben explained to the second graders what *caring* means, and Karla and Nick explained haiku (see Figure 9.6).

Next, we read aloud *Tomas and the Library Lady* (Mora 1997) to the entire group. Tomas is a Mexican American boy in the United States during the 1950s. His parents are migrant farmworkers. When they arrive in a small town in Iowa, Tomas, who loves to read, becomes friends with the local librarian, who is white. Without a library card Tomas cannot check out books, but the library lady allows him to take books out in her name. She welcomes him into the library every day, encouraging him to fall in love with books and reading. At the end of the book, you find out that Tomas is a real person, Tomas Rivera, who went on to become chancellor of the University of California at Riverside. We used this book to model how to identify acts of caring in a story.

Figure 9.6 Karla and Nick teach haiku to the second graders.

We wanted the sixth graders and the second graders to create something together in response to their books. But with only an hour, our options were very limited, so we decided to create "caring haiku." Japanese haiku is usually about nature. But our haiku would be about caring.

After reading *Tomas and the Library Lady*, we did a mini-lesson about haiku. Earlier I had made a few posters of example haiku. The first was from Matsuo Basho, the famous seventeenth-century Japanese poet. Everyone counted the necessary syllables as we read the three lines aloud. Next was a haiku I wrote in response to *Tomas and the Library Lady*. We counted those syllables too, with the second graders and their sixth-grade buddies eagerly clapping along in syllabic rhythm.

The kids paired up and spread out to read their picture books (see Figure 9.7). Nick was putting tremendous emotion into his reading of *Stone Soup*

Figure 9.7 Hailey reads to her second-grade partner, Martha. (Hailey's partner, Nick, and their other second-grade buddy are off camera.)

(Muth 2007). All four boys who so often pushed the behavior boundaries did their readings with maturity and grace. Walter was going out of his way to help his second graders understand empathy: "It's when you are seeing through *their* eyes. It's when you really *feel* what they are feeling."

After reading the picture books, we placed large sheets of butcher paper on the lunchroom tables so the students could write their caring haiku together. We then displayed the sheets in Gina's classroom, and each group took turns reading their poems. Their poems showed us that all of the groups were able to find acts of caring in their books, and some of them went beyond typical examples, such as caring for books, caring to help girls get an education, and caring for trees. This is exactly what we wanted for all the kids: to have their vision of caring expanded and enriched. Here are five of their haiku:

She cared for her books
She risked her life to save books
She got her books saved

Not fair, so not fair
Girls not allowed in school
She needs lots of help!

Nobody trusts trusts
Monks cared about happiness
The town had a feast

She loves to plant trees.
She plants sugarcane and trees
She loves Africa

I enjoy poems
Poems help me to relax
They are wonderful

READING: *Leon's Story*

NEW YORK TIMES ARTICLE: "Unearthing a Town Pool, and Not for Whites Only"

To connect the picture book project to *Leon's Story*, we went back to the picture book *Freedom Summer*, which we had read a few days before. We passed out an article from the *New York Times* that I had in my files, titled "Unearthing a Town Pool, and Not for Whites Only" (Nossiter 2006). We began by going over a few vocabulary words from the article and showing the class the state of

Mississippi on the map of the United States. We read the article as shared reading. It is the same story as *Freedom Summer*—but a *true* version. Two men who grew up in Stonewall, Mississippi, discovered the town's swimming pool that had been filled with dirt and buried more than thirty years before. They excavated the pool to reopen it. The story captivated the kids, making *Freedom Summer* (and history) breathe with truth.

MINI-LESSON: Timeline of *Leon's Story*

To understand *Leon's Story*, the students needed some background knowledge. *Freedom Summer* and the newspaper article helped build some of that knowledge. But we wanted to place the history of African American civil rights in historical context so the students would have a deeper understanding and see the "big picture" of history that is so often lost in the endless trivia of social studies textbooks. We drew a timeline on the board with Leon's birth year (1936) on the left end and the current year on the right. We asked the students when they were born and added 1998 to the timeline. Then we added when their parents were born, around 1970, and their grandparents, about 1940.

This way they saw that their grandparents and Leon were born around the same time. Leon was probably just a bit older than their grandparents. They also saw that the story in this book is not "ancient history." In fact, Leon was still alive! (As I mentioned previously, he died the year after we taught this unit.) We did the math and saw that he was seventy-four years old. Much of the class was astonished. As we read the book, knowing all of this made Leon's story more real and relevant. Some students pointed out that surely some of the people who treated Leon so horrendously were also still alive.

READING: *Leon's Story*

The story, which reflects Leon's gentle voice, propels the reader forward. Two-thirds into the book we are confronted with the true horrors of racism in our country's recent past. Natalie and I knew this was going to be the emotional epicenter. It is Leon's fifteenth birthday. He is walking with his family down a road. Driving down the road, two white teenagers purposely run down his father and drag him two blocks under their car. Then they stop the car, get out, pull his dad out, put the car in reverse, and run over his father again, killing him.

After I read this aloud, I paused. Silence enveloped the classroom. With disbelief and shock, Alex said what everyone was thinking: "How could people do that?" Some of them could not believe this was a true story, that people could be so cruel. A few asked—even though we had emphasized it many times—"So, this is a true story? This *really* happened?" Yes, it really happened. And many, many more times than just to Leon. It is ugly and painful historical truths like these that middle-grades students must be trusted to embrace and explore for them to feel historical empathy and use that understanding to make them better people and socially responsible citizens.

In a flash, our reading was done. I love that the book ends with Leon's participation in the nonviolent protest marches of the civil rights movement. There were many ideas we would have loved to explore with this amazing book, but spring break was just hours away. We had just enough time that afternoon to do two activities.

ACTIVITY: Venn Diagram

Natalie and I wanted her students to explicitly connect *The Tiger Rising* and *Leon's Story*. Although they are different books in many ways, they also have much in common, especially Rob and Leon, who are both struggling in profoundly difficult times. We gathered the class together one last time to create a Venn diagram, comparing the fictional Rob and the real Leon. We also felt this would be a good way for the kids to see how both of these books come together under the larger umbrella of empathy and caring and how people deal with adversity. We created one Venn diagram as a class.

JOURNAL-WRITE: Responding to *Leon's Story*

Our last activity was a journal-write. Again, we wanted to give Natalie's students some choice in what to write about. We gave them two prompts:

1. *After reading a good book we can be changed. In what way has reading* Leon's Story *changed you? Has it changed how you see the value of learning history and knowing people's stories? Has it changed how you see empathy or caring?*

2. *Imagine Leon visited the school and you spent some time alone talking. What would you want to say to him? What did the story of his life make you think and feel and learn? Write exactly what you would say to him.*

Below are two responses, one from each prompt. Although they are rather short (it *was* practically spring break), the writings give us insight into how Leon's story influenced the students' thinking and feeling. Shiondrell's writing shows us that she understands we can learn from history, that we must know the injustice and oppression so many people have endured, that some of these people stood up for what is right and just and, perhaps most notably, that she now empathizes—yes, she used that word—with her own African American history:

Yes, I feel like Leon's Story *changed me, because in every history story it tries to make a point, teach a lesson. To show how things used to be, to show us how far we come. And I feel like we should be very grateful that people before us took a stand, saying, this is not right, life shouldn't have to be this way. And the people who took a stand knew what they were doing. They knew if I go against this I am risking my life, but for a good cause. I now realize that history is very important to know, because without history we wouldn't know our background history. I now feel like I can empathize with the people in my history, black history. And I personally feel very, very grateful, because without people like Leon, I wouldn't be standing here today.*

Alex wrote to Leon. His brief writing emphasizes that he has never had to endure the racism and brutality of Leon's life, which is clearly part of empathy. It also shows, just like Shiondrell, that he's had a change of heart about the value of learning and reading history. And finally, we see just how much reading about the killing of Leon's father affected Alex.

I would tell him: That story about you really got to me and it touched me. I have never been a victim of any racial situation, but I can empathize with you. Your story really made me think. Wow, how can people be so racist, and I learned a lot about the time of segregation. I wasn't much into learning history, but since I read your book I totally changed my opinion. I felt horrible when I read the part when your dad was murdered. I mean, the teen's dad went up to your house and all he said was, "Stuff like this happens," and then he gave your mom $100, and I thought, money doesn't make up death.

And what about Leslie? Before we read the book, she wrote that learning history was not important. What did she think two days later, after *Leon's Story*? Maybe she changed more than she realized:

I didn't really change my opinion on history much. Although now I think it really depends on what you're learning and how you're learning it. This story also made me feel like every time I see someone getting beat, hurt, teased, etc., I'm going to help. Empathy, it's a hard thing to do, but I can empathize with Leon. I can see things the way he does. The way they treated him, it was just horrible.

Reading for Caring and Empathy

In Chapter 1, I asked a question: Why read? One of the very best reasons to read, especially fiction, is that it makes us more caring and compassionate people. Indeed, psychology researchers believe that reading fiction makes us more empathic. Reading novels is a kind of simulation for real human interactions. The researchers write, "The simulations of social experience that literary narratives afford provides an opportunity for empathic growth. It trains us to extend our understanding toward other people, to embody (to some extent) and understand their beliefs and emotions . . . and ultimately to understand ourselves" (Mar and Oatley 2008, 181). There has even been a phrase coined, *narrative empathy*, for this connection between reading fiction and empathy (Keen 2006).

While I was writing this chapter, my thirteen-year-old son, Max, was reading the historical novel *Between Shades of Gray*, about Stalin's ruthless purges in Lithuania. Watching him engrossed in that book, hearing him talk about it, listening to him insist on reading aloud passages to my wife and me, I have no doubt I was witnessing narrative empathy.

Remember the excerpt from President Obama's speech that we had Natalie's students read? Obama said that our country was suffering from an "empathy deficit." Research backs this up. A widely publicized University of Michigan study shows a significant decline in empathy in America. Researchers have been surveying college students since 1979 to gauge their level of empathy. Since 2000 students have self-reported a *40 percent* drop in their levels of concern. They offer a variety of possible causes: people spending less time in social situations, our huge rise in media usage, the violent content of media, the popularity of reality TV, changes in parenting styles, smaller families with fewer siblings, and an increased focus on economic success. They also point out that while research shows our empathy is decreasing, it is also showing that are our *narcissism* is increasing (Konrath, O'Brien, and Hsing 2011).

There might also be another cause: the steep decline in the number of Americans reading fiction. Researchers believe (and so do I, by the way) that as a result of declining readership of fiction, millions of people are missing out on literary experiences that cultivate empathy and caring (Zaki 2011). That point is worth considering when teachers want to justify the importance of creating inquiry units that aim to open students' hearts and minds. Why immerse adolescents in reading good books? Yes, it certainly helps them become better readers and thinkers, but it also makes them more caring people, and that cultivates a better world.

All of the resources for this unit are included on the companion Web site, stenhouse.com/caringhearts.

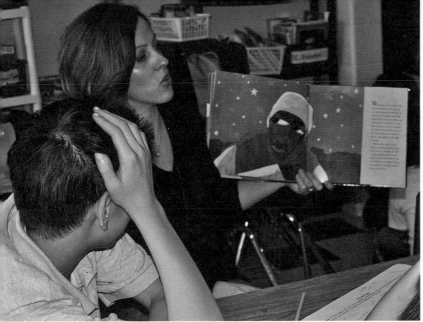

Chapter 10

Why Should I Care About What Is Happening Around the World?

When I asked Dika why they bombed her house and why they put her in prison, she said, "No reason. No Reason. Only the hate."

—*Red Glass*

I'm inside schools a lot, working with teachers of every subject, from kindergarten to eighth grade. I visit urban schools and suburban schools. How often do I see students investigating or reading about a country other than the United States? Very rarely.

It is also uncommon for American students to read fiction set in another country, unless the author's name is Shakespeare (Ivey and Broaddus 2001; Pitcher et al. 2007). Sixth-grade social studies classes usually focus on ancient history and religion, but because that study is limited to the *ancient* world, students learn little of the *present* world. The National Assessment of Educational Progress, which the media likes to call our "nation's report card," asked fourth graders in 2010 how often "world affairs" is part of their classroom. Eighty percent said "not at all" or a "small extent" (2010, 12).

A much-publicized report by the National Geographic Education Foundation included this statement:

The survey demonstrates young Americans' limited understanding of their world within and beyond their country's borders. Respondents answered just over half (54 percent) of the questions correctly, and they don't appear to value skills that would enhance their knowledge. In fact, fewer than three in 10 of those surveyed think it is absolutely necessary to know where countries in the news are located. (2006)

Here are a few of the results of the survey:

♦ Nearly one-third could not locate China on a world map, and nearly one-half could not locate India.

♦ In 2006 after nearly five years of the United States at war in Afghanistan, 88 percent could not find that country on a map.

♦ Most did not know that Sudan and Rwanda—the locations of the world's two most recent genocides—are in Africa.

Now let's face a harsh truth here: American kids are not alone in global illiteracy. When American adults eighteen to thirty-four years old answered a fifty-six-question survey about current events, international issues, map reading, and geography skills, they got an average of only twenty-three answers correct (National Geographic Education Foundation 2002).

Our children are following in our footsteps. They see the world on TV and online, listen to global music, watch worldwide sports, and buy endless stuff manufactured around the planet, yet they have little knowledge of the countries that contribute to global commerce, politics, and information, or of the rich cultures spread across our world. They also have limited understanding of how personal and political choices in one country affect so many others. For example, the United States has 5 percent of the world's population but uses about one-third of Earth's natural resources and causes a third of the world's pollution. The world devotes $2.2 trillion each year to military spending, and the United States spends *one-third* of that sum. Thirty percent of the planet lives in extreme poverty. These issues raise inquiry questions students can explore: What are the ethical uses of natural resources? How much money should we spend on the military? How do other people around the world live? What moral and economic responsibilities do wealthy countries have to help poor countries? (The inquiry unit in Chapter 11 is, in part, about global poverty.)

A long list of prestigious education organizations have called for the inclusion of global literacy in school. These include the National Geographic Society, the Harvard Think Tank on Global Education, the professional development organization World Savvy, the aid organization Oxfam, the Partnership for 21st Century Skills, Coverdell World Wise Schools (part of the Peace Corps), the Asia Society, and the One World Youth Project. (Most of these have resources for teaching global awareness on their Web sites.) The Association for Middle Level Education writes in its position paper "What We Believe: Keys to Educating Young Adolescents" that middle-grades teachers should help their students do the following:

♦ Become actively aware of the larger world, asking significant and relevant questions about that world and wrestling with big ideas and questions for which there may not be one right answer.

♦ Respect and value the diverse ways people look, speak, think, and act within the immediate community and around the world. (2010)

Teaching global awareness goes beyond simple geography lessons or cultural studies, especially if one of your goals is to teach social responsibility. A short list of topics or themes could include the following:

- Gender issues
- Global economics and poverty
- Environmental issues and global ecosystems
- Cultures and languages
- Wars, violence, and global peace efforts
- International current events
- American foreign policy
- Quality of life and happiness
- Global arts, drama, movies, music, and pop culture

It is especially exciting to explore this knowledge with middle schoolers because of their budding ability to think abstractly and their growing consciousness of the larger world. Daisaku Ikeda, the distinguished humanistic educator and Buddhist philosopher, writes that there are three vital qualities of the global citizen:

- Wisdom—the ability to perceive the interdependence of all life
- Courage—the courage to respect one another's differences and use them as an impetus to creative living, rather than rejecting or excluding others on the basis of differences of culture, nationality, and race
- The ability to empathize with and share the pain of every person and all of life. (2007, x)

Having students read textbooks full of facts will give them barely a surface understanding of the world. We need deeper explorations of the planet and its diverse and fascinating people. Ikeda's global citizenship qualities of wisdom, courage, and empathy are high standards to reach, but understanding and compassion are central to becoming caring, smart, and moral people. One of the best ways to teach those qualities is by coming together as communities of readers to share globally conscious books.

Reading the World

There is a small sign on the hallway wall just outside Karen's classroom: "Reading is breathing in . . . writing is breathing out. Just breathe." This simple sign paints a picture of the classroom through that doorway, led by a teacher who wants her students to see and think about life inside books. Karen was in her tenth year of teaching seventh and eighth grade in a Chicago public school when we decided to work together on an inquiry unit with her twenty-eight lively eighth graders. They were a culturally diverse group, but largely Mexican American, with strong opinions and a zeal for their voices to be heard.

Karen had taught a literature unit using the novel *Red Glass* the previous year, but it's fair to say she had not focused on global awareness or inquiry. Karen loved this book with its transformative story of the main character, Sophie. She also knew her eighth graders would enjoy the subplot of Sophie's first romance. In addition to featuring that crowd-pleasing theme, we added two new goals: raising her

NEW YORK TIMES OP-ED PIECE: "The Karma of the Killing Fields"

Over the course of the unit, Karen and I wanted her students to read about a variety of "journeys"—both fictional and nonfictional—especially taking place around the world, as a way to integrate global awareness. This also connected to *Red Glass* because many of the characters go through (or went through) their own harrowing global journeys.

We read an op-ed piece from the *New York Times* that I had in my files. "The Karma of the Killing Fields" (Siv 2005) recounts the author's harrowing journey to escape the genocidal "killing fields" of Cambodia in 1975. He began his escape with fifteen family members, yet he was the only survivor. He later became the U.S. ambassador to the United Nations. We knew this article would later connect to the war and genocide that Dika and Mr. Lorenzo experience in *Red Glass*.

NONFICTION PICTURE BOOKS: *Global Stories* and *Journeys*

We divided the class into groups of about four students each. Each group was given a picture book about a real person who experienced a "remarkable journey." Continuing to thread our global awareness theme through the unit, we included some books about people in other countries. We also wanted stories of both men and women. Here are the picture books we used:

- *Planting the Trees of Kenya* about Wangari Maathai, who won the Nobel Peace Prize for starting the Green Belt Movement in Africa (Nivola 2008)
- *The Wall*, Peter Sis's (2007) autobiographical story of growing up in Czechoslovakia
- *Grandfather's Journey*, Allen Say's (1993) story of his grandfather's immigration to the United States from Japan
- *Anne Frank* by Josephine Poole (2007), an outstanding telling of Frank's story with beautiful yet somber illustrations
- *Harvesting Hope: The Story of Cesar Chavez* by Kathleen Krull (2003), another well-told story with stunning illustrations
- *When Harriet Met Sojourner*, about Harriet Tubman and Sojourner Truth (Clinton 2007)

We gave each group a large piece of paper and asked the students to write the book title in the center. We did a variation of "silent conversation." As one of the students read aloud, the other kids jotted down words and phrases that captured the person's journey. We did not have a lot of time on this day, so after their reading, we asked a volunteer from each group to talk briefly to the class about the person they read about and their remarkable journey.

Extended Ideas

In an ideal world, I would advocate international travel for every high school student, but if we can't get students to other countries, we can bring other countries to them. Here are four ways to do that:

- Digitally connect them to students all over the world through epals.com and globalschoolnet.org. These Internet hubs link classrooms in different countries to work on joint projects. You might also be able to Skype (if the time difference works) to have the students meet and talk in real time. Jenna, a student teacher I worked with, arranged for her second graders to become e-pals with first and second graders in Nairobi, Kenya, and Vietnam.
- Ask students to interview recent immigrants to the United States to learn about their native countries and cultures. Ideally, they would create a project in response to the interview, such as writing and drawing (or photographing) a picture book, writing and performing a monologue, creating an iMovie of the interview, or writing the interview as a biography.
- Show them the remarkable 360-degree panoramic global photos at 360cities.net.
- Assemble a panel of people who were raised in other countries and invite them to the classroom to talk about their lives. You can have students prepare questions in advance, and you also might want to have the panelists split up to talk to smaller groups of students.
- Contact the Coverdell World Wise Schools organization. Their Correspondence Match program connects a Peace Corps volunteer in another country to your classroom. Their Speaker Match program brings returning Peace Corps volunteers right into your classroom to speak with your students. You can find them here: peacecorps.gov/wws/. The Web site is loaded with great stories, podcasts, photographs, and videos by Peace Corps volunteers.

THE CLASSROOM WALL: World Map

We hung a large world map on the classroom wall. Throughout the unit, each time a country came up—either from the picture books, *Red Glass*, or another text—Karen placed a small arrow on the country. We started with arrows on Cambodia for Sichan Siv's op-ed piece and added more for the picture books the students read. Over the course of five weeks, we spent on the unit we read about or discussed fifteen countries:

Japan	Czechoslovakia	Germany
Cambodia	Kenya	Poland
Yugoslavia	Mexico	United States
Bosnia	Guatemala	Rwanda
Honduras	Afghanistan	India

WRITING ASSIGNMENT: Six-Word Journeys

Early in the unit we had a short discussion with the class to introduce the idea of journeys. We asked the students, "Who has been on a journey? Any kind of journey." Hands shot up in the air. Not surprisingly, these eighth graders grasped the idea of emotional journeys. April said her emotional journey had to do with some of her oldest friends who were getting into drugs. She had to make the decision to break away from them. Destiny mentioned that she was getting into fights with her mom until she realized that many of their conflicts had to do with her fears.

Inspired by the students' insights, Karen and I created a small assignment. An online magazine, smithmag.net, started a popular phenomenon called "six-word memoirs." People submit a memoir that sums up their life or a critical experience in just six words. Two volumes of six-word memoirs have been published as books, one written by adults and one by teenagers (Fershleiser and Smith 2008, 2009). We brought them to class and read some examples, and then asked the students to write "six-word journeys." To say they loved this assignment would be a grand understatement. The following day one girl came to class with thirty written journeys. Here are some examples from the class:

Love hurts,
People die,
Parents yell.

found out
   i have
      two brothers.

He left
   to Neverland.
I'm empty.

Must know
   how
     to
       control
         time

My journey stopped
in purgatory: sins

Soon to be
Freshman
I'm terrified.

Karen and I wrote and shared our six-word journeys too. Here is Karen's: "Came alive plucking chickens in Mexico." Here is mine: "Emergency room. Mom. Hospice. Mom. Gone."

This assignment was a perfect addition to our unit. These whispers of writing helped the kids quickly and eloquently express their fears, struggles, joys, and heartaches. Sure, some of the writing was melodramatic, but so is adolescence! These feelings are real, and it was remarkable to sit and listen as the students took turns sharing glimpses of their humanity and humility. The next day Karen posted the writing on the classroom wall to honor and share their emotional journeys.

READING: *Red Glass*, Chapters 6 and 7

Middle school teachers know the marvelous, expansive, and sometimes convoluted and mind-boggling directions their students can take in classroom conversations. Start talking about the weather, and soon a kid has connected that to his dog and another kid to her favorite band and yet another to a friend who moved away to California. Sometimes these paths lead nowhere and other times they are pure gold. That's what happened when we were all crowded into a corner of the classroom, books in hand, as Karen read Chapters 6 and 7 aloud. Some of the students were on the floor with Karen, others pulled up a chair, others sat at a nearby desk, and a few were on top of a desk. It was a tight group—close in more ways than just physical space (see Figure 10.3).

Figure 10.3 Karen Tellez's eighth graders pack in close to read and discuss *Red Glass* and life.

Karen began with shared reading, and then asked student volunteers to read aloud. When someone is part of the flow of conversation as I often was, it can be difficult (and sometimes impossible) to capture and convey the scope of a discussion. That's what happened after reading these two chapters. In the course of about thirty minutes, the conversation—all the comments connected to and revolving around the novel—was like a pinball game. It was thoughtful and important and rather electric. All of these topics were part of this discussion:

- Self-confidence
- Self-esteem
- Wondering if celebrities like Brad Pitt have self-doubt (all the kids together: Yes!)
- Our fears
- The murder of Emmett Till
- Wondering if it's okay for middle school boys to cry (everyone again: Yes!)
- Appreciating the "little things" in life more after a near-death experience, such as the taste of berries

This conversation bounced around with the refreshing energy and spontaneity that middle school teachers crave. When facilitating a discussion about books, teachers have to make split-second decisions about what paths to follow and what paths to avoid, all while honoring the unique (and occasionally disjointed) directions in which adolescents can take us. Sometimes the best course of action is to let the talk flow and see where it leads. Such conversations show the tremendous power that literature has to offer and the remarkable connections readers can make to good books.

But good talk like this around books does not happen on a whim; it takes good teachers like Karen to cultivate good talk. She honors her kids' voices and encourages their participation, but also strives to keep their talk confined to important matters. She really trusts her students to take their talk seriously, and she knows just when to let go a bit and allow their talk to drift, seeing where it will go. That's how we ended up with this amazing conversation. And equally important, Karen embraces the humor that is as natural to middle school as crazy hormones and socializing. One sign of a good and healthy middle-grades classroom is laughter.

BOOK EXCERPT: *Three Cups of Tea*
VIDEO: The Girl Effect

In 1992, Greg Mortenson, an emergency room nurse and lifelong mountain climber, was on a three-month expedition to climb K2 in Pakistan, the second-highest mountain in the world. He got lost and was rescued by the people of Korphe, a remote village. When he saw that the village school was a patch of dirt where the students wrote with sticks, Mortenson promised he would return to build them a real school. He did that and wrote a best-selling book, *Three Cups of Tea* (2006).

We went online to show the class the Web site of Mortenson's organization, the Central Asia Institute (ikat.org). It has a map of Afghanistan and Pakistan, showing the regions of his work and the schools he has built not just in Korphe, but in more than 100 other places as well. A murmur raced through the classroom. The kids were amazed. Talk about a journey! Then we read the first three chapters of the Young Reader's Edition of *Three Cups of Tea* (Mortenson and Relin 2009).

In 2011, it came out through well-known author Jon Krakauer and the television news show *60 Minutes* that some of Mortenson's story was fictitious and that some of his schools had not been built or were not operating. (Mortenson refutes those claims, and many of his schools are open.) Of course, we did not know about these problems at the time of our unit. However, as Krakauer himself said on *60 Minutes*, Mortenson has probably done more to expose the education rights of girls in impoverished countries than anyone else. No one doubts the very real plight of millions of girls around the world being denied an education. Would I use his story and book if I taught this unit in the future? Probably not. I would find other great resources on the same topic. But if I did use the book, I would choose an excerpt from the adult version of *Three Cups of Tea,* because the Young Reader's Edition is too easy for middle school students.

Educating girls and women in underdeveloped third-world countries has been in the spotlight, in part because of the so-called girl effect. Sending a girl in a poor country to school has profound effects, like tipping a domino. An educated female can read to her children, raise a healthier family, participate in local government, and get the knowledge and empowerment to start a small business. There are two remarkable videos about this process at thegirleffect.org. We showed the first video to the students, and they were amazed by it. Many of the kids applauded at the end. This is an example of the caring that Nel Noddings passionately advocates, the caring for "strangers and distant others" (1992).

GRAPHIC JOURNALISM: *Safe Area Gorazde*

In *Red Glass*, Sophie's aunt Dika survived the Bosnian War. Glimpses of the horror of the war and genocide are found in Chapter 11, titled "Explosions," when fireworks in the middle of the night terrify Dika, reminding her of the bombs of Bosnia. Sophie recounts what her stepfather, Juan, told her about what happened to her aunt, including that she was in one of the notorious Bosnian prisoner-of-war camps.

To help the class understand what Dika went through—and to emphasize the war and violence that is happening today around the world—we read a chapter from Joe Sacco's (2002) journalistic account of the brutal Serbian attacks in the Bosnian War, *Safe Area Gorazde*. Sacco is famous for his books, in part because they are not written in prose, but are graphic journalism. They look like graphic novels, but Sacco's books are nonfiction. They are remarkable to read.

We began with a mini-lesson on the Bosnian War, explaining how Yugoslavia fell apart after the end of the Cold War, with Serbians launching a campaign of genocide against the Croatians and Muslims. We read a chapter from *Safe Area Gorazde* about an attack on the Kokino Selo neighborhood in Gorazde and the residents' harrowing escape. To avoid being shot, some of them spent *nine hours* hiding in a river. Many people died, and the chapter ends with them returning to their homes and burying the dead.

ACTIVITY: Silent Graffiti

We chose the "silent graffiti" activity from *Less Is More* by Kimberly Hill Campbell (2007). We placed five large sheets of butcher paper around the classroom and in the hallway. Each sheet had a question on it, and the students had to walk to each sheet in silence and write responses. By having five or six students start at each sheet and then rotate to another open sheet, we were able to keep the space open for everyone to write. We encouraged the kids not just to write their own thoughts but also to read and respond to what others had written and connect the comments with arrows. After they wrote for about thirty minutes, we gathered around the sheets for discussion.

PHOTOGRAPHS: Sawdust Carpets
ASSIGNMENT: Beautiful Memories

One of the wonderful benefits of reading books set in other countries is learning about different cultures. Teachers benefit as well as students. In Chapter 11, Sophie, Angel, and Pablo are in Mexico, taking a walk. They see a parade, and along the streets are gorgeous "sawdust carpets." When I first read the novel, I had no idea what a sawdust carpet was. I immediately went online to investigate. Sawdust carpets are an annual ritual in many Latin American countries. As part of the festival celebrating the Virgin of Guadalupe, people spend hours dyeing sawdust in a rainbow of colors, and then they sprinkle it on the streets in elaborate designs of flowers, plants, animals, and symbols. These artistic representations look real, as if carpets had been stretched down the road.

In *Red Glass*, Sophie and Angel see a parade coming down the street, destroying the sawdust carpet in its wake. Angel joins a group of children, stomping on a carpet. Sophie is aghast:

> "I can't believe they're doing this!"
>> Angel spoke calmly. "But I think that's the point."
>> "What?" I felt faint. I took a gulp from my water bottle and tried to keep my eyes glued on Pablo. "To make something incredibly beautiful, and then, before you even get to enjoy it, mess it up?"
>> He gave me a puzzled look. "What about the memory? You'll have that."
>> I glared at my reflection in his glasses. "Memory isn't something real. Something you can touch."
>> "But the memory changes you, right? It makes you a different person." (108)

Karen and I prized Angel's point about memories, so we designed an assignment. First, we went online and showed the class pictures of sawdust carpets. Very few of the students had ever heard of them. Then, we explained the assignment: bring in something that represents a "beautiful memory." We discussed different meanings of *beauty*, so the students would know it does not relate only to visual beauty. An experience could be beautiful; so could a person's character or actions.

Three days later we gathered around the rug in the corner of the classroom and shared our beautiful memories. Jacob brought in part of a pancake-mix box for his memory of making pancakes with his friends. Olga had a small jar with three dead butterflies to represent her memory of traveling by horse in Mexico to see the migration of monarch butterflies. Charles brought a baby picture of himself as a memory of his past and how "I have grown up and matured." Destiny brought in a poem she wrote in fifth grade, which taught her at the time to "Not give up on myself, and to focus on the positive, not the negative, which I tend to do." Karen and I brought in memories too. It was a wonderful sharing that resulted in both some laughter and some tears.

PHOTOJOURNALISM: Enrique's Journey

In Chapter 11, Angel tells Sophie and Dika how he and his dad escaped from Guatemala, a journey rife with peril. When they got to Mexico, they hopped on top of a freight train along with many others from Mexico and Central America. Each year thousands of children make this journey in search of their parents, a treacherous passage that a reporter and photographer from the *Los Angeles*

Times documented in 2002. See the Pulitzer Prize–winning articles at pulitzer.org/works/2003-Feature-Writing. The magnificent photographs can be found at latimes.com/news/local/photography/la-ph-pulitzer-enrique-html,0,4727213.htmlstory. Sonia Nozario wrote a book based on her work, *Enrique's Journey* (2006).

We showed the class the book, and then projected photos from the newspaper series. The photos show trains with desperate people hanging from the sides, sitting inside cars filled with coal, and hopping from car to car as the train speeds through the countryside. It is not uncommon for riders to slip and fall beneath the wheels of the train. The class gasped when we showed them the photo of a seventeen-year-old boy who lost his left leg and right foot when he slipped off a train. They call these freight trains *mata gente*, "the people killer."

New Resources

La Linea, by Ann Jaramillo (2006), is a very good middle-grades novel that mirrors *Enrique's Journey* and can teach students about global awareness and illegal immigration. *La Linea* is the story of a brother and sister trying to get from Honduras to the United States to find their mother. Part of their journey is on a freight train. A similar novel is *Crossing the Wire* by Will Hobbs (2006).

HARPER'S MAGAZINE ARTICLE: "Death Squad Diary"
WEB SITE TEXT: Frontline: *"Guatemala: The Secret Files"*
BOOK EXCERPT: *Banana: The Fate of the Fruit That Changed the World*

Sophie's aunt Dika, a survivor of the Bosnian genocide, has a boyfriend, Mr. Lorenzo (Angel's father), who is a survivor of war and torture in Guatemala. In one scene, they talk about the scars on his body. Previously, when the class read about and discussed the Bosnian War, they saw the scars of war on Dika's psyche. Dika and Mr. Lorenzo are drawn together, in part, by their common experiences of the madness of war and violence.

We used Mr. Lorenzo as a window to explore the history of Guatemala's civil war, which began in 1960 and finally ended with a peace agreement in 1996. For more than thirty years, the Guatemalan National Police and military kidnapped, tortured, and killed 200,000 people. Fifty thousand Guatemalans are still known as "the disappeared." (Leslie, the teacher in Chapters 8 and 11, read to her class Gloria Whelan's [2006] novel, *The Disappeared*—which is about Argentina's "Dirty War"—as part of a unit on South America. She also played the song "Mothers of the Disappeared" by U2 for her class.)

We had the class read an article from *Harper's* magazine titled "Death Squad Diary" (Doyle 1999). This article features four pages of annotated photographs of Guatemalan police records showing civilians who were murdered. Students were assigned to read specific annotations, explaining different parts of the police record and the history of the war. We had the students use "think marks" on sticky notes as they read the article (Fountas and Pinnell 2001). I like how Stephanie Harvey and Harvey Daniels (2009) refer to this process as a way for students to "leave tracks of their thinking" (120) and how Cris Tovani uses it to help students annotate a text as they read (2011).

One question dominated the discussion: Why did this happen? The students could not understand why Guatemalans—or anyone, for that matter—would systemically brutalize so many people, especially their *own* people. Connections were made to the Bosnian genocide discussed earlier, as well as to the Holocaust (which had briefly been discussed earlier through the picture book about Anne Frank).

The next day I put a banana on a chair in the middle of the classroom. I said, "Bananas are a key factor in what happened to these people in Guatemala. Bananas are partly responsible for it. How do we get from bananas to the killing of 200,000 Guatemalans?" The students were intrigued.

Karen and I put three vocabulary words on the board—*coup*, *agrarian*, and *communism*—and defined them. We passed out a concise summary of the beginning of Guatemala's civil war from the PBS Web site for the program *Frontline*. The text came from the episode "Guatemala: The Secret Files" from the section titled "U.S.-Backed Coup—Civil War Starts, 1954–1965." We read it as shared reading. Here's a key quote:

> On July 2, 1954, the U.S.-backed coup, commanded by Guatemalan exile Colonel Carlos Castillo Armas, overthrew the democratically elected President Jacobo Arbenz. Castillo installed himself as president, and the U.S. administration cast him as a hero for his victory over communism. In September of the same year, Castillo was formally declared president. Once in office, he removed voting rights for illiterate Guatemalans and cancelled the new agrarian reform law, which forced peasants to give up their newly acquired lands. (Frontline/World, 2008)

Informational texts like this require so much background knowledge and specialized vocabulary that for many students they might as well be reading a foreign language. We needed to take the time to unpack this history and help Karen's kids understand this at a deeper level. What was that "new agrarian reform law"? I showed them the book *Banana: The Fate of the Fruit That Changed the World* (Koeppel 2008). Chapter 23 is titled "Guatemala" and helps us understand the term *banana republic*. Here's a bit of the history of bananas and mass murder: In the 1950s, the U.S. company United Fruit (now known as Chiquita) owned 70 percent of the arable land in Guatemala to grow bananas. The new and democratically elected president, Jacobo Arbenz, wanted to force United Fruit to sell some of this fallow land to the government so they could give it to the peasants, who were largely Mayan. (Angel, in *Red Glass*, was born in a Mayan village.) United Fruit did not want to sell any of its land to the government, and it had connections to the Eisenhower administration.

Under a plan orchestrated by the CIA and authorized by President Dwight Eisenhower, President Arbenz was labeled a "communist" and removed from office in a military coup. The new president, Carlos Castillo Armas, thrust the country into thirty-six years of war, torture, and death.

The *Frontline* Web site that I quoted earlier includes this: "In the next three decades the U.S. continued its war against communism in Guatemala and throughout Latin America, in supporting right wing military governments that openly violated human rights." And that's how we get from bananas to mass murder.

The students were silent, trying to make sense of killing tens of thousands of people, in part for bananas, but also for the money those bananas would make for a corporation, as well as to nullify a political and economic ideology the United States government did not like. Just as we began to contemplate these vital issues, the P.A. system blared for a tornado drill. Welcome to teaching.

CLASS DISCUSSION: "The Higher Moral Path"

WEB SITE: Human Rights Data Analysis Group: Guatemalan National Police Archive Project

Not wanting a tornado drill to end the discussion of such important history, we went back the next day to the *Harper's* article for some shared reading and to focus on one particular sentence. The article quotes President Ronald Reagan's ambassador to Guatemala, Fredric Chapin. During the atrocities Chapin sent a cable to Washington. He wrote about the "horrible human rights realities in Guatemala" and added this: "We must come to some resolution in policy terms. Either we can overlook the record and emphasize the strategic concept or we can pursue a higher moral path" (53). We asked the students, "What does it mean to 'take the higher moral path'?" This is a good example of how teachers can select just one sentence from a text and take the time for students to unpack it to gain deeper understanding.

Because the students did not grasp the meaning of this sentence, Karen connected it to *Red Glass*. In Chapter 16 (page 169), Sophie, who is in Mexico, gets a call from Mr. Lorenzo in Guatemala. He tells her that Angel was badly beaten in a mugging and went to the hospital. Everything they had was stolen, so he needs Sophie to wire him money and mail him photocopies of their passports.

Sophie, who is now in love with Angel, thinks, "At the heart of things, Angel needed me, I could feel it" (176). Confronting her deepest fears, she decides to go to Guatemala by herself. She hops a ride in the back of a pickup truck to get to the bus station. After a few harrowing encounters as well as good experiences with kind strangers, Sophie makes it to the hospital. While caring for Angel, she sees some teenage boys who are rushed to the hospital after a car accident. Eventually, Sophie learns that these are the boys who robbed and savagely beat Angel. One of the boys, Mercurio, is wearing Angel's necklace. Once again facing her fears, Sophie confronts Mercurio, demanding to know what he did with Angel's belongings. Feeling guilty, as well as fearing Sophie's wrath, he tells her. One of the nurses then tells Sophie that they are not going to contact the police. She tells Mercurio that his thirteen-year-old friend Raul was killed in the crash. Mercurio is distraught. The nurse says, "Justice has been served. Let this be and move on" (232).

To help the class make sense of that notion of a "higher moral path," we asked the class, "*Has* justice been served?" One girl said yes because Mercurio "didn't mean to hurt him." Karen and I were stunned. Of course he meant to hurt him, we thought; he *attacked* him! But we didn't say that; we both just said, "*Really?*" Karen pushed everyone to think further by asking, "Do you think Mercurio's done that before? Beaten people up?" Murmurs of "yes" rippled through the class. So we asked, "Couldn't *he* have taken the higher moral path?" We let that thought sink in for ten seconds. "What would that have been?" Some kids responded, "To not do it. To not beat him up." Exactly. The higher moral path for Mercurio is the same as the U.S. ambassador was alluding to about Guatemala. To do the right thing. To cause as little harm as possible. To end the suffering and war—and maybe not start it in the first place.

Karen and I then offered our own opinions but not before we had given the students time to frame their own thoughts. We said we both believed the nurse *should* call the police so Mercurio would be held accountable for his actions. This did not mean that we, the teachers, were right, and the students were wrong. It means we have different opinions, and that's exactly what healthy civic discourse is all about.

The conversation continued a bit longer, and then we asked about forgiving Mercurio. Most of the class was okay with this. But we asked if there are limits to forgiveness. A chorus of "yes!" blasted through the room. Genocide was unforgivable, they thought. The Holocaust was unforgivable. So was the Bosnian genocide we had just read about. (Ninth-grade English teacher Tracy Wagner [2003] designed an entire unit on forgiveness.)

To bring the discussion to a close, we showed the class a Web site featuring the work being done today in Guatemala by the Human Rights Data Analysis Group. In 2005, people in Guatemala City stumbled upon a building containing 80 million pages of Guatemalan National Police records. Bundles of documents—including logbooks with photos of civilians who were murdered by the police—stacked to the ceiling, some of them wet and moldy, are being documented one page at a time. You can find the pictures at hrdag.org/about/guatemala-police_arch_project.shtml. We asked the class, "The war is over. Why do this? Why take the time and energy and feel the pain of doing all of this work?" The kids knew why. To expose the truth. To educate the world and Guatemalans. To bring some closure to the families of the 200,000 dead and disappeared. Doing this work is a living example of a higher moral path.

PROJECT: Dream Journeys: Where Do You Want to Go?

As we progressed through our inquiry unit, we continued to add things to the world map we hung on the wall. We labeled each country we read about, and Karen added some pictures of book covers and Web sites. To bring us back to the theme of personal and global journeys, Karen and I designed a small research project. Each student had to choose a country that he or she hoped to visit in the future. Where in the world would they want to take a journey?

The students had to research their chosen country and write information on a large index card. After three days of research, both in the classroom and at home, the students turned in their cards so Karen and I could add them to our map. Figure 10.4 shows the entire completed project.

We gathered around the map and took turns talking about our dream journeys. I made a card about Morocco, where I was actually going that summer with my family. As we discussed the information from our countries, students immediately identified some gender disparities, such as the startling differences in literacy rates in India: 79.8 percent for males and 41.3 percent for females. This connected to our earlier discussions about *Three Cups of Tea* and *The Girl Effect* video that we watched.

Variations in national income levels were also enlightening. The per capita income of a wealthy country, such as France, is around $42,000, whereas that of a poor country, such as Haiti, is less than $1,000. Information such as this goes beyond simply knowing how others live. The more knowledgeable we become about the lives of people around the world, the more understanding, perspective, and humility we gain. This knowledge is at the core of social responsibility.

Figure 10.4 Our completed world map with everyone's global dream research cards.

ESSAY ASSIGNMENT: Which Experiences Most Contributed to Sophie's Transformation from Sophie La Delicada to Sophie La Fuerte?

This prompt was our last assignment for the unit. Karen wanted her students to write a formal essay on how the main character, Sophie, changed from Sophie "the delicate" to Sophie "the strong." This emphasized both the idea of a character (and a real person) changing and the power of a personal journey in that change. Karen asked her students to use specific examples from the novel as supporting evidence. These essays went through a writing process, from brainstorming to drafting to editing. Here are the opening paragraphs from two students. Josilyn wrote:

Sophie, the protagonist in the book Red Glass, *is a 16-year-old germ-phobic girl who is on a trip to Mexico. If it wasn't for her journey, she wouldn't have been able to be brave and stand up for herself. The experiences that contributed from Sophie's transformation from Sophie La Delicada to Sophie La Fuerte were the risks she took and the people she came across.*

When Sophie was going to Guatemala to save Angel, she came across a risk and handled it perfectly. She went into a filthy bathroom with waste all over the floor, and instead of screaming like she usually would have, she started laughing! That shows she is really growing in self-confidence and bravery. Would Sophie La Delicada be so nonchalant about being in a filthy bathroom? I don't think so. I know if I would have walked into that bathroom, I know I would have freaked.

Jacob wrote:

Sophie, the protagonist in the novel Red Glass, *is a teenage girl who is not confident in herself. She is extremely terrified of germs and she has to put lime on everything she eats. Sophie is not only afraid of germs, but she is also afraid to open up to love. Everything changes when she takes a physical journey to return Pablo, an orphaned Mexican immigrant who lost both parents while crossing the border. Her physical journey results in a mental journey that leads to a transformation from Sophie la ehhh to Sophie la errr!*

Sophie transformed when she met Pablo because she dedicated her time and read to him. Sophie became a mom to him because she cared. Before he came into her life, she was alone and didn't have a reason to get up in the morning. When they finally reached Pablo's village and he raced furiously fast to his grandmother's arms, Sophie says, "Holding on to his hand gave me purpose." This showed how when he came into her life, she had a purpose to get up in the morning. She changed from an amoeba to a fully developed, growing person.

These essays showed Karen and me that her students had not only empathized with Sophie and her transformation, but that they also were able to pull evidence from the book to support a character's change. I especially like that Josilyn and Jacob selected different aspects of the story to support the same conclusion.

AUTHOR VISIT: Laura Resau

At the conclusion of our unit, *Red Glass* author Laura Resau visited the school. She spoke to all of the seventh and eighth graders, had lunch with Karen's students, and then visited Karen's classroom. It is fair to say that she was quite impressed with all the thoughtful and creative work these kids had done around her book. She posted pictures of her visit on her Web site at lauraresau.com.

Living in the Global Community

As teachers, we are not able to take our students to other countries, but that does not mean we should abandon the cause of teaching them about global understanding and compassion or sharing knowledge about the countries, cultures, and people in every corner of the planet. On a practical level, the life of the twenty-first-century citizen and worker will be a global one. Our elected government representatives make global decisions—often deeply serious and forceful, and sometimes hostile and deadly—in our name. If adolescents and young adults remain ignorant of these realities, they will not fulfill the promise of a "government of the people, by the people, and for the people." As educators, it is our social responsibility to empower our students with the knowledge and habits of mind to participate in that daily worldwide decision making. As the professional development organization World Savvy concluded, "With a globally illiterate population, the U.S. will not produce the workers it needs to compete, lead or cooperate to resolve global problems in the 21st century" (2012).

On a more personal level, this global education might spark a passion to explore. That was one of the purposes of the culminating research project Karen and I designed for her students. There is a remarkable world out there. They need to experience it. (See the companion Web site, stenhouse .com/caringhearts, for the unit resources.)

Chapter 11

Why Care About Poverty?

"Esperanza," said Mama, "We have little money and Hortensia, Alfonso, and Miguel
are no longer our servants. We are indebted to them for our finances and our future.
And that trunk of clothes for the poor? Esperanza, it is for us."

—*Esperanza Rising*

Reading historical fiction can give students a lens through which to examine contemporary issues within the context of past events. Historical novels situate the past in a story, revealing the intimate and complex decisions that shape the world. Rycik and Rosler (2009) add that "Good historical fiction creates an emotional connection between children of today and their historical counterparts" (163).

Consider a stellar work of historical fiction that I've mentioned previously, *Between Shades of Gray* (2011), which describes the forced deportations of hundreds of thousands of people living in the Baltic States (Latvia, Lithuania, and Estonia) during the 1940s. Soviet leader Josef Stalin ordered soldiers and police to arrest the people, stuff them into boxcars, and send them to Siberian labor camps for years of hard labor. The novel's protagonist is fifteen-year-old Lina Vilkas, whose mother uses her strength, intelligence, and compassion to help her children and others survive. One scene details the savage conditions inside a crowded boxcar where dirty, exhausted, and brutalized passengers must relieve themselves through a small hole in the floor. After a newborn baby dies, the passengers decide they must toss her out of the train because of the toxic smell. In the midst of such madness and despair, what does Lina's mother do? She puts on lipstick, refusing to allow the Russians to break her spirit and pride.

Instead of the flavorless "factual stew" of knowledge (VanSledright 1995, 330) that so many social studies textbooks feed to students, good historical fiction such as *Between Shades of Gray* offers context and meaning, characters to care about, and global issues reduced to a personal scale. Being with Lina's mother in that boxcar and visualizing her applying lipstick enabled me to grasp a small moment of humanity within the sweeping scope of history. This is the intellectual and emotional experience that Leslie Rector and I hoped to offer as we began shaping a unit around Pam Munoz Ryan's well-known novel *Esperanza Rising*. Leslie is wonderful at using historical fiction in her teaching as a natural way to connect social studies and literacy and to make the past breathe with life for her students.

We chose the book, which is set during the Great Depression, to connect the cataclysmic events of the 1930s to the contemporary challenges of American and global poverty. Understanding that more than 46 million Americans—22 percent of the nation's children—currently live below the official federal poverty and that *2 billion* people worldwide live on less than two dollars a day (Tavernise 2011) puts our lives into perspective, reminding us that for many people around the world, survival truly is a daily struggle. We also used the book to encourage Leslie's sixth graders to appreciate knowing history.

Leslie and I did not want to tell her students what to think about poverty, offer simple solutions, or dictate moral stances. Instead, we hoped they would recognize that each of us has the social responsibility to acknowledge poverty, understand its complexity, form our own moral and political opinions, and take action to reduce it. Because Leslie's school does not departmentalize in the sixth grade, we could easily design an inquiry unit that integrated literature, writing, social studies, and even math. Here are some of the guiding questions that framed this inquiry unit:

♦ Why is it important to know history?
♦ What is historical empathy?
♦ What was the Great Depression?
♦ Why are people poor?
♦ What does *poor* mean?
♦ Why are there such high percentages of African Americans and Latinos in poverty?
♦ Do we have a responsibility to help the poor?
♦ What is life like for the poor in the United States and around the world?
♦ How important is money to our happiness?

Figure 11.1 shows the flowchart for our unit.

Esperanza Rising by Pam Munoz Ryan

It is 1930, and the Great Depression is tightening its grip on the United Sates. Thirteen-year-old Esperanza lives in Aguascalientes, Mexico. Her father is a wealthy rancher who spoils Esperanza with luxury. She openly disparages her father's "hired help." After bandits murder her papa, his stepbrothers demand to take over the ranch, and one of them wants to marry Esperanza's mother. When she refuses, they burn down the house.

With few options, Esperanza and her mother flee. After being smuggled into the United States, they become migrant farmworkers, the kind of people Esperanza once scorned. Not surprisingly, this is a very difficult change for Esperanza, whose privileged worldview is challenged. Hard work is new to her. Esperanza's struggle is heightened by her budding romance with Miguel, the son of her father's ranch foreman, who left Mexico with them to find work.

The story is based on the life of Pam Munoz Ryan's grandmother. A beautifully written book, flowing with imagery and cultural symbolism, *Esperanza Rising* offers a rich story that is both historical and relevant. Using this historical book to frame the conditions of poverty today, we were connecting the past to the present, which makes learning history infinitely more meaningful and interesting.

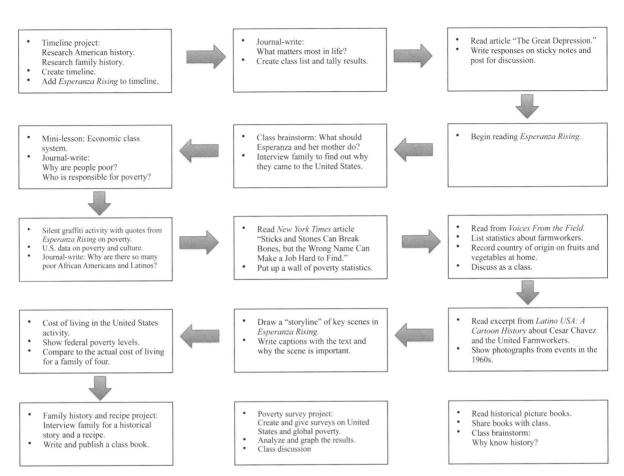

Figure 11.1 Flowchart for the inquiry unit based on *Esperanza Rising*.

OPENING MINI-RESEARCH PROJECT: American History and Family History Timeline

Too often teachers convey history without helping students see the big picture, such as how the Great Depression fits into the larger landscape of U.S. history. Leslie and I thought that the best way to provide context for sixth graders who are transitioning to more abstract thinking was to connect history to what they know best—themselves.

Working in groups, students conducted quick research on specific major events in U.S. history and summarized the information on 4-by-6-inch index cards, which they then placed on a large timeline on butcher paper. They also interviewed family members so they could add important personal events to the timeline. Finally, each group glued a photocopied cover of *Esperanza Rising* onto the timeline. That way they could see that the story is not "ancient history," but took place around the time that their grandparents were born.

The project had the added benefit of enhancing students' comprehension of informational texts. To help them organize their notes—and to keep their notes concise—we created a sheet that included four categories: who, what, where, and why (and the dates of the event). (See Figure 11.2, as well as Appendix N, also included on the companion Web site, stenhouse.com/caringhearts.) Every group had to research the Great Depression and the Mexican Revolution. We included the latter event because so many of Leslie's students were Mexican American, and we wanted to honor and integrate culturally relevant history.

Additionally, we asked each group to become class "experts" by researching two more of the following major topics from American history:

- Declaration of Independence
- American Revolution
- U.S. Constitution
- American Civil War
- World War I
- World War II
- Civil Rights movement
- Vietnam War
- War in Afghanistan
- War in Iraq

American History + Family History Timeline Project

Name _____

Event	Who?	What?	Where?	Why?
Event: Dates:				
Event: Dates:				

Figure 11.2 Students collect notes for our American History + Family History Timeline.

Figure 11.3 shows students using laptop computers to research the topics on the Internet. Using a "jigsaw" organization, groups summarized their historical topics on index cards, made copies for all the groups, and then distributed the cards so each group had a collection of cards for every topic that they could display on their timelines.

We also asked Leslie's students to add some technological inventions (airplanes, television, cell phones, and so on) to the timelines so they would understand how people lived then and now, and to be sure they knew that there was no texting during the Great Depression!

Figure 11.3 Leslie Rector's sixth graders research topics in American history.

ACTIVITY: What Matters in Life?

The first page of *Esperanza Rising* includes this Mexican proverb: "The rich person is richer when he becomes poor, than the poor person when he becomes rich." We had Leslie's kids write the proverb on the cover of their journals because its meaning connected directly to the poverty themes of the unit.

Next, we wrote the question, What matters most in life? on the dry erase board and asked students to list five answers in their journals. Admittedly, students often respond to prompts like this by writing what they think adults want them to think, but most of Leslie's students took this prompt to heart. We gathered on the rug to tally the results and discuss them by categories. Among Leslie's twenty-six students, twenty-three listed family, fifteen mentioned education, and just seven included money. When talking about the importance of family, Yazmin told the class this wonderful sentiment: "You can buy a house, but you can't buy a home."

JUNIOR SCHOLASTIC MAGAZINE ARTICLE: "The Great Depression"

Because we had primed the students' background knowledge with the timeline, Leslie and I thought it was the perfect time to have them independently read an article from *Junior Scholastic* that was geared to their grade level. As they read the article, they were to jot down one important fact they learned on a blue sticky note and list one additional thought they had while reading on a pink sticky note. We gathered and displayed the notes (see Figure 11.4), and then the students shared their questions and connections to history.

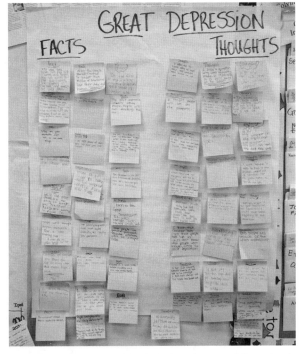

Figure 11.4 Students jotted their thoughts on sticky notes in response to an article about the Great Depression to prepare for a class discussion.

Teaching Tip

With so many resources to choose from, how do we decide which ones to use as supplemental texts for our students? Here are some suggestions:

- *Medium*: In an inquiry unit, it's ideal to have a mix of resources. That way, students can watch a video clip one day and read a newspaper op-ed the next. They can look at photographs on Tuesday, read a short story on Friday, and so on. Variety makes school (and teaching) more interesting.

- *Time and Length*: I prefer to complete the reading of a short text in one sitting, and I usually choose resources that we can read in ten to thirty minutes. Some of the best short texts, such as newspaper editorials, are very short. Remember, with certain longer articles you do not have to read the entire piece. Sometimes a section will suffice.

- *Difficulty and Use*: A resource can be easy or difficult for students, depending on how we plan to use it. For example, a short story might be above the students' independent reading level but appropriate for shared reading.

- *Student Interest*: Every student will not like every resource. Part of school is encountering things you may not enjoy. But we should choose resources that students will likely find thought-provoking and sometimes provocative.

- *Quality*: Our job is to find creative, intellectual, captivating, well-written, and accurate resources to share with students. We need to know that we can trust the resource and that the information is accurate and honest. For example, when I use a statistical graph or chart, I point out the source (usually included in the fine print). I want students to *see* and understand how and why we check the reliability of information.

New Resources

Using the previous criteria, I would include these three spectacular resources for teaching about the Great Depression:

- As part of President Franklin Roosevelt's New Deal, the Farm Security Administration hired photographers to document American life during the Depression. This project resulted in a remarkable collection of 175,000 photographs. All of those images— some taken by Dorothea Lange, Gordon Parks, Walker Evans, and other renowned photographers—are available in a searchable Library of Congress database: loc.gov/pictures/search/?st=grid&co=fsa.

- I love using editorial cartoons with middle school students because they must use inference skills to understand them. Students also benefit from the brilliant creativity and good humor found in many cartoons. Examples are easy to find online by searching "Great Depression editorial cartoons" and clicking for images.

> ◆ Studs Terkel, the prized Chicago writer known for his books of oral history, wrote *Hard Times: An Oral History of the Great Depression.* Students can read excerpts from the book or we can have them listen to a treasured resource: the audio interviews Terkel conducted for his book are online at studsterkel.org/htimes.php.

ACTIVITY: What Should Esperanza and Her Mother Do?
ACTIVITY: Why Did We Come to the United States?

We read the first thirty-eight pages of the book as shared reading. (The book does not have numbered chapters; each one is named after a food item. Food is important to both the story and Mexican culture, and we used this theme for our final unit project.) We assigned the chapter "Los Higos (Figs)" for homework and asked the students to write in their journals, listing at least three reasons why Esperanza and her mother should stay in Mexico and three reasons why they should go to California. We also asked them to briefly interview an adult in their families and find out why their families came to the United States.

The next day we compiled a list of the reasons. Creating a list that compares options is a good way to teach critical thinking because it helps students see the complexity and nuance involved in decision making. This strategy also teaches the skills of argumentation. The activity had the added benefit of checking students' comprehension, because we asked them to support their choices based on the text.

Leslie flipped over the chart paper on the easel and wrote the question, Why did we come to the U.S.? This also connected back to the family history part of their timelines. From the notes of their interviews, the students offered some of the reasons:

- ◆ To have a better life
- ◆ To get a job
- ◆ To get a better education
- ◆ Needed more money
- ◆ Had a lot of children to feed
- ◆ Better life for their children
- ◆ More freedom and better rights

It was fascinating to do this activity with Leslie's students for them to see the obvious parallels between their own histories and Esperanza's story. In a sense, their lives in the United States justified Esperanza's mother's decision to go to America.

MINI-LESSON: Socioeconomic Class System
JOURNAL-WRITE: Why Are People Poor?

I did a mini-lesson on socioeconomics, focusing on class systems. I drew a diagram and included the labels *poor, working poor, middle class, upper middle class,* and *rich.* We had the kids bring their journals to the rug to take notes.

Leslie and I knew that most of her students qualified for federal lunch subsidies, but we felt sure that most of them would not know how much money their families made. Near the end of the mini-lesson we told the students to put a star next to the class level that best represented their families; nearly every student marked middle class. Our realities begin with ourselves. If we feel we're middle class, then that is our definition of *middle class*. So, if they saw themselves as middle class, how did they define *poor* and *working poor*? We posed two questions for them to write on in their journals:

- ◆ Why are there rich and poor people in the world?
- ◆ Are people in control of their economic class, or is it decided for them?

Rather than tell the students the answers to these questions—after all, the questions don't have single correct answers, and social responsibility involves independent thinking—we wanted to know what they thought. What are their theories about economic class and poverty? What do they base their theories on? Do they see racism or systemic forces as factors in where people land on our socioeconomic ladder? Do they consider the American economic class system fair? Yes, these are hard questions; people write dissertations about these topics. But that doesn't make the topics off-limits for sixth graders. Quite the contrary. These are important and intellectual questions for middle school kids to explore. If we don't engage them with high-level ideas, how will they ever learn to think and care and be active participants in our democracy?

The students' writing showed us two things. First, they really had very little to say about why there are rich and poor people in the world. Their writing was simplistic and minimal, which was not surprising, given their age and limited background knowledge. For example, a boy wrote, "I think there are rich people because people decide they want a good life so they take the advantages. I think there are poor people because they decide not to take the advantages in life." Second, although a few students alluded to systemic factors in determining economic class, most of them believed that people are in charge of their own economic destiny. Here are typical responses:

I think that people are in control because they decide if they want to make a change. They decide if they want to work hard and make a change and decide whether to be successful or not.

Are people in control of their socioeconomic class? . . . Yes, because they have control on what they are going to do in their life. Also they are poor because they are lazy, they don't want to do homework and they don't want to look for a job. And the rich they work hard but they have no feelings for other people and they [are] smart to get rich because they work for a lot of education, and the poor, they don't really work hard.

There are so many reasons why people are poor and rich. One reason is because people don't finish school and some do. There are so many rich people in the world because the rich people study and work hard to get their grades high. They work hard to get their diploma and get any job they want.

The emphasis on doing well in school echoed their earlier writing about what matters most in life (education came in second), and one of the reasons why their families came to the United States (to get a better education). To Leslie's students, education and "hard work" are *the* keys to economic success, which is a very good thing for them to believe. But although doing well in school is certainly part of moving up the economic ladder, their thinking raises some important issues. They did not see racism or any other systemic factor, such as a very unequal American system of school funding, as playing a role in poverty.

Brazilian educator Paulo Freire wrote *The Pedagogy of the Oppressed* (1970) to explain how countries make poverty systemic. Freire argued that unequal societies keep the poor ignorant to keep them poor. Instead of teaching the poor to think critically or to question, they educate them with a "banking system" of schooling of memorizing facts and testing students for "withdrawals." In some ways, "banking" education in the United States has improved a lot since the seventies, yet in other ways, it has barely changed at all. Many underprivileged schools spend far more time teaching discrete skills and doing test prep than teaching complex thinking and questioning. The eminent researcher Jean Anyon (1981) did seminal studies showing the huge differences in curriculum based on socioeconomic class, and I still see those differences in many schools I visit today.

It would be difficult to ignore the fact that Leslie's students were echoing the very stereotype that contributes to their own poverty—that the poor are lazy. They are also repeating the rags-to-riches Horatio Alger myth that success requires only hard work; if you're poor, it's because you did not work hard enough. Freire addresses this in his book:

> Self-deprecation is another characteristic of the oppressed, which derives from their internalization of the opinion the oppressors hold of them. So often do they hear that they are good for nothing, know nothing and are incapable of learning anything—that they are sick, lazy, and unproductive—that in the end they become convinced of their own unfitness. (1970, 49)

Freire argues that schools and teachers with minority children have a responsibility to help their students develop a "critical consciousness" to the realities of oppression and how power is used and abused. I'm sure Freire would say affluent children need this too, and so would I. Everyone must critically understand the use of power in order to question it and create change. This is the essence of "critical literacy," which I consider an important part of teaching for social responsibility. (For more about teaching for critical literacy, see Hinchey [2001], Cowhey [2006], and Apple [1990].)

ACTIVITY: Silent Graffiti

After reading a section of the book where some of the characters comment on socioeconomics, we asked the students to reflect. Adapting the silent graffiti activity described in Chapter 10, we wrote a quote from the novel on four sheets of chart paper and then wrote a question after each quote. Instead of taping the sheets to the walls and having the kids walk around to write their responses, we placed the chart paper on four tables around the classroom, which allowed more students to gather and write at the same time (see Figure 11.5).

Figure 11.5 Students write during the silent graffiti activity.

Teaching Tip

In Chapter 3, I mentioned George Lucas's Edutopia Web site. An article by Mariko Nobori (2011) articulates some strategies for critical thinking. The first suggestion is to ask "questions, questions, questions," the very heart of inquiry-based teaching. Of course, the *kinds* of questions we ask are key. We must move far beyond basic comprehension questions to those that require analytical reasoning and synthesizing. Some of the other suggestions are:

♦   Start with a prompt and unpack it.
♦   Model critical thinking skills.
♦   Encourage constructive controversy.
♦   Choose content students will invest in.
♦   Encourage students to challenge each other's thinking.

DATA: U.S. Poverty Statistics
JOURNAL WRITING: Why Are So Many African Americans and Latinos Poor?

To help her students develop critical-thinking and questioning skills, as well as to further build their knowledge to use in their decision making, Leslie and I pulled data on poverty in the United States from the Internet. We wanted specific and easy-to-read sources that would break down poverty by race. You can find excellent resources with this data on many Web sites, including the Children's Defense Fund and the Annie E. Casey Foundation Kids Data Center. We used convenient one-page sheets from statehealthfacts.org, part of the Kaiser Family Foundation. These sheets also had charts that compared poverty rates by state and race/ethnicity.

The pages we handed out were filled with long rows and columns of numbers, so we had to help the students locate specific data. After determining that the percentage of poor African Americans and Latinos dwarfs the percentage of whites and pointing out that in some states nearly *half* of minority families are poor, Leslie and I asked her students to write about the possible reasons.

To our delight, this prompt resulted in a flood of good writing and thinking. The students' ideas were insightful, including being critical of their own culture. One boy wrote, "In my opinion straight up blunt most of the gangbangers I see are black, Mexican, and Puerto Ricans. I've seen some white girls out there, but almost always see those." This is candid thinking and a very valid point about personal responsibility. Of course, this can lead us to ask, Is he seeing the cause or the effect of poverty? Or is it both?

Three theories stood out from their writing. First, many students wrote about the past, arguing that throughout history minorities have been at a disadvantage. For example, Adonis, who is African American, wrote this:

Because of the past! Before just because of their race. Blacks, Hispanics, Native Americans, they didn't get as much money as white people did. Children didn't get [an] education either because of their race! Like, before African Americans couldn't go to school, which effected what jobs they got or if they even got jobs! It's extraordinary on how your ancestors health affects the way you live. What they didn't get affects you all the way. Like the Cherokee tribe, they had money, they had their land, but white people wanted it and war raged, which obliterated the Cherokee tribe. And children didn't have any money to buy food, which killed them! If it weren't for the way our ancestors were treated we could have been rich just like the white people. It's all because of the way our ancestors lived or made their choices [and how] it affects our health, our pride, and the way we live!

The second theme was immigration. Students noted that newcomers have not had as many opportunities for success. This put them at a disadvantage compared with whites who have lived in the United States longer. However, some students continued their earlier point, arguing that immigrants often compound the problem by not choosing to get an education.

Finally, the third theory was racism, both in the past and in the present. Luisa put it bluntly: "I think that this is because they are being racist to those people because of their color or country they come from." Valeria echoed her thoughts, writing, "Some people just think that some races are better than others." Cristal identified a mix of causes:

I think there are higher percentages of African Americans and Hispanics than whites living in poverty because of immigration. There are many Hispanics that come from their country here to the United States to find better jobs and better lives. For example, us Mexicans. We come from Mexico to the United States to get jobs. But because we are immigrants they don't let us have good jobs. They don't let us work to earn money to feed our families . . . There's other reasons why African Americans live in poverty. Because of racism. There's many jobs that have racist managers. And because of the racism people don't get jobs.

Picking up on Cristal's points about racism and jobs, Leslie and I decided to continue this conversation with one more activity.

NEW YORK TIMES ARTICLE: "Sticks and Stones Can Break Bones, but the Wrong Name Can Make a Job Hard to Find"

I remembered a research study from the University of Chicago and M.I.T. and hopped onto the *New York Times* Web site to find an article. "Sticks and Stones Can Break Bones, but the Wrong Name Can Make a Job Hard to Find" (Krueger 2002) explains that researchers chose 1,300 help-wanted ads from newspapers in Boston and Chicago and sent out multiple résumés and cover letters for the same jobs from fictional people. The applications were identical except for one change: the first names. Among the roughly 5,000 applications, some had first names more common among whites (Brad and Kristen), and others had first names more common among African Americans (Tyrone and Tamika).

The results? The "white" applications received 50 percent more invitations for interviews. Within racial groups, there were no differences by sex. As the article says, "Their most alarming finding is that the likelihood of being called for an interview rises sharply with an applicant's credentials—like experience and honors—for those with white-sounding names, but much less for those with black-sounding names."

Although this is a short article, it is not easy reading for sixth graders. The article includes some tough vocabulary and requires background knowledge that we had to fill in before reading. Once the front loading was done, we read the article aloud so the students could focus on the meaning and Leslie and I could model the fluency. Leslie created a simple two-column graphic organizer, with the photocopied article on the left side and a blank section on the right, which the students used to jot a few notes.

READING: *Esperanza Rising*: *Comprehension Struggles*

Early in our shared reading of *Esperanza Rising* it was apparent that many of Leslie's students were struggling with comprehension. They weren't confused about the plot, but rather the meaning of some of Ryan's expressive writing. For example, soon after Esperanza and her mother arrive at the farmworkers' camp, they must do chores in addition to working in the field. Because she always had servants in Mexico, Esperanza does not know how to perform basic housekeeping tasks such as washing diapers or sweeping a room. Clumsily, she holds a broom, "as if willing it to behave." She sees a group of workers laughing at her, saying, "*La Cenicienta*!" or Cinderella. "Burning with humiliation," Esperanza drops the broom and runs back to the cabin (117).

Later that night when the workers are mildly complaining of their aches and pains as they prepare dinner, "Esperanza chopped *tomates* for a salad and hoped no one would mention the sweeping. She was glad this day was over. Her bruises had been to her pride" (121–122).

We asked Leslie's students to write about this passage in their journals, explaining the metaphor the author used to describe Esperanza's emotional injuries. Their writing showed what Leslie and I had suspected about their limited ability to make textual inferences. Here are some examples:

I think what Esperanza means is that all her hard work paid up. When you give all your hard work and pride it sooner or later pays up.

This to me would mean that she was tired because she had been working hard that day.

I think it means she doesn't care if she got bruises. She is just happy she worked and felt pride.

I think the quote "Her bruises had been to her pride" means that out of all of the work she has done, her bruises have probably increased her pride. I also think her life is getting better.

If students couldn't understand that Esperanza was humiliated and embarrassed, they wouldn't realize that these experiences are *changing her*, helping her see the world through different eyes and a new heart. Leslie and I did three things to build her students' skills. We continued to pull similar sentences from the book to discuss and "take apart." We usually did this sitting around the rug, sometimes having the students write in their journals and other times just talking about the ideas.

We also started to explicitly teach vocabulary before shared reading. If you were to look at my copy of *Esperanza Rising,* you would see that I circled a range of tricky words—*pretentious*, *devious*, and *monotonous*, to name a few. Spending just a few minutes to go over three to five words before we read gives students the contextual clues they need to understand the text. It also means we usually won't need to stop during our reading to define the word, interrupting the flow. (We probably should have created an *Esperanza Rising* word wall.)

Last, we started to focus on Esperanza's character and her transformation. Leslie created a quote sheet for the students to use when briefly reflecting on selected sentences. "What does this quote tell you about Esperanza?" we repeatedly asked. This idea is similar to Kelly Gallagher's (2004) "shift charts" that have students identify key parts of a story that cause a character to change or "shift." The benefit of doing this became clear when students later were able to expand on references they previously had not understood. A week after he had misunderstood the quote about Esperanza's pride, for example, Moises explained it correctly, writing, "Her pride was embarrassed and a little disgraced."

Reflection

What should teachers do when students are struggling to understand a text? Kylene Beers points out that students may struggle with a particular text for a variety of reasons and that comprehension and fluency depends on which text they are reading. (Of course that's true for adults too.) Beers writes:

> What I want to do is to teach them *how to struggle* with a text, how to develop the patience and the stamina to stick with a text, how to figure out on their own what is separating them from success with the text, and what they should do to fix it. In short, I want to teach students how to struggle *successfully* with a text. (2003, 16)

We need to help students acquire the tools and strategies they need to learn how to become strong independent readers. Perhaps most important, we need to *model* good reading and make the usually invisible process of reading (that happens inside our heads) very visible for students. Doing "think-alouds" is a good example of modeling. Teachers need to find the just-right balance between teaching skills and cultivating kids' enjoyment of reading. Yes, we need good readers, but we must never forget that we also want students who love to read.

As I have mentioned throughout this book, two of the key reasons middle-grades students struggle with informational texts is their lack of background knowledge and vocabulary. The best way to solve this is to engage kids with a variety of real-world resources that are about issues that matter to them and use those materials for good discussion and debate. (Think about how much kids can learn in the talk around a dinner table.) We also need to help them with vocabulary, but without hitting them over the head with many exercises. Nancie Atwell (1998) limits her middle school students to five spelling words a week, and each student chooses words that they can't spell.

Another reason so many students struggle with informational reading is that they don't do enough of it in the younger grades (other than through boring textbooks). Nell Duke (2001) did a study of first graders and found that they read informational texts for a mere 3.6 minutes per day. As middle-grades teachers, we must start raising the bar, which is (in part) what the Common Core State Standards are directing.

CLASSROOM WALL: U.S. and Global Poverty Statistics

Leslie and I created a wall of poverty statistics (see Figure 11.6), which we referred to throughout the unit. One side featured data about poverty in the United States, and the other side focused on global poverty. We made the signs using a large, bold font, so kids could easily read them. We also did mini-lessons on some of this data, in part because it was going to connect to our end-of-the-unit project. Leslie added some pictures and a quote by Gandhi: "Poverty is the worst form of violence."

Figure 11.6 The poverty statistics wall.

BOOK: *Voices from the Fields*

Food and farming are important in *Esperanza Rising*. Not only is food a cherished part of Mexican culture, but Esperanza and her mother must work as farmworkers to survive. This is the manual labor that Esperanza looked down on at the start of her story. She has been forced to become one of the very people she disparaged. Leslie and I wanted her students to understand that, although this story takes place during the Great Depression, the fruits and vegetables we eat today must still be picked by farmworkers. In addition, we wanted to help her students appreciate the backbreaking (and low-paying) labor involved in this work. Finally, we wanted the class to understand our country's long history of struggle for the rights of farmworkers.

We began with the nonfiction book *Voices from the Fields* (Atkin 2006), which the students knew about from our previous unit on the environment with the novel *The City of Ember* (see Chapter 8). This book features real children of migrant farmworkers. We read aloud some excerpts and photos and took notes on chart paper. First, we listed what we learned about the kids from the book, dividing them into two categories: their Challenges & Struggles and their Hopes & Dreams. Then we listed some of the essential facts of farmworkers today:

- There are 2–3 million farmworkers in the United States.
- 75 percent earn less than $10,000 per year.
- 52 percent are undocumented immigrants.
- 22 percent are U.S. citizens.
- 24 percent are legal permanent residents.
- 77 percent are Mexican.
- 9 percent are U.S.-born Hispanic.
- 7 percent are U.S.-born white.
- 1 percent are African American.

ACTIVITY: Looking at Our Fruits and Vegetables

How closely do you look at your fruits and vegetables? If you have ever scraped off one of the tiny stickers that grocers put on produce, you have probably noticed the four-digit PLU codes (which stands for "price look-up"), which the cashiers use to determine the item's price. However, you may not have noticed the tinier print that identifies the product's country of origin. Most people, I assume, just peel off the sticker and toss it into the garbage without much thought. We wanted Leslie's students to stop and think about the farmworkers (and sometimes their children) who picked and packaged the food just like the characters in *Esperanza Rising*. We asked the students to go home that night, examine their fruits and vegetables, look at that tiny print, and record the countries of origin.

We made a sheet so it would be easier for the students to collect this information (see Figure 11.7). The next day we examined the results. When I saw Daizy's sheet—with its Del Monte banana sticker with GUATEMALA printed on it—I knew right away that we should have included a column on the sheet for the students to actually put the stickers. Our purpose here was simple. We wanted to raise the middle schoolers' consciousness about all the people who labor in the fields to feed us.

Name: Marycruz M.

✳ Esperanza's family became migrant farm workers in California. They picked the fruits and vegetables that many families around the country eat. Look in your kitchen at home. What fruits and vegetables do you have? If there is a sticker on your produce, look at it to see where it came from. Leave the 3rd column blank and we will fill it in as a class.

List your Fruits/Vegetables	Where did it come from?	Most popular place of origin
Papaya	Mexico	3,342 Hawaii
Mango	Mexico	6,766 Florida
Apple	USA	54,177 Washington
Banana	Colombia	87,985 Hawaii
Sandia	Mexico	4,076 Flordia
Grapes	California	California
Oranges	Florida	8,425 California
Potates	Idaho	168,973 Idaho
Broccoli	California	California
Pineapples	Hawaii	15,247 Hawaii
Carrots	California	9,762 California
Peaches	California	7,110 California
Strawberries	California	14,315 California
Blueberries	Michigan	1,900 Michigan
Tomatoes	Flordia	25,283 Flordia

Figure 11.7 Marycruz's data collection of the fruits and vegetables at her home.

STORYLINE PROJECT: *Esperanza Rising* in Pictures

Esperanza Rising is filled with beautiful imagery. Leslie and I wanted to take some time to help her students appreciate how visually appealing good writing can be, so we asked them to draw a visual "storyline" of the book. In this way, we could integrate art into the unit and point out vivid scenes while we read.

Leslie listed scenes we selected from the book, wrote short descriptions on scraps of paper, and asked the students to choose them randomly. They had to reread the chosen passages several times, draw the scene, write a key line of the text from the scene on the bottom, and then write why they thought the scene was important. This was not a quick project; we wanted high-quality drawings and thoughtful written responses. The students completed all of this work during class so we could help them. Once they were finished, we displayed the pictures in the hallway (see Figures 11.8 and 11.9).

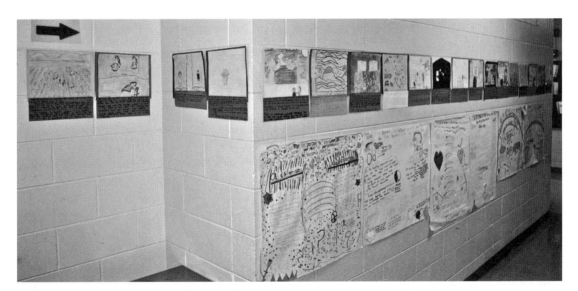

Figure 11.8 The class storyline of *Esperanza Rising*.

Figure 11.9 Students contributed these three panels to the class storyline.

This project was successful for many reasons. The visual storyline helped us look back at the entire story and gave the students another opportunity to interact with the book besides writing or talking. The pictures also enabled them to see the transformation of Esperanza from a spoiled rich girl to a caring person. In addition, their written explanations of why each scene was important let Leslie and I evaluate their comprehension of the scene and its thematic connection to the story.

ACTIVITY: Cost of Living in the United States

Each year the federal government sets our "official" poverty levels. In 2012, the poverty level was $11,170 for a single adult and $23,050 for a family of four. That means single Americans who earned $11,200 were not considered poor. So, when the government says that 46 million Americans are poor, the number does not include the millions of "working poor" whose earnings are above the federal poverty guidelines but below what many people would consider a livable wage.

We wanted Leslie's sixth graders to gain a beginning understanding of our country's poverty levels. I say "beginning" because this is an extremely complex topic requiring wide background knowledge, and we did not intend to spend a large amount of time on it. Then the unexpected happened. We showed the students a chart with the current federal poverty guidelines (which, at the time was $22,050 for a family of four). Their reaction led to one of those moments in teaching when you instantly wonder, "What were we thinking?"

The kids thought $22,000 was a *lot* of money. Leslie and I knew otherwise, of course, but we didn't tell that to the students, because we wanted their opinions, and we knew that their assumptions were based on incomplete knowledge.

After doing a bit of research online, Leslie and I found data for the average cost of living for a family of four (I've forgotten the Web site). It divided costs into categories such as rent and mortgage, food, utilities, and medical expenses. Added together, the total cost of living for a family of four was $44,000 a year—nearly double the federal poverty level. Immediately the students could see that it would be very difficult for a family to live on half that amount. Now those official poverty guidelines had new meaning. The kids were shocked that it costs so much to live.

PROJECT: Family Stories and Recipes

We were able to do two culminating projects at the same time, completing one during writing workshop and the other during Leslie's math block. The first project continued the food-and-family thread of the unit. We wanted the class to publish a magazine that combined family recipes and family stories of coming to the United States, similar to how Pam Munoz Ryan told her grandmother's story through *Esperanza Rising*.

We began with a series of mini-lessons. Leslie first demonstrated how to write a recipe, using her own family's version of Polish nalesniki (crepes or blintzes). She explained how to write the ingredients and directions for cooking, which is a form of expository writing. The next mini-lesson explained how to share a family story. For students whose families had immigrated more recently (most of them, actually), we talked about the kinds of questions students could ask their relatives, such as what their lives were like before they came to the United States, why they left their native countries, whether they had encountered any struggles during immigration, and how their family values had endured or changed.

When the students had completed their family histories and recipes at home, they worked on the writing during class so we could observe them and offer suggestions. Much of this writing was very good, and some of it was exceptional. One of the crafts of writing is how we choose to open a story, what Nancie Atwell calls our "leads" (1998). We used this writing assignment to have the kids focus on their openings. Here are some examples:

Have you ever witnessed a hopeless human being get burned because of tradition and race? My grandma witnessed this horrifying moment in a German tent in Poland. It is shocking that she could live through this moment in time.

Picture yourself leaving a country you've lived in your entire life. You're learning a language you've heard, but cannot understand it. This is the life of my grandparents.

It's 1978. You and your children are trying to not get caught, scared that your abusive husband will come and get you. You don't know how life will be in Chicago. All you know is that you will live there.

Imagine living en el Rancho and working en al Campo, and doing hard work each and every day. Never even getting to spend time with your family because you need money to support them. Imagine working in the real hot weather with nothing to drink. My grandpa, Ricardo Vazquez, was born on April 3, 1942 and lived in Guerrero, Mexico. My grandpa had to work like that.

And here is Karina's opening page to her family story titled "A Road to a New Discovery." I just love the literary quality of her lead and how it pulls the reader in. Her lovely writing has an informal, almost conversational essence to it. And it shows that through this assignment, Karina learned about her own parents, that she empathizes with their difficult past and clearly appreciates them today.

From past to present, to now and then. To rich and poor and big and small. We have our family history. Rising again from your bed and having a relaxing time—it's now. For mom and dad, relaxing didn't exist in Mexico. One small picture can mean anything. Three letters tell a story. Four phone calls can bring back memories. Five videos can say a lot. Six emails are still warm in your heart. Seven, eight, nine, ten and you start all over again. And two, two is the number of families you have—two pieces of discoveries, but only two parents you have—too much to tell.

Meet my dad, Raul Salgado. He was born in Guerrero, Mexico. I had no idea there was a place named Guerrero. My dad worked on a farm. I wonder if he was picking vegetables. Wasn't it tiring? My back would probably hurt if I worked on a farm. My dad only finished high school. There weren't any colleges around his hometown. I felt bad for him; he didn't even get a chance to try. He only remembers seeing corn and beans. Was it because they were significant to him?

Let me introduce you to my mom, Misaray Sanchez, born in Guerrero, Mexico. I can't understand why Mexicans have such weird names. My mom is always exhausted, never relaxing. She didn't finish high school, only elementary school. My mom didn't have the privilege to go to school because she didn't have enough money. I worried about her because I had in mind that without education, you're nothing. When my mom was thirteen, she began to cook. I remembered she once said, "It was so stressful." I bet it was. I can't even imagine how she felt. She worked on a farm too. Her parents didn't have the best of luck. They had trouble with economic problems. It was hard to earn money. I wish they had a better life.

My parents met on a farm where they both worked. They decided to come to the United States. Oh, what love does to you! It wasn't easy; they left their families and their culture for us. They came because there were better opportunities. I would do the same.

"Oh, what love does to you!" How delightful is that?

A week later we brought in a pile of copies of our beautiful class magazine, *Back to the Past: A Collection of Unique Family Stories and Delicious Recipes.* Everyone sat around the room reading and enjoying our stories and recipes. Publishing students' writing brings a vital and exciting authenticity to their work in school. No longer are they merely fulfilling an assignment to get it done for a grade; instead, they are producing something genuine and personally meaningful for a real audience.

PROJECT: Poverty Survey

I'm a big fan of having students conduct surveys. They get to create their own resources for learning, and by venturing into the community, they discover that education doesn't happen just at school. Surveys integrate math, research, critical thinking, and writing, and engage students in investigating people's opinions about important issues. Surveys also bring a variety of perspectives into the classroom, making democracy and social responsibility thrive.

We had Leslie's students work in small groups and survey people about U.S. and global poverty. This not only allowed the kids to learn from the public but also put them in the empowering position of informing people about what they have learned. Surveys enable students to become teachers, appreciate diverse perspectives, and understand that many people are poorly informed about significant social issues such as poverty.

We began with some mini-lessons about types of survey questions we could use, such as closed-ended questions (choosing yes or no, or circling a specific number) and open-ended questions, which require a narrative answer. We also explained Likert scales, when you give a range of options to choose along a line. In addition, we explained how students could include demographic information on the surveys, which we could use to look for patterns by age, sex, culture, and education level, and then graph the results. We also defined the word *demographic* ("picture of the people") and explained professionalism and privacy issues, so students would understand why it is inappropriate to ask for names or specific ages or incomes. (We did include age ranges to circle.)

Next, we hung a ten-foot-long sheet of butcher paper on the dry-erase board. We asked the class for possible survey questions about poverty. The fact that they had just spent six weeks studying poverty and reading *Esperanza Rising* gave them the knowledge they needed to begin the brainstorming process and pose good questions. Leslie and I took turns facilitating, which I consider to be a kind of collaborative thinking process. I equate this to doing a "think-aloud" with a text, only in this case you are thinking about possible survey questions as an entire class. As students offered their questions, we wrote them on the sheet, but we also shared our thoughts and used arrows to draw connections between ideas. As we talked our way through this process, we also eliminated questions. Figure 11.10 shows our completed sheet.

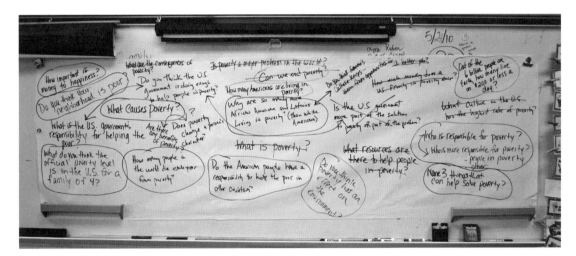

Figure 11.10 Our class brainstorm sheet to create a poverty survey.

To expedite the process, I typed the survey (see Figure 11.11). Each student had about a week to give the survey to at least ten people who were eighteen years or older.

Teaching middle-grades students to analyze surveys—especially when they include open-ended questions—is a serious undertaking. There were too many questions to analyze and graph collectively, so each group was responsible for one closed-ended and one open-ended question. Each group also had to graph data for one of the questions for the entire class, so that meant rotating the surveys from group to group. For the second question, each group graphed just its own data. We also did math mini-lessons explaining how to convert the data into percentages and choose the graphs appropriate for different sets of data. Figure 11.12 shows one group busy with the hard work of data analysis.

We used mini-lessons to teach the class how to analyze open-ended questions. Because these questions have narrative answers, students had to carefully read through each survey, creating categories. This required judgment, critical thinking, and teamwork. Once the data was tallied, we reviewed different kinds of graphs again and then took the kids to the computer lab so they could plug their data into an online graphing program. After about an hour, the graphs starting flying out of the printer. In the end, they had made more than two dozen graphs.

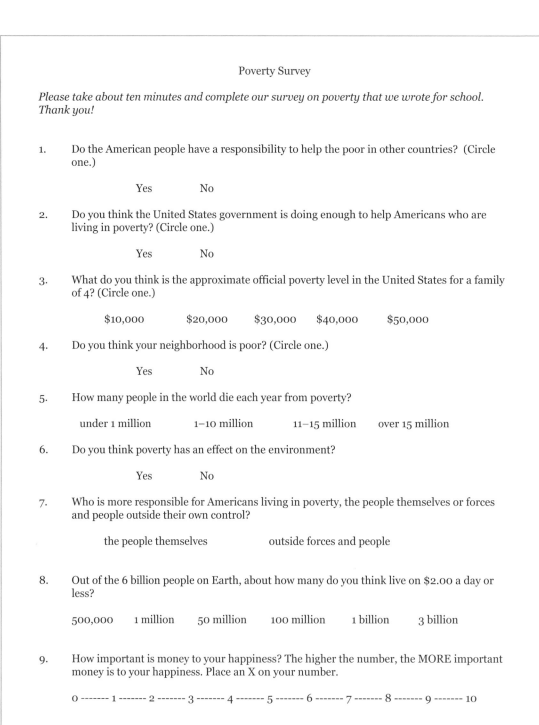

Poverty Survey

Please take about ten minutes and complete our survey on poverty that we wrote for school. Thank you!

1.   Do the American people have a responsibility to help the poor in other countries? (Circle one.)

              Yes   No

2.   Do you think the United States government is doing enough to help Americans who are living in poverty? (Circle one.)

              Yes   No

3.   What do you think is the approximate official poverty level in the United States for a family of 4? (Circle one.)

          $10,000 $20,000 $30,000 $40,000 $50,000

4.   Do you think your neighborhood is poor? (Circle one.)

              Yes   No

5.   How many people in the world die each year from poverty?

          under 1 million   1–10 million   11–15 million   over 15 million

6.   Do you think poverty has an effect on the environment?

              Yes   No

7.   Who is more responsible for Americans living in poverty, the people themselves or forces and people outside their own control?

          the people themselves   outside forces and people

8.   Out of the 6 billion people on Earth, about how many do you think live on $2.00 a day or less?

      500,000   1 million   50 million   100 million   1 billion   3 billion

9.   How important is money to your happiness? The higher the number, the MORE important money is to your happiness. Place an X on your number.

      0 ------- 1 ------- 2 ------- 3 ------- 4 ------- 5 ------- 6 ------- 7 ------- 8 ------- 9 ------- 10

Figure 11.11a Our class survey on poverty.

10.   What is your gender? (Circle one.)   Male   Female

11.   What is your age group? (Circle one.)

      16–18   19–29   30–49   50–69   70+

12.   What is your highest level of education? (Check one.)

      ☐ less than high school
      ☐ high school
      ☐ community college
      ☐ college degree
      ☐ graduate college degree

13.   Name three things that can help solve poverty.

14.   What causes poverty?

15.   Why are so many more African Americans and Latinos living in poverty compared with white Americans?

Figure 11.11b Class survey on poverty continued.

New Resources

After we taught this unit I found some terrific online tools teachers can use with students to explore the cost of living. The Economic Policy Institute's "Basic Family Budget Calculator" (epi.org/resources/budget/) lets you select family size, state of residence, and community, and then click "calculate budget" for an estimate. Penn State University has a similar "Living Wage Calculator" at the Web site livingwage.geog.psu.edu/. The site also lists typical hourly wages for many jobs.

    If I were to have students do a survey project again I would use Google Drive, the free online file creation, storage, and sharing service from Google. Students can use a spreadsheet to aggregate and share their data, a "Google Doc" to write about the results, and the Presentation function to create a formal slide show to share their graphed data.

Reading the Past, Seeing the Present, Creating the Future

Figure 11.12 Crystal, Luisa, and Ruben analyze their group poverty surveys.

In his essay "Why Study History?" historian Peter Stearns writes of the many benefits of exploring the past. These include helping us understand how people and societies function, how the past shapes and influences our lives and the world today, how our family and cultural identities were formed, and how the stories of the past can give us insight into the human condition from other times and places (2008).

    Stearns writes that "History also provides a terrain for moral contemplation. Studying the stories of individuals and situations in the past allows a student of history to test his or her own moral sense, to hone it against some of the real complexities individuals have faced in difficult settings." Helping students cultivate their moral identities is at the core of teaching for social responsibility. Stearns addresses this point directly. He says that knowing the past is indispensable for good citizenship, writing, "Studying history encourages habits of mind that are vital for responsible public behavior, whether as a national or community leader, an informed voter, a petitioner, or a simple observer" (para. 12–15).

    I see immediate connections between the benefits of studying human history and the value of reading good books. They both tell stories, connect to our emotions, help us untangle the complexities of life, connect us to people and places around the world, and contain the hope of making us better people and inspiring us to create a better world. That may sound like a bit of romantic musing, but isn't that why we teach? (The unit resources are included on the companion Web site, stenhouse.com/caringhearts.)

Reading for Heart and Mind (in the Age of Testing and Standards)

"The place of the cure of the soul."
—Etched in the stone wall in the Library of Alexandria, 300 BCE (Manguel 2006)

Books change us in unique, profound ways. And I don't just mean reading *Moby Dick* or *Anna Kare-nina* or *To Kill a Mockingbird*. I mean reading books, from Mal Peet's brilliant young adult novel *Life: An Exploded Diagram* to David Mas Masumoto's memoir of organic farming, *Epitaph for a Peach;* from *Lord of the Flies* to *Diary of a Wimpy Kid;* from Daniel Boorstin's sweeping history *The Discover-ers* to Jacqueline Woodson's middle-grades novel about the friendship of three girls, *After Tupac and D Foster*. And I don't really mean any single book or even a handful of books. I mean an entire school year immersed in books and a lifetime buried in the words and ideas and emotions of others. Have a seventh grader enter a classroom in September, spend that year reading and thinking and talking, and in June out comes a different kid, a better kid.

And that better kid makes a better world.

Sven Birkets says that books are the "unformulated stuff of the self." He writes, "Sometimes I think the long-term work of reading is to discover, one by one, the books that hold the scattered elements of our nature, after which the true consummation can begin" (2007, 23).

Middle school English teacher Claire Needell Hollander puts it another way. In her *New York Times* op-ed piece "Teach the Books, Touch the Heart," she laments that the standardized test-based "school reform" movement is turning the teaching of reading good books into making students reading-test takers. The process destroys the greatest benefit we get from reading books, she says: the emotional human connection.

We cannot enrich the minds of our students by testing them on texts that purposely ignore their hearts. By doing so, we are withholding from our neediest students any reason to read at all. We are teaching them that words do not dazzle but confound. We may succeed in raising test scores by relying on these methods, but we will fail to teach them that reading can be transformative and that it belongs to them. (2012)

We all know what's at stake here. We are fighting for the hearts and minds and souls of children. We want to cultivate a vibrant democracy with citizens who possess the critical-thinking skills to participate in it. Our quest is to teach *democracy* as a verb, full of action and purpose and vigor, creating a more thoughtful and caring and connected world. It is about fostering a lifelong love for reading and embracing those transformative powers. It is about having a student bound into your classroom Monday morning, sparkling with excitement about the fantastic book he or she read over the weekend.

Listening to the voices of the teachers in this book, we hear their passion to make good books an essential part of their classroom. In a sense, they are speaking as one. As Mary says:

I want my kids to learn about life from books. To find that they are not alone because they can connect to the characters they encounter. I want them to have "a-ha" moments when they relate a book to another text, print or nonprint. I want them to make positive life choices as they enter adolescence based on what they have read, to see the good in life, to learn that people can and do change, that they make mistakes and learn from them. I want my students to feel "normal" when they are figuring out their identity at this critical age. I want them to care more about the world and the future… I guess the biggest difference is that in September they pick up a book because they have to. In June they pick up a book because they want to.

Leslie says:

I want every student to love reading. I want my students to have the passion to read and to crave it. I want them to think of reading as a lifelong journey and not just a school subject. I want them to read because they want to not because they're forced. When my students leave me in June I want them to choose to go read outside under a tree instead of staying in playing video games . . . I want them to be thinkers and have rich conversations regarding critical issues in the text and be able to formulate opinions regarding these issues. I want them to be exposed to the outside world and know that reading goes beyond the classroom walls.

Ron is right along with them:

I want them to become lifelong readers and enjoy the love of reading a book to expand their critical thinking skills. I want them to learn from these novels and adapt the ideas and opinions of the author into their lives. I want books to help them think situations through and understand and agree or disagree with ideas or characters in the novel. Students use novels to understand themselves and through the characters they learn how to make better decisions in their own lives.

And here's Karen:

I know from experience that a great book changes the reader. For me, books have helped me escape, fall in love, recover from heartbreak, and have broken open my mind from the age of twelve . . . I hope they gain better reading comprehension, confidence as a reader, connections to the characters and events, a curiosity for the world, and tolerance for others.

I love how Karen says that books "broke open her mind." What all of these terrific educators are talking about is raising teaching to a new level. Every teacher wants students to acquire excellent reading skills, but we cannot just help them pass a reading test or comprehend a plot or define a new word. That is primarily about the *mechanics* of reading. The teachers featured in this book take their practice far beyond the basic requirements of the job to explicitly connect students' reading to learn critical thinking, develop their unique selves, become compassionate people, be involved citizens, shape their moral identities, and understand the world through books.

There is a word for all of those ideals. It's called an *education.*

Any real education would never be about primarily preparing workers and test takers. To educate is not an economic thing or even a future thing; it is a life thing and a human thing. Adolescents live in the here and now, so they want their education to be significant today, not some distant time in their adulthood. We must teach in ways that value what Michael Smith and Jeff Wilhelm call the *immediate experience* of reading and learning, not for students doing their homework later that night or passing a test in March or graduating high school in five years (2007).

Making Reading Relevant

Let us confront some reality here. Students are *bored* in school. They are bored by what they read and what they study and how they study it. They do not see it as being relevant to their lives. I do not presume that this is a new insight. I suspect most kids were bored in school when my grandma Gertie was in the middle grades a hundred years ago. And my grandma did not have a smartphone in her pocket buzzing with a new text message.

Karen Tellez says the biggest challenge she faces as a teacher has nothing to do with testing or administrators or dealing with the emotions of adolescents. It is her competition with technology:

Our students are admittedly staying up texting, dead tired in school, addicted to their cell phones, and quite frankly not interested in reading. It gets harder and harder to hold their attention for longer than ten minutes. When we can get their attention with great books, some students have difficulty with the stamina it takes to read intensely for long periods of time. I am not sure what the answer is to this problem, but I know that great books are needed to get them to take notice and read again.

Good teachers have many strategies in their pedagogical toolbox to motivate their students and suck them out of that boredom and their fixation with media. Here is a very important one: *Make school about ideas that matter.* The ideas are inside those great books Karen is talking about. They are on the pages of every newspaper each morning. They are inside the life experiences of every student. They are in every local community and every global culture.

The notion that focusing on ideas rather than discrete skills will water down the curriculum and push important content to the sides is simply wrong. We help students learn the skills so that they can explore the ideas. This is not a linear process; it is a *symbiotic* one. The ideas, questions, emotions, and personal connections are the engine leading the work. Rather than being a fact-memorizing and skill-building factory, schools must become communities of learners and thinkers and innovators who are *using* skills and knowledge to explore questions about the real world. When schools achieve that aim, they become vibrant workshops of democracy and problem solving. We don't read a novel about racism just to teach students comprehension skills and assess them on reading a novel. We do it to explore racism and intolerance, understand ourselves, and change the world, to make it less prejudiced and more kindhearted and open-minded.

It's perfectly understandable for teachers to say they don't have time in their overflowing curriculums to teach the big questions of life. It seems every day they are given yet another mandate to cover. But I think we do have the time—at least *some* time. We just need to rethink how we see our curriculum and how we use the school day. By shaping our units around ideas of substance, we can build into them the teaching of necessary skills and knowledge. When Leslie's sixth graders surveyed people about poverty, they learned much more. They learned to work collaboratively; care about current social problems; ask good questions and listen to different opinions and perspectives; use reading to connect to their lives, shape their own beliefs, and expand their background knowledge; and build vital critical-thinking skills. All of that was packed into a single inquiry project. Nel Noddings writes about focusing our teaching on the essential issues of life:

> Where should these matters be discussed? Surely, they are relevant topics for study in social studies, literature, and science. But with a curriculum already groaning under the demands of high-stakes testing, how can we add still more? My answer is to get rid of the trivia and spend time on topics that really matter. (2004, 491)

As educators we can choose to be bystanders and allow others to define our teaching and curriculum, or we can choose to be active participants and activists in the transformation of our schools and society. Put another way, we don't need teachers on the sidelines; we need teachers leading the team. The best way for all of us to do that is to practice—in whatever big and small ways that we can—the teaching that is in our hearts. This requires courage, collaboration, creativity, the willingness to make bold decisions, and the knowledge to back them up. It also requires compromise, which is not easy for teachers with passion and determination. But one thing we know for certain is that we will not create classrooms rich with a passion for books and reading and thinking about life without teachers leading the way.

Teaching for Caring Hearts and Critical Minds (in the Age of Standards and Tests)

How did fostering thoughtful, empathetic, smart readers get turned into creating test takers? Who would ever think that teaching for a robust and caring democracy—that is, preparing children for our extraordinary and complex twenty-first-century lives—would ever be considered "progressive" or controversial? Politicians and everyday Americans sing the praises of our democracy endlessly. You would think teaching for social responsibility and its accompanying twenty-first-century literacies would be part of the foundation for any education reform policy. And how did we ever create a school system that has children reading far more textbooks and basal readers than good books and captivating real-world resources?

Unfortunately, many educational and political leaders still see creative teaching and good test scores as being mutually exclusive. With so much pressure to teach to standards and increase student achievement, how should teachers respond to these expectations and professional responsibilities? How do they satisfy their *own* passions and purposes while also fulfilling the long list of requirements from the powers that be?

All of the teachers in Chapters 7–11 deal with the realities of testing and standards. They must confront the onslaught of data. None of them offers any easy answers, and some of them face very real limitations on their instruction or see their practice as being subversive. (Good teaching often *is* subversive.) There are no magic wands we can wave to make these requirements disappear. Of course, if we disagree with something—from a federal education policy to a district requiring the use of textbooks to a school without block scheduling to a grade-level team having students read only novels with white protagonists—we can let our voices be heard. Good change can happen, but only if we speak up.

Exactly how the teachers in this book respond to these expectations varies widely. They are, after all, in different schools with different students and administration. Their opinions and experiences run the gamut from not thinking much at all about testing to genuine concern and even some self-doubt about their teaching. I should preface this with the fact that most of the teachers in these pages do not have students with sky-high reading test scores. All of these teachers work in lower-income schools with a primarily nonwhite student population. Based on their State of Illinois school report cards, most of their students' reading scores fall in the range of 70–80 percent at "meets or exceeds" state standards. Although those figures are considerably better than at many urban schools, the averages are quite below affluent schools.

As many people have forcefully argued, such as Diane Ravitch (2010), it is a Herculean task for any teacher to overcome the devastating effects of poverty. But for me, the very first task in helping students succeed, no matter what their socioeconomic status, is to make going to school an *interesting, thought-provoking, creative, authentic,* and *highly social* experience. We are not going to transform the system of education overnight. But we can actively participate in the process, because that transformation happens one school and one classroom at a time. One of those classrooms can be yours.

Consider my son's former school, Burley Elementary in Chicago. Burley has one of the most dedicated literature-based and inquiry-based curriculums I have ever seen. In 2011, the school's middle-grades reading test scores were very close to *100 percent* "meets and exceeds state standards." About one quarter of Burley's students are from low-income families, far lower than the Chicago Public Schools average. Yet I would still argue that Burley and schools like it have shown that teaching through inquiry, immersing students in a world of good books and authentic literacy, and integrating content that matters to adolescents is most certainly not bad for test scores. On the contrary, I have seen firsthand that it cultivates thinkers, readers, and adolescents with a rich imagination and a spirited intellectual curiosity, all of which helps students succeed on tests. In all of his years at Burley, my son never brought home a textbook.

Most of the teachers in this book are struggling to varying degrees with following school district expectations to prepare their students for standardized testing. Some of them have explicit expectations or school structures that limit their choices. Natalie has a strictly required guided-reading time each day that seriously cuts into her time for teaching with literature and other authentic resources. She says, "There's a lot of pressure from testing, especially at my school, because we have not made AYP [Annual Yearly Progress] in several years. The district wants to have more control over what we do."

Leslie, who is now in a different school, no longer has the big chunks of time she had previously, making it more difficult to implement in-depth literature units. She also says that "each year the pressure to raise students' test scores increases."

Ron offers this dose of reality: "Everyone wants to see test results, and that's what makes people seem happier whether students are learning or not. All of the administration and teachers are under extreme pressure to keep test scores high, so I try my best to mix the test prep with high-interest authentic literature."

Karen adds these sobering words:

We are now conducting five separate standardized tests in eighth grade that consume seventeen days for testing alone. This doesn't include the time needed to prepare them for the tests and reintroduce them into units that were stopped to conduct the tests. It's mindboggling that this is what teaching looks like now. I do the best I can with the time limitations and had to drop an entire unit this year due to the excess testing. As for the pressure to teach to the test, I never really bought into that and continue to believe that in order for kids to perform on standardized reading tests, they need to read, read, and read more.

Mary says that although she feels some pressure from her administrators, she does not let concerns about her students' test scores dominate her thinking She tries not to put too much emphasis on them:

I believe that good teachers will prepare students for standardized tests simply by motivating them to read. The more students read, the better they will get at reading, and that will translate onto their test scores. I have unofficially noticed my students who read more books show more improvements over the course of the year on their Scantron tests. I try not to let myself get too stressed out about these tests because my stress would filter down to my students and that wouldn't help them.

Mary also believes that having a strong independent reading structure in her classroom pays off big dividends. Independent reading time is "sacred" in her classroom. She adds, "It's the best feeling of the day to see 33 students all absorbed in their individual novels or journaling about them. That time is all about choice: choice in reading material and how they respond."

When it comes to meeting standards, I see a glimmer of hope. Most of the teachers I work with believe the new Common Core State Standards are actually allowing them to design good literature units. Ron, for example, is now working in his sixth- to eighth-grade teams to design integrated units that align with the new standards. Natalie commented, "I like the Common Core more because I think it's at a higher level and there are less standards overall. Common Core curriculum maps focus on a couple of novels and give examples of all kinds of other texts to use during the unit." In fact, the Common Core Curriculum Mapping Project that Natalie refers to not only brings together literary and informational texts in units, but frames the units with an "essential question."

Karen says, "I'm excited to see that the new Core Standards and the framework for teaching is moving toward a curriculum much like the one you designed in our unit. They want to see a balance of short texts and literature that's compelling to students and helps them understand the world." Here is a teacher who is designing her own units and using the Common Core State Standards to validate her teaching with literature.

Mary (who is at the same school as Karen) also feels strongly that teachers can *use* these new standards to justify teaching through inquiry and integrating real-world resources into their teaching:

The new standards for literacy have three shifts that are very conducive to teaching with novels. One, they want us to use "complex texts" and "academic vocabulary." A basal doesn't really allow for students to get deeply into a text . . . Another shift emphasizes the use of nonfiction and informational text, which is also lacking in the basal. The novels that we put at the center of the unit we can then connect to articles, poetry, picture books, and so on. The last shift emphasizes citing the text, which I find is also novel-centered. I plan to integrate the novels that I'll use as core texts with informational texts that are connected, relevant, and engaging.

Mary goes on to mention the new focus on "cognitive rigor" that she learned about in her school's professional development. Karin Hess has developed a "cognitive rigor matrix" that uses a revised Bloom's Taxonomy and Norman Webb's Depth of Knowledge levels (Hess et al. 2009). There are plenty of critics of Bloom's Taxonomy (including me) and its notion of a strictly neat and linear progression of thinking. But rather than seeing this as a hindrance to her teaching with good books, Mary told me, "You have to use literature if you're going to get to the levels 3, 4, and 5 in terms of rigor, and that's what the big buzzword is, rigor, rigor, rigor." This is a very important point. Just like Karen, Mary is not letting the push for standards and test prep stop her from using great literature, engaging children with the world, and inquiry-based teaching, because more and more of those expectations are being connected to deeper thinking, stronger readers, and building students' background knowledge—all of which are vital elements in her literature units.

So, although these teachers feel pressure when it comes to testing, all of them to varying degrees are continuing to make literature an essential part of their classroom. Karen told me that the biggest insight she gained from our working together was the idea of not making her units strictly about the novel:

> *The novel became one component of the unit that was driven by inquiry. It has completely changed the way that I approach designing my curriculum. For example, I used to teach a unit on* To Kill a Mockingbird. *Now I teach a unit on civil rights that encompasses a variety of primary sources, articles from the past and present, documentaries, nonprint texts, and the novel. We begin by inquiring whether or not Martin Luther King would be proud of our advancements in civil rights if he were alive today. Our essential question drives our unit and results in a debate that includes evidence from all the materials we've read, not just the novel. The result is a much richer experience for the students and for me.*

Karen adds these words of defiance for all teachers to live by: "Dragging my students through five standardized tests this year is our reality, but it won't overwhelm my curriculum."

What does all of this mean for teachers who want to teach for social responsibility and excite their students with in-depth inquiry with good books? It means we have our work cut out for us. It means we must become part of the pedagogical and political *push* to bring sanity and humanity into our classrooms. It means we must literally study our schools and curricula and figure out any and every way we can to make this infinitely more meaningful and important vision of what it means to be an educated human being a reality in our classrooms. And it means that we must become educated ourselves about all the standards and education organization position statements that we can use to justify good teaching, great books, and an invigorating curriculum. None of it will be easy. At times we will be stressed and frustrated and feel like crying or screaming. But we can't give up. Because we also know that even with all of these limitations and crazy expectations, we can make good things happen with a classroom full of energized adolescents. I know this is happening. I see it happening. We just need to take the lead and make it happen.

And let's own up to one more vital tool in our secret box of teacher tricks for making our passions come alive inside our classrooms: we play the game. Teachers politely listen to their administrators, go to their school in-service meetings, read the memos, complete the paperwork, fill in the rubrics, and then go into their classroom, close the door, and *teach*. I like to tell my college students to put all of those district mandates, school directives, and curriculum requirements into three mental buckets. The first bucket holds the things you must do, the second bucket holds the things you somewhat have to do, and the third bucket holds the things you can ignore. Yes, these days, with accountability measures and computers full of data, that last bucket has gotten a bit emptier. But teachers know that sometimes the key to good teaching is as simple as closing the classroom door.

Chapter 13

Becoming a Teacher of Inquiry

I have come to teach by searching, and by searching, teach. My classroom has become
a place where we are all wonderfully menaced by a compelling curiosity.
—Phyllis Muldoon (1990)

Reading through the units in this book can be a bit overwhelming. They sure seem like a lot of work. Well, they *were* a lot of work! But teachers work hard all the time. So yes, it does take time to find good books, brainstorm good questions, design thought-provoking activities, locate those fantastic real-world resources, and fit them together into a cohesive unit. And it's not like teachers have tons of free time. So, how do we make this happen?

Start small.

Remember when I equated designing an inquiry unit to my mom spending weeks (or months) fitting together a 1,000-piece jigsaw puzzle? Well, to begin you don't need to design a 1,000-piece unit. You can start with a 100-piece unit. This is the advice Leslie offers:

Start with a book that you've taught before, but reread it with a different lens. Find key ideas that you want your students to explore and gather a few supplemental texts and develop a small and large project.

That's right. Don't think you need to create a seven-week unit on *Speak* or a six-week unit on *The Wednesday Wars,* and have to design ten activities and find fifteen resources and fill up an entire page with teaching ideas. Even for experienced teachers who embrace literature wholeheartedly and want to take their teaching to a higher level, this can be a daunting task. If you're ready for that, then by all means, jump right in. But if you're not, take these seven steps instead:

1. Choose a novel that includes an important issue of social responsibility. Come up with an interesting title for your unit based on that issue. Consider making it a question. That title is what your unit is about.

2. Read the book (or read it again). Mark up the book to brainstorm specific parts that you can use to get students thinking and talking about ideas and issues that matter. Remember, these topics don't need to be about the morality of war or the evils of racism. They can also be about everyday acts of kindness, the complexity of friendship, the struggles of poverty, or a character making an ethical decision.

3. Write ten stimulating questions you could ask in a class discussion or use for journal writing.

4. List five mini-lessons you can do at various points in the unit. Remember, these will be just ten to fifteen minutes long. These lessons can become easy ways to cover standards. If you need to integrate more standards, then add to your mini-lesson list. Every good book includes a long list of possible mini-lessons.

5. Locate three interesting and different kinds of real-world resources that connect to the book and social responsibility, such as a newspaper op-ed piece, a song, and a video; or a short magazine article, a poem, and photographs. Mix them up. You need to find only three so find three *great* resources. If in your search you come across another one, grab it.

6. Create one very good (and very real) writing assignment. This could connect to your issue of social responsibility or even directly to a main inquiry question.

7. Design one smaller project to be done after the book is completed—I'd suggest a project that could be done in a week or so.

Plug these puzzle pieces into a calendar on your computer or tablet and you are well on your way. Depending on the book you choose and how much time you have each day, a unit such as this would most likely be done within four weeks. I bet, as you are teaching, that you will end up doing more, because new ideas will come to you as your class is engaged in exploring critical issues and discussing a really good book. And these ideas will *excite* you, so you will be pulled like a magnet to do more, and that is a very good thing. Go with the flow. Explore new paths. Be bold (even in a small unit like this). Perhaps most important, become the model *thinker* in your classroom. Let your students see you as the epitome of social responsibility, asking and grappling with complex questions, seeking multiple perspectives, caring for the world, and using literature to explore important ideas.

Actually, I would do one more thing. I would spend some extra time carefully designing my opening activity and the resource I use for it. The *immediate experience* of that activity helps set the tone for the entire unit. It can either pull kids right in or push kids right out. It can turn their hearts and brains on or shut them off. A unit does not succeed or fail on the first activity, but a good opening sure helps.

Here's an example. Imagine I wanted to design an inquiry unit around the historical novel *Chains* by Laurie Halse Anderson. This wonderful book is about the American Revolution and slavery. The main character, Isabel, is a slave for a family in New York and becomes a spy for the Rebels. How might I begin? There are many good options. But I'm thinking back to Karen's point about her struggles to compete with technology. Forget competing with it; I would welcome it into the classroom. Most important, I would not start in the past, but *today*. I would not say anything to my students about the American Revolution or slavery. I would flip on the computer, go online, and project onto the screen the remarkable videos and pictures of the Arab Spring protests across the Middle East. This is Revolution 2.0. It is images of 100,000 people packed into Tahrir Square in Cairo; it is throngs of angry and impassioned people by the thousands marching through the streets of Yemen; it is police and soldiers fighting back protesters in Syria. There are videos with the voices of the people and others set to music. Some of it is raw and brutal and bloody and chaotic. But it is all the emotion of humanity speaking out for change. Just like many of the colonists in the American Revolution. Just like abolitionists with slavery.

Or what if I wanted to design a unit around Coe Booth's novel *Tyrell*? That book has more mature content, and some would argue it's more for high school students, but I think it has much to offer older middle-grades students. Tyrell is fifteen years old, African American, and struggling to survive in inner-city America. When his dad goes to prison for selling drugs, the family loses its apartment and Tyrell must go to a homeless shelter with his mom and younger brother. With his mom refusing to work and pressuring him to sell drugs to support the family, Tyrell has no easy answers. *This book has no easy answers.* How might I begin this unit? Here's one idea: have the class sit together on the rug or packed in around sofas and chairs and pillows. I would pass out the lyrics to Lupe Fiasco's song "Kick, Push" for us to read together. We'd discuss possibilities for what the song is about. On one hand it's simply a song about the love of skateboarding ("Kick, push, kick, push, kick, push . . . coooooast . . ."). Or is it about inner-city kids being pushed from place to place with nowhere to really go? Or is it a metaphor for urban youth trying to find themselves? Or is it about a young kid selling or "pushing" drugs? Singer Lupe Fiasco grew up on the South Side of Chicago in a neighborhood just like Tyrell's. I would play the song. Students would have a lot to say about all of this. That conversation could last all day.

Once you design and teach that first inquiry unit, what's next? I suggest making a pile of the books you will teach or think you will teach during the school year. Most teachers have an idea of at least some of the books they'd like to use. Look through the books. Do any of them resonate with themes of social responsibility? Remember, I do *not* think every literature unit you teach and every book you read aloud should be connected to social responsibility. Sometimes we need to read a book simply to enjoy a good story and be entertained. That's it. No more work necessary. But ask yourself if any of your books would work well as an anchor text of a future unit focusing on social responsibility. Your next unit may be sitting in that pile. Of course, I strongly encourage you to go beyond the books that you have already been teaching and seek out new ones to design a unit.

You can also choose a specific theme of social responsibility, such as different forms of government, moral decision making, war and peace, current social problems, racism in America, global gender issues, homophobia, how power is used and abused—the list goes on and on. Once you identify a theme or topic—perhaps it connects to another part of your curriculum, such as social studies—you can seek out a good book as the unit anchor text.

There are really no rules set in stone when it comes to designing an inquiry-based literature unit. The only absolute is the book. Everything else I've written about must be seen as being flexible and changeable, so teachers use whatever ideas they like and make the themes work for their students and their schools. That means you can "start small" the entire school year and focus on creating a series of smaller inquiry units. Or you can wait until later in the year (maybe after testing) and teach one large unit. When it comes to engaging adolescents and young adults in issues and questions that matter to them and the world, something is always better than nothing. But once you start, you will not want to stop. You will be *pumped* to design your next unit! After Mary Tripp and I finished our unit with the novel *Black and White* that explored racism and friendship, she told me—after having taught with literature for fourteen years—"I will never teach a book the same way again."

What Would I Do Differently?

How, besides giving me a dose of humility, did my journey back into the classroom change me? Let me put that another way; if I were to go back into the classroom again, what would I do differently? What am I now exploring with my education students and teachers about designing and teaching inquiry-based literature units? About teaching for social responsibility? About bringing the wonder of reading and books to middle-grades students? I will limit my thoughts here to five that stand out in my mind.

Critical Thinking and Problem Solving

Life has become amazingly complex. We read texts and see images and hear sound bites *everywhere*. We have political perspectives coming at us from every direction and ideology. We are plugged into media practically 24/7. We have information and *misinformation* clamoring for our attention. We have the amount of all that information *doubling* every two years. We have companies selling us stuff constantly. We have war and melting ice caps and staggering poverty and urban violence and intractable intolerance. I can't imagine many skills and habits of mind that have greater importance than the ability to think critically about all of this.

Without the abilities and the *interest* to critique information and perspectives—and quite honestly the fine art of manipulation—any real hope of informed and reasoned social responsibility may be lost. Our democracy needs citizens (young and old) who can take apart and interrogate ideas, question perspectives, and think in innovative and creative ways. I cannot imagine how our democracy can sustain itself in any healthy and productive way in the twenty-first century without a citizenry steeped in the skills of thinking critically.

Critical thinking is usually coupled with problem solving, and if our nation and our world need anything, it's people who can solve problems. When we design our units, we can connect books to real-world problems, guide students toward understanding them, and challenge them to work together to solve the quandaries. This is known as *problem-based teaching*, and it takes inquiry to an entirely new level. Our classrooms and schools really can become workshops and think tanks for solving problems—from bullying on the playground to the destruction of ecosystems to genocide in Africa—and literature can help humanize these issues. Given all of this, I would strive to integrate critical thinking and problem solving into my inquiry units more explicitly.

The generic view of critical thinking involves the ability to discern fact from opinion; see multiple perspectives; question assumptions; and use reasoning to analyze, synthesize, and critique information. Ron Ritchhart and his colleagues at Harvard's prestigious Project Zero have spent years studying the teaching of *thinking* (Ritchhart, Church, and Morrison 2011). From their own work, as well as the work of other researchers, they compiled a comprehensive list of specific "thinking moves" that we can engage students in:

1. Observing closely and describing what's there
2. Building explanations and interpretations
3. Reasoning with evidence
4. Making connections
5. Considering different viewpoints and perspectives
6. Capturing the heart and forming conclusions
7. Wondering and asking questions
8. Uncovering complexity and going below the surface of things
9. Identifying patterns and making generalizations
10. Generating possibilities and alternatives
11. Evaluating evidence, arguments, and actions
12. Formulating plans and monitoring actions
13. Identifying claims, assumptions, and bias
14. Clarifying priorities, conditions, and what is known (11–14)

We can add to this a couple ideas that every teacher is very familiar with: inference skills and wide background knowledge. A list like this can be either exciting or daunting. Either way, these specific "thinking moves" can help teachers design activities and find good resources with which to engage students in real thinking about real issues in the real world. You can see examples of this in our units in this book: When Ron's seventh graders debated bioethical options, when Leslie's students closely observed their trees, when Natalie's students explained their rankings of items on the priority list, when Karen's eighth graders considered different options and opinions during silent graffiti, and when Leslie's students brainstormed questions for and analyzed responses to their poverty survey.

Notice that all of the thinking moves involve *action*. They all begin with a verb because we want students to *do* thinking and *show* their thinking. Ron Ritchhart advocates "making thinking visible." This involves designing activities and assignments for students to make their normally invisible thinking very visible so we can all *see it*. That visible thinking leads to more thinking. Ritchhart and his coauthors write, "When we make the thinking that happens in classrooms visible, it becomes more concrete and real. It becomes something we can talk about and explore, push around, challenge, and learn from" (30). Ritchhart has worked with sixth-grade teachers who have their students keep a "visible thinking portfolio" with examples of their thinking moves.

Here's another example of making critical thinking visible in an inquiry-based literature unit. In a unit that I cotaught with Ron Sledge (that is not in this book), we divided his seventh graders into three book groups, each of which read a different novel that fit under the larger unit umbrella of "social problems." One group read *Monster* to look at our criminal justice system, another group read *Make Lemonade* to examine teenage pregnancy, and the last group read *La Linea* to explore illegal immigration. For one activity, we had each group divide into two smaller groups and create pro/con charts for a specific issue within their topic. The *Monster* group focused on the death penalty, the *Make Lemonade* group focused on teen pregnancy and abortion, and the *La Linea* group chose closing or opening our immigration policies (see Figure 13.1). This activity required the students to consider multiple perspectives, including ones with which they did not agree. It pushed them to consider nuance and moral dimensions. By posting all of the chart papers on the wall and having the students discuss their work, we helped them make their thinking visible and used that to engage the class in intellectual and, at times, heated debate, which fueled even more thinking.

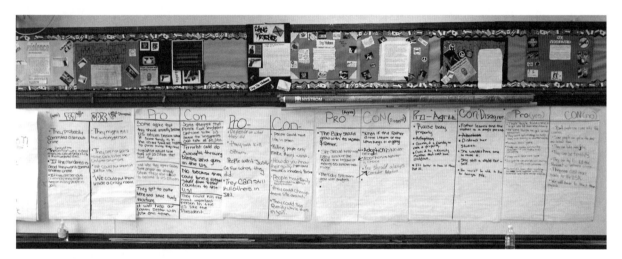

Figure 13.1 Ron Sledge's seventh graders create pro/con charts on current social problems.

Reading Informational Texts

In our units, students read a lot of informational texts. Let's take the "social problems" unit I just mentioned. For *Make Lemonade*, we read part of a report by the National Campaign to Prevent Teen and Unplanned Pregnancy (Moore 2008). For *Monster*, we read an excerpt from the Pew Center on the States report, "One in One Hundred: Behind Bars in America 2008." For *La Linea* and illegal immigration, we read newspaper editorial cartoons. They also looked at statistics on incarceration and teen pregnancy, which is a different kind of informational text. (And it *shocked* Ron's students— who were largely Latino—to read this: 53 percent of Latina teenagers will get pregnant before they are twenty years old. After we read that sentence, ripples of girls' voices went through the classroom: "Not me . . . Not me . . . Not me . . .")

We read nearly all the informational texts in all these units as shared reading. This was too much! I'm a big believer in shared reading for the reasons that I explained earlier. But students must also read these texts on their own. Most students struggle mightily with reading informational texts. I saw this firsthand when teaching these units. But as Janet Allen (2000) writes, shared reading should be a *path* to independent reading. That means using that shared reading to help students gain the skills they need to tackle more complex texts on their own.

Writing

I am inside classrooms a lot, and here is a tragic fact: much of the writing I see is dreadful. Our schools don't really value good writing; they value *technical* writing. As many have pointed out, when it comes to writing instruction, there is a very large disconnect between school writing and real writing in the real world (Daniels, Zemelman, and Steinke 2007). That's why kids are still stuck in education agony, filling in vocabulary worksheets, writing five-paragraph essays, and being drilled endlessly on writing "extended responses" for standardized tests. (I have never met anyone outside of school who wrote an "extended response.") As long as we teach writing solely as a "school thing" and rarely as a craft and thinking thing for *life*, we will continue to struggle to cultivate good writers. There is only so much junk writing people can do before they turn off their brains and write like robots. And school is exceptional at teaching kids to turn off their brains.

As I wrote in the introduction, I need to get better at integrating meaningful and *finished* writing into these inquiry units. By "finished" I mean writing that students are expected to craft with care and attention and take through a writing process—including complete editing steps—to produce beautiful final work that ideally is made public, such as by publishing it in a class magazine, blog, or Web site, or simply by displaying it on a hallway wall.

The only way this will happen is if teachers have students read good writing; explicitly teach good writing through mini-lessons and writing conferences; assign carefully chosen, purposeful, and selective writing projects; give them time to write; and honor students as real writers who publish their work for a real audience. The problem is that all of this requires *time*, which is where compromise comes in. Adding more in-depth writing to a unit might mean I have to cut something else. I do have other options, however, such as seeing if another teacher on my team would be interested in sharing some of the unit activities. That's what Mary did in our unit with *Black and White*. We gave the seventh graders an assignment to write an essay explaining racism to a space alien. Mary did not have the time for us to do this in her reading class, so she spoke to the language arts teacher, and he was happy to have the kids write the essay for his class.

Teaching for social responsibility gives us an endless array of substantive issues for students to write about. I would make a minimum of one finished piece of writing an almost nonnegotiable part of any unit in the future.

Works of Excellence

Ron Berger is really on to something. He's the former fifth-grade teacher I mentioned in Chapter 7. Currently he's with Expeditionary Learning, a nationally known professional development organization and network of schools that promotes hands-on, creative, project-based learning. Berger wrote the book *An Ethic of Excellence* about helping students produce the highest-quality work. He writes:

> At its core, my consulting with schools and districts is an effort to share the power and the pride of this ethic of craftsmanship. Most students, I believe, are caught on school treadmills that focus on *quantity* of work rather than *quality* of work. Students crank out endless final products every day and night. Teachers

correct volumes of such low-quality work; it's returned to the students and often tossed in the wastebasket. Little in it is memorable or significant, and little in it endangers personal or communal pride. I feel that schools need to get off this treadmill approach and shift their focus from quantity to quality. (2003, 8–9)

We need to teach students how to produce works of high quality, excellence, and craftsmanship. This applies to a piece of writing as much as it applies to a mural, survey, podcast, or math project. A few of our units had too many projects, which caused the quality to suffer. Some of the other work was done too quickly. If I had to choose between having students do two or three mediocre projects or one high-quality project, I would opt for the one with excellence.

Students' Questions

More than twenty years ago, when I was starting my career as a teacher, I was perusing the shelves in a used bookstore. I came upon an old copy of *Freedom to Learn* by Carl Rogers (1969). I don't remember if I knew who Rogers was at the time, but I bought the book, because when I flipped through the pages, I knew immediately it would resonate with my newly forming educational beliefs. That book was a seminal reading experience for me as I tried to figure out what to do with my sixth graders. I still have that book on my shelf. I'm still trying to figure out what to do with sixth graders.

Carl Rogers was the great humanistic psychologist who strongly advocated student-centered schooling. His book is filled with sparkling gems of wisdom. Compared with our traditional industrial schools, many consider Rogers's education thinking "radical." I consider it brilliant, caring, and humane. Rogers wanted schools to truly honor the uniqueness of each child and help them reach their greatest (and often untapped) potential. At the beginning of his book, he chose an epigraph by Albert Einstein:

It is in fact nothing short of a miracle that the modern methods of instruction have not yet entirely strangled the holy curiosity of inquiry; for this delicate little plant, aside from stimulation, stands mainly in need of freedom; without this it goes to wrack and ruin without fail. (iv)

Reading this quote it's not surprising that Rogers believed wholeheartedly in giving children the freedom to learn on their own terms. School must be a place where the innate curiosity and wonder of children are allowed to blossom. He believed that letting students pursue their interests was central to their meaningful learning. I agree with all of this. I immediately began working to turn Rogers's ideas into actual classroom practice. My first book, *A Democratic Classroom* (Wolk 1998), was in part about my efforts to do that. I quoted Rogers multiple times in that book. Here is a taste of that:

If I distrust the human being then I must cram him with information of my own choosing, lest he go his own mistaken way. But if I trust the capacity of the human individual for developing his own potentiality, than I can provide him with many opportunities and permit him to choose his own way and his own direction in his learning. (114)

I still agree with most of what Rogers wrote in *Freedom to Learn*. But a handful of years into my teaching, something happened. The politics of schooling and curriculum crashed into my student-centered beliefs. Allowing kids the space in the school day to ask their own questions was essential, but I also had to teach the critical knowledge about life and the world that I felt they had to understand.

In the units in this book, I did not give students any real opportunities to ask their own questions. Carl Rogers would be disappointed in me. Of course, we engaged in a great deal of dialogue and debate, and the kids had the freedom to make personal connections and construct their own meaning, and they certainly did much of that. But how should inquiry units that are specifically designed around social responsibility also give students the space to ask and even study their own questions?

Here is one rather sad example: In all of these units, how many times did I have students read the novel and respond in their journals to *anything they wanted*, as opposed to giving them a specific prompt? Honestly, maybe *once*. Why didn't I do that more often? I suspect it was because I was too focused on teaching social responsibility and not focused enough on allowing students to interact freely with a novel.

Progressive, student-centered teaching has an extensive history, and teachers have long struggled with finding the dividing line and balance between the knowledge they want (and need) their students to study and their students' personal knowledge and interests. Of course, the answer is to do both. I can select a novel because it resonates with specific themes and ideas; however, I must also allow students the space to meet that book on their own terms and interpret the story through their own meanings. I can design a unit around social responsibility, but also have students ask their own questions, explore their own ideas, and engage in their own discussions, and see where it all leads. This "freedom to learn" must be genuine; we must be willing to step aside from our own purposes and allow students to discover and develop their own significance.

I think back to some of our delightful and thought-provoking class discussions in these units, and I see where the students really did have the space and freedom to forge their own paths in our conversations. Was it enough? No. But one of the wonderful things about teaching is that we have the next unit and we have the next year. By studying our practice and asking good questions—to regard our teaching as inquiry itself—we can improve our important work with students and do our jobs better the next time.

Why Teach Reading?

We must ask ourselves what we are doing to help every student find purpose and meaning in books and reading. Instead of teaching "Reading," which is a school "subject," how about we just teach reading filled with the real purposes and experiences and emotions of life? Let's turn reading "class" into reading life.

If we want to have students fall in love with reading, we must have them read to enjoy good stories. We want them to find relevance in what they read. We must choose books with characters and cultures and life situations they can identify with. Maybe the test of our success with this comes from Mary's earlier comment: "In September they pick up a book because they have to. In June they pick up a book because they want to." That is a goal for every teacher to aspire to. Our work to make that happen begins on the first day of every school year. They do not need to read any specific book or author or genre to love reading. They just need to read a lot because they want to, and ideally with some variety.

I have many other hopes and goals for how adolescents can grow from reading in school.

I want them to understand that some reading is a form of bearing witness to life. This applies to fiction as much as nonfiction, because good novels show us the truths of being human.

I want them to see the beauty of good writing, to appreciate the words themselves.

I want them to know that books can show us that we are not alone, even when we feel alone.

I want books to challenge their assumptions and take them outside their comfort zones.

I want them to connect to the world from books.

I want them to own the idea that reading makes people more tolerant and less racist, more empathic and less self-centered.

I want them to read to cultivate imagination and creativity. I am referring here to people who think "outside the box," see in new ways, ask divergent questions, criticize conformity, and can be *visionary*, even at twelve years old. We can use imagination and creativity in all parts of our lives, from solving social problems to designing a new product to figuring out how to get more Americans involved in our daily democracy. This also includes what Maxine Greene calls *social imagination*, which she defines as "the capacity to invent visions of what should be and what might be in our deficient society, on the streets where we live, in our schools" (1995, 5).

I want them to believe that reading is a vital way to participate in democracy.

I want their reading to shape their moral identities.

I want them to read a book that moves them to tears.

I want them to read *Captain Underpants* and *Diary of a Wimpy Kid* and *The True Meaning of Smekday* because they are hilarious and clever.

I want them to read *The Chocolate War* and argue about what the ending means.

I want them to read *The Lord of the Nutcracker Men* and walk with soldiers into the battles of World War I.

I want them to read *The Disreputable History of Frankie-Landau-Banks* and have all of them—girls and boys—ask questions about gender and power and adolescence and society.

I want them to understand that there are millions, actually billions, of people around the world *right now* who do not have the freedom or money to walk into a library or a bookstore or a school and pluck a book off a shelf and read it.

I want them to know that slaves were denied literacy to keep them ignorant and powerless.

I want them to know that throughout history, and still today, people are imprisoned and killed for possessing banned books and for *reading*. Hazel Rochman, an editor for *Booklist,* is white and grew up under the systemic racism of apartheid in South Africa. She writes:

[Nelson] Mandela spent twenty-seven years in prison. And during those dark years, it was a crime to quote his words. To keep the apartheid system going you had to have fierce censorship. You had to control what people saw and thought. It was a police state. There were borders and barriers everywhere, barbed wire around our homes and in ourselves. There was blanket censorship of books and newspapers. Radio was state controlled. Until 1976 there was no television at all. The "public" library was for whites only. Most black writers were banned, banished, imprisoned. (1995, para. 12)

I want students to know what Hazel Rochman did to read. She had to hide her books from the government by burying them in her backyard.

I want them to know that there are people banning books in the United States.

I want their reading to rouse them to *care*. By this I mean going outside themselves, their own interests and wants, and having compassion and concern for people, the Earth, and the human condition. This includes the *common good*, putting the good of the group and community before the good of oneself, and having empathy for those in need and victims of oppression. Hazel Rochman writes, "The apartheid government with its rigorous censorship was right about one thing: books matter. The stories you read can transform you because they help you imagine beyond yourself" (1995, para. 13).

None of these goals are represented on any standardized test. Teaching them is a form of *resistance* to the people who regard reading in school as little more than a stack of data and a job requirement.

Having these ambitious goals also means that I must do all I can to avoid practices that work against them. I can't make kids read books and complete assignments that run the risk of turning them off to reading and caring and teach them to think like a toaster. Part of my teaching is damage control, limiting the damage our factory-minded schooling and industrial reading can inflict.

As teachers stand in their classrooms each day, they are in the center of deciding why their students go to school. Many teachers assume the real power is outside the classroom, made by bureaucrats who pass down mandates, publishers who write the textbooks, and testing companies who create the tests. Well, we all know that there is certainly some truth to their power and influence.

But they are not inside classrooms. And teachers make decisions every day that communicate to their students what it means to be educated, the responsibilities we have to people and the planet, and why they should read. Even in student-centered classrooms the teachers are the final gatekeepers of what happens in that space. As they stand each day in the center of their classrooms, they are not really alone. They stand with every author they can invite in. Henry David Thoreau wrote, "I have great faith in a seed. Convince me that you have a seed there, and I am prepared to expect wonders."

We have seeds. They are called books. Our wonders await.

Appendix A

100+ Novels for Teaching Social Responsibility

Keep in mind that many middle-grades novels are also good choices for young adults, just as many YA novels are also great for middle schoolers. This is NOT a list of the "best" 100 books. That would be impossible for me to write. I will just say that these are all good books. Besides, I mixed some older books, some newer books, and some classics into the list.

Middle Grades

After Tupac and D Foster by Jacqueline Woodson
Any Small Goodness by Tony Johnston
Bamboo People by Mitali Perkins
Between Shades of Gray by Ruta Sepetys
Bone by Bone by Bone by Tony Johnston
Bread and Roses, Too by Katherine Paterson
Breaking Stalin's Nose by Eugene Yelchin
Chains by Laurie Halse Anderson
Crossing Jordan by Adrian Fogelin
Counting on Grace by Elizabeth Winthrop
The Day No Pigs Would Die by Robert Newton Peck
The Ear, the Eye, and the Arm by Nancy Farmer
Elijah of Buxton by Christopher Paul Curtis
Freak the Mighty by Rodman Philbrick
Heat by Mike Lupica
Holes by Louis Sachar
Homeless Bird by Gloria Whelan

Hoot by Carl Hiaasen

Inside Out & Back Again by Thanhha Lai

Jefferson's Sons by Kimberly Bradley

The Lions of Little Rock by Kristin Levine

Locomotion by Jacqueline Woodson

The Loud Silence of Francine Green by Karen Cushman

Love That Dog by Sharon Creech

Maniac Magee by Jerry Spinelli

The Misfits by James Howe

Money Hungry by Sharon G. Flake

A Monster Calls by Patrick Ness

Nory Ryan's Song by Patricia Reilly Giff

Nothing but the Truth by Avi

Now Is the Time for Running by Michael Williams

Okay for Now by Gary D. Schmidt

The One and Only Ivan by Katherine Applegate

One Crazy Summer by Rita Williams-Garcia

Operation Redwood by S. Terrell French

The Outcasts of 19 Schuyler Place by E. L. Konigsburg

Rules by Cynthia Lord

The Skin I'm In by Sharon G. Flake

Stargirl by Jerry Spinelli

Things Not Seen by Andrew Clements

Totally Joe by James Howe

Trash by Andy Mulligan

Waiting for Normal by Leslie Conner

The Wednesday Wars by Gary D. Schmidt

Wonder by R. J. Palacio

Yellow Star by Jennifer Roy

Young Adult

The Absolutely True Diary of a Part-Time Indian by Sherman Alexie

All the Broken Pieces by Ann E. Burg

Autobiography of My Dead Brother by Walter Dean Myers

Before We Were Free by Julia Alvarez

Black and White by Paul Volponi

The Book Thief by Marcus Zusak

Boy Meets Boy by David Levithan

Bronx Masquerade by Nikki Grimes

Buried Onions by Gary Soto

Chanda's Secrets by Alan Stratton
The Chocolate War by Robert Cormier
Code Name Verity by Elizabeth Wein
Copper Sun by Sharon M. Draper
Dairy Queen by Catherine Gilbert Murdock
Daniel Half Human by David Chotjewitz
Deadline by Chris Crutcher
Delirium by Lauren Oliver
Diamonds in the Shadow by Caroline B. Cooney
The Disreputable History of Frankie Landau-Banks by E. Lockhart
Divergent by Veronica Roth
The Drowned Cities by Paolo Bacigalupi
The Earth, My Butt, and Other Big Round Things by Carolyn Mackler
Elsewhere by Gabrielle Zevin
Ender's Game by Orson Scott Card
Feed by M. T. Anderson
The First Part Last by Angela Johnson
The Giver by Lois Lowry
The Goats by Brock Cole
How to Save a Life by Sara Zarr
Hurricane Song by Paul Volponi
I Am the Cheese by Robert Cormier
Keesha's House by Helen Frost
Leverage by Joshua Cohen
The List by Siobhan Vivian
Little Brother by Cory Doctorow
The Loud Silence of Francine Green by Karen Cushman
Make Lemonade by Virginia Euwer Wolff
Mexican WhiteBoy by Matt de la Peña
Milkweed by Jerry Spinelli
The Moves Make the Man by Bruce Brooks
My Mother the Cheerleader by Robert Sharenow
Never Fall Down by Patricia McCormick
Parrot in the Oven by Victor Martinez
Perfect by Ellen Hopkins
Scrawl by Mark Shulman
Seedfolks by Paul Fleischman
Ship Breaker by Paolo Pacigalupi
Speak by Laurie Halse Anderson
Sold by Patricia McCormick

Spite Fences by Trudy Krisher
Stupid Fast by Geoff Herbach
Touching Spirit Bear by Ben Mikaelson
Tree Girl by Ben Mikaelson
Tyrell by Coe Booth
Uglies by Scott Westerfeld
Unwind by Neal Shusterman
We All Fall Down by Robert Cormier
Whale Talk by Chris Crutcher
Whirligig by Paul Fleischman
Will Grayson, Will Grayson by John Green and David Levithan
You Don't Know Me by David Klass

Appendix C

Middle-Grades and Young Adult Short Story Anthologies

Am I Blue? Coming Out from the Silence edited by Marion Dane Bauer

Athletic Shorts: Six Short Stories by Chris Crutcher

Baseball in April and Other Stories by Gary Soto

The Color of Absence: 12 Stories About Loss and Hope edited by James Howe

Cornered: 14 Stories of Bullying and Defiance edited by Rhoda Beleza

Dear Bully: Seventy Authors Tell Their Stories edited by Megan Kelley Hall and Carrie Jones

Face Relations: Eleven Stories About Seeing Beyond Color edited by Marilyn Singer

First Crossing: Stories About Teen Immigrants edited by Donald R. Gallo

Free? Stories About Human Rights edited by Amnesty International

Geektastic: Stories from the Nerd Herd edited by Holly Black

Guys Write for Guys Read: Boys' Favorite Authors Write About Being Boys edited by Jon Scieszka

How Beautiful the Ordinary: Twelve Stories of Identity edited by Michael Cart

How They Met and Other Stories by David Levithan

Join In: Multiethnic Short Stories edited by Donald R. Gallo

Leaving Home:15 Distinguished Authors Explore Personal Journeys edited by Hazel Rochman and Darlene Z. McCampbell

Living Up the Street by Gary Soto

Necessary Noise: Stories About Our Families As They Really Are edited by Michael Cart

No Easy Answers: Short Stories About Teenagers Making Tough Choices edited by Donald R. Gallo

145th Street: Short Stories by Walter Dean Myers

On the Fringe edited by Donald R. Gallo

Owning It: Stories About Teens with Disabilities edited by Donald R. Gallo

Petty Crimes by Gary Soto

Places I Never Meant to Be: Original Stories by Censored Writers edited by Judy Blume

Steampunk! An Anthology of Fantastically Rich and Strange Stories edited by Kelly Link and Gavin J. Grant

Sudden Flash Youth: 65 Short-Short Stories edited by Christine Perkins-Hazuka, Tom Hazuka, and Mark Budman

Tales from Outer Suburbia by Shaun Tan

13: Thirteen Stories That Capture the Agony and Ecstasy of Being Thirteen edited by James Howe

This Is Push: New Stories from the Edge edited by David Levithan

Twice Told: Stories Inspired by Art by Scott Hunt

What a Song Can Do: 12 Riffs on the Power of Music edited by Jennifer Armstrong

What They Found: Love on 145th Street by Walter Dean Myers

Who Am I Without Him? Short Stories About Girls and the Boys in Their Lives by Sharon G. Flake

You Don't Even Know Me: Stories and Poems About Boys by Sharon G. Flake

Appendix D

Middle-Grades and Young Adult Books of Poetry

Cool Salsa: Bilingual Poems on Growing Up Latino in the United States edited by Lori M. Carlson

Dizzy in Your Eyes: Poems About Love edited by Pat Mora

Falling Hard: 100 Love Poems by Teenagers edited by Betsy Franco

Heart to Heart: New Poems Inspired by Twentieth-Century American Art edited by Jan Greenburg

Here in Harlem: Poems in Many Voices by Walter Dean Myers

I Heard a Scream in the Street edited by Nancy Larrick

I Lay My Stitches Down: Poems of American Slavery by Cynthia Grady

I Wouldn't Thank You for a Valentine: Poems for Young Feminists edited by Carol Ann Duffy

A Maze Me: Poems for Girls edited by Naomi Shihab Nye

19 Varieties of Gazelle: Poetry of the Middle East edited by Naomi Shihab Nye

Paint Me Like I Am edited by Writerscorps

The Pain Tree and Other Teenage Angst-Ridden Poetry edited by Esther Pearl Watson and Mark Todd

Poems by Adolescents and Adults: A Thematic Collection for Middle School and High School edited by James Brewbaker

Poetry Speaks Who I Am: Poems of Discovery, Inspiration, Independence, and Everything Else edited by Elise Paschen and Dominique Raccah

Red Hot Salsa: Bilingual Poems on Being Young and Latino in the United States by Lorie Maria Carlson

River of Words: Young Poets and Artists on the Nature of Things edited by Pamela Michael

Salting the Ocean: 100 Poems by Young Poets edited by Naomi Shihab Nye

The Surrender Tree: Poems of Cuba's Struggle for Freedom by Margarita Engle

Teen Ink series edited by Stephanie H. Meyer

Tell the World edited by Writerscorps

Things I Have to Tell You: Poems and Writing by Teenage Girls edited by Betsy Franco

This Same Sky: A Collection of Poems from Around the World edited by Naomi Shihab Nye

Time You Let Me In: 25 Poets Under 25 edited by Naomi Shihab Nye

Tough Boy Sonatas by Curtis Crisler

War and the Pity of War edited by Neil Philip

What Have You Lost? edited by Naomi Shihab Nye

You Hear Me? Poems and Writing by Teenage Boys edited by Betsy Franco

You Remind Me of You: A Poetry Memoir by Eireann Corrigan

Appendix E

Picture Books for Teaching Social Responsibility

The Auction by Jan Andrews. An aging widower tells his grandson about his life on the family farm as he is preparing to sell it at auction.

The Pot That Juan Built by Nancy Andrews-Goebel. Through rhythmic text and stunning illustrations we learn how famed Mexican potter Juan Quezada makes his famous Mata Ortiz pottery.

Home by Jeannie Baker. A remarkable book that tells a story with no words. Through the use of just pictures—which are actually three-dimensional paper cutouts—the reader sees the transformation of an urban neighborhood (and a family) over an entire generation through a single window of their home.

Zoom and *Re-Zoom* by Istvan Banyai. Without any words this book (and the sequel) uses amazing imagery to send the reader on a journey of time and perspective. *Re-Zoom* is the sequel to *Zoom*.

Through My Eyes by Ruby Bridges. Ruby Bridges, the first African American girl to desegregate Alabama schools, tells her story of breaking through the racist barrier.

Voices in the Park by Anthony Browne. Four people (portrayed as gorillas) go to a park, and each person tells of the experience from his or her perspective. Browne gives each of the four—a man and his daughter and a woman and her son—their own personalities while confronting issues of class. This may be the perfect book to help kids explore the idea of perspective.

Piggybook by Anthony Browne. A father and his two sons (gorillas again) do not appreciate the hard work of their mother. This is a great book through which to explore issues of gender with even the youngest students.

Between Earth & Sky by Joseph Bruchac. Little Bear, a Native American, learns about Native American sacred places from his uncle Old Bear. The book explains what Native Americans call the "seven directions." Bruchac is Native American and has written many books.

A Day's Work by Eve Bunting. A Mexican American boy and his grandfather look for an honest day's work in this simple yet profound story.

Smoky Night by Eve Bunting. During the Los Angeles riots after the Rodney King verdict, Daniel and his mother must escape the madness, and unexpectedly make some new friends.

Someday a Tree by Eve Bunting. People join together to try to save an old oak tree that has been poisoned by chemicals.

Fly Away Home by Eve Bunting. A boy and his father are homeless and live in an airport. The father works as a janitor but doesn't make enough money for a home.

Cheyenne Again by Eve Bunting. This book tells the history of when Native American children were sent to boarding schools to "remove" their culture and learn the "white man's ways."

A River Ran Wild by Lynn Cherry. The Nashua River went from pristine natural beauty in the days of Native Americans to an industrial polluted wasteland in modern days—and then back to a natural wonder when people cleaned it up.

What Planet Are You From, Clarice Bean? by Lauren Child. Clarice Bean's wacky family works together to protest the destruction of a neighborhood tree.

Redwoods by Jason Chin. This is a story about the remarkable redwood tree and forests.

Woody Guthrie: Poet of the People by Bonnie Christensen. The great singer used his music to champion the common person and the land.

Si, Se Peude! Yes, We Can! by Diana Cohn. In this story based on actual events in Los Angeles in 2000, a boy's mother (a janitor) helps to lead the janitors' strike. In English and Spanish.

White Socks Only by Evelyn Coleman. An African American grandmother tells the story of when as a girl she first confronted the cruelty of the Jim Crow laws of the South.

The Cello of Mr. O by Jane Cutler. Amid the madness of war Mr. O insists on making music to bring peace and beauty to everyone.

Gandhi by Demi. This is a beautiful biography of the great nonviolent activist who helped bring India its independence.

The Greatest Power by Demi. A Chinese emperor sends children on a quest to find the "greatest power" in this gorgeously illustrated book. Although nearly every child insists it is weapons, money, beauty, or technology, one little girl stands alone with a very different vision.

City Green by DyAnne DiSalvo-Ryan. A girl gets the residents of her neighborhood to join together to clean up an empty lot and plant a garden. This is similar to Paul Fleischman's short novel *Seedfolks*.

The Long March by Mary Louise Fitzpatrick. This true story of the Choctaw tribe sending $170 to the starving people of the Irish potato famine in 1847 is a wonderful example of the common good.

The Life and Death of Crazy Horse by Russell Freedman. The story of the great Oglala Sioux chief.

Teammates by Peter Golenbock. This book tells the story of the horrible racism endured by Jackie Robinson and the courage of Pee Wee Reese, the only white teammate to stand by his side.

The Journey: Japanese Americans, Racism, and Renewal by Sheila Hamanaka. This story is based on Hamanaka's large mural of the history, oppression, and struggle of Japanese Americans.

Hey, Little Ant by Phillip Hoose and Hannah Hoose. This is one of my favorite picture books. A boy has his foot raised and is about to stomp on an ant. The ant pleads with the boy not to lower his foot. This is a great story for exploring power and decision making, especially with younger kids.

Now Let Me Fly: The Story of a Slave Family by Delores Johnson. A fictional story follows the capture of a girl in Africa in 1815 and the brutality of her life as a slave.

Walt Whitman: Words for America by Barbara Kerley. A biography of the great poet and his life during the Civil War.

Harvesting Hope: The Story of Cesar Chavez by Kathleen Krull. Chavez was the great activist leader of the United Farm Workers union.

Families by Susan Kuklin. Kuklin is a writer-photographer, and for this book she took portraits of all different kinds of families: mixed culture, divorced, Orthodox Jewish, gay, and so on. The written text comes from the kids in each family.

John Muir by Kathryn Lasky. A biography of the great environmentalist.

The Great Migration by Jacob Lawrence. This book is based on the Great Migration series of paintings by the late African American artist Jacob Lawrence. The paintings tell the story of the migration of African Americans from slavery to Jim Crow, and the migration from the South to the North.

Learning to Swim in Swaziland by Nila K. Leigh. An American girl has written and illustrated this true story about her stay (and her learning) in Swaziland, in southern Africa.

From Slave Ship to Freedom Road by Julius Lester. The story of slavery is told, from the capture of slaves in Africa to their enslavement and fight for freedom on the Underground Railroad. This book (which has graphic illustrations) directly asks readers to put themselves in the shoes of slaves and the oppressors.

Caring Hearts and Critical Minds: Literature, Inquiry, and Social Responsibility by Steven Wolk. Copyright © 2013. Stenhouse Publishers.

Pearl Moscowitz's Last Stand by Arthur A. Levine. Grandma Pearl chains herself to a gingko tree to save it from being cut down.

Vherses: A Celebration of Outstanding Women by J. Patrick Lewis. These short biographies—written in verse—tell of women of great accomplishment, from Rachel Carson and Ella Fitzgerald, to Fannie Lou Hamer and Venus and Serena Williams.

This Land Is My Land by George Littlechild. Littlechild, an artist, is a Seminole. In his words and pictures, he tells the story of the oppression of his people.

The Flower Man by Mark Ludy. With not a single word, this story tells about one old man who moves to a town overcome with bleakness and by passing out flowers, spreads happiness.

Erandi's Braids by Antonio Hernandez Madrigal. Erandi, a little girl in the village of Patzcuaro, Mexico, volunteers to sell her hair to the barber so her poor family can buy a new fishing net. It is based on historical fact: in the 1940s and 1950s, merchants drove around Patzcuaro to buy the beautiful hair of the Tarascan women who needed money.

Hiroshima No Pika (The Flash of Hiroshima) by Toshi Maruki. At 8:15 a.m., August 6, 1945, the atomic bomb was dropped on Hiroshima. The story is of a little girl, Mii, running from the destruction with her mother and badly injured father. Based on a true story told to the author.

Peaceful Protest: The Life of Nelson Mandela by Yona Zeldis McDonough. A gorgeous biography of the antiapartheid activist, who after twenty-seven years in prison, became president of South Africa.

Richard Wright and the Library Card by William Miller. This fictionalized story is based on an actual comment that Richard Wright, the African American novelist, made about getting his first library card. Because he could not get a library card as an African American, a white coworker secretly let Wright use his.

Baseball Saved Us by Ken Mochizuki. During their imprisonment at Japanese internment camps during World War II, Japanese American boys escaped their anguish by playing baseball. Once a boy is freed, he confronts prejudice on a Little League baseball field.

Tomas and the Library Lady by Pat Mora. With the help of a local librarian, the young son of Mexican American migrant farmworkers falls in love with books and reading.

The Paper Bag Princess by Robert Munsch. In this book for younger kids, a princess rescues her prince in distress—and then dumps him after he insults her.

Stone Soup by Jon J. Muth. The wonderful retelling of the classic story, this time with Zen monks, is a great way to teach kids about living as a community.

Zen Shorts by Jon J. Muth. This is one of my favorite picture books. Three kids meet Stillwater, a panda bear, who uses "Zen shorts" (very short stories) to encourage them (and us) to "reexamine our habits, desires, concepts, and fears." Breathtaking illustrations.

Zen Ties by Jon J. Muth. This continues the story started in *Zen Shorts*. Brilliant and beautiful.

The Three Questions by Jon J. Muth. A boy seeks the answers to three questions: When is the best time to do things? Who is the most important one? and What is the right thing to do? Based on a story by Leo Tolstoy.

Wings by Christopher Myers. Ikarus has wings and can fly. But his peers and the adults around him tease him and treat him as an outcast because he's "different."

Malcolm X: A Fire Burning Brightly by Walter Dean Myers. This biography of the civil rights leader is by one of the best children's authors.

Patrol: An American Soldier in Vietnam by Walter Dean Myers. We follow one soldier in the jungles of Vietnam as his visceral fear echoes the senselessness of war. Myers's brother was killed in Vietnam.

Planting the Trees of Kenya by Claire Nivola. Wangaari Mathai, founder of the Green Belt Movement in Africa and winner of the Nobel Peace Prize, has helped women plant 30 million trees.

The Seed by Isabel Pin. A seed drops from the sky and two tribes of insects prepare for all-out war to claim it.

In Our Mother's House by Patricia Polacco. A wonderful story about two lesbian partners who adopt three children and raise a happy, loving family.

Pink and Say by Patricia Polacco. Two boys who are friends, one white and the other black, are both fighting for the Union during the American Civil War in one of the most emotionally moving read-alouds a teacher can choose.

Aunt Chip and the Great Triple Creek Dam Affair by Patricia Polacco. Eli and his Aunt Chip live in Triple Creek. Once the big TV tower was built years ago, people stopped reading books. All people do in Triple Creek (except Aunt Chip) is watch TV. Aunt Chip teaches Eli how to read and shows him the wonder of books.

The Patchwork Quilt by Patricia Polacco. The story of a quilt as it passes through the generations of Polacco's family.

Why? by Nikolai Popov. This book has no words but tells the story of two frogs that have an innocent disagreement, which escalates into complete war and destruction. It's a profound idea told in a way that even young kids can understand.

How to Make an Apple Pie and See the World by Marjorie Priceman. A humorous story of a girl who wants to make apple pie and must travel the world to get the ingredients.

And Tango Makes Three by Justin Richardson and Peter Parnell. Two male penguins in the Central Park Zoo raise a baby penguin in this account based on a true story.

John's Secret Dreams: The Life of John Lennon by Doreen Rappaport. Biography of the Beatle.

If a Bus Could Talk: The Story of Rosa Parks by Faith Ringgold. A telling of Rosa Parks's activism when she refuses to give up her bus seat to a white man.

It Doesn't Have to Be This Way by Luis Rodriguez. Poet and activist Rodriguez tells a story of the pressures to join gangs in the barrio.

Tikvah: Children's Book Creators Reflect on Human Rights, published by SeaStar Books. *Tikvah* means "hope." More than forty children's book authors and illustrators have written short essays and created a wide variety of illustrations on different human rights issues from around the world.

Whitewash by Ntozake Shange. A racist incident on a little girl draws the support of her friends and family.

Ten Amazing People and How They Changed the World by Maura D. Shaw. Short biographies of ten people who devoted their lives to making the world a better place, from Black Elk and Malcolm X, to Mother Teresa and Thich Nhat Hanh.

Americans Who Tell the Truth by Robert Shetterly. A collection of portraits of, and quotes from, fifty American activists such as Jane Addams, Chief Joseph, Helen Keller, Frederick Douglass, and Walt Whitman.

The Wall by Peter Sis. This is a story about the author's life growing up under a Communist government in Czechoslovakia.

Madlenka by Peter Sis. A little girl, Madlenka, has a loose tooth. She runs around her block in New York City and tells all her friends who run the local shops, all of whom have immigrated from another country. A gorgeously illustrated story about the goodness of a culturally diverse world.

How I Learned Geography by Uri Shulevitz. The author was a war refugee in Kazakhstan during World War II.

When Gogo Went to Vote by Elinor Batezat Sisulu. The author lives in Capetown, South Africa, and her book tells the story of Thambi's great-grandmother, a black South African, who goes to vote for the first time in 1994.

If the World Were a Village by David Smith. Imagine if the entire world population of 6 billion people were proportionally reduced to a village of 100 people. For example, twenty-five villagers—that's a quarter of the entire planet—would not have easy access to clean drinking water.

Alia's Mission by Mark Alan Stamaty. The same true story as *The Librarian of Basra* by Jeanette Winter, about Alia Muhammed Baker, a librarian in Bara, Iraq, who saved thousands of books before the library was destroyed in the war.

One Well: The Story of Water on Earth by Rochelle Strauss. The miracle of water, as well as pollution, the lack of access to clean water, and the science of water and the water cycle are covered in this nonfiction work.

Madam President: The Extraordinary, True (and Evolving) Story of Women in Politics by Catherine Thimmesh. This longer book consists of short biographies of women from the United States and around the world who have worked in politics, interspersed within a story of a girl who wants to be president—and others telling her she can't be.

Subway Sparrow by Leyla Torres. Four people from different cultures sit apart in a subway car. When a sparrow flies into the car, they work together to catch the bird and set it free.

Faithful Elephants by Yukio Truchiya. During World War II, Japanese government officials were concerned that if the country were bombed, the wild animals in the Bonzai Zoo in Tokyo would roam free. They ordered all the zoo animals to be killed. A true story.

Freedom on the Menu by Carole Boston Weatherford. A girl witnesses the lunch counter sit-ins in the South, which were held to protest the Jim Crow segregation laws.

Freedom Summer by Deborah Wiles. This beautiful story about two boys who are best friends—one is white and the other is black—tells about the day the 1964 Civil Rights Act goes into effect. The boys love to swim and can't wait to go to the newly integrated public pools but are shocked by what they find.

Caring Hearts and Critical Minds: Literature, Inquiry, and Social Responsibility by Steven Wolk. Copyright © 2013. Stenhouse Publishers.

A Chair for My Mother by Vera B. Williams. Rosa, whose mother is a waitress, tells the story of her family saving coins to buy a new chair after all their furniture is lost in a fire. Much goodness emerges when the neighbors help Rosa's family after the fire.

The Librarian of Basra by Jeanette Winter. Based on the true story of an Iraqi librarian who worked tirelessly to save the library's books from destruction as the United States began its war in 2003.

Wangari's Trees of Peace by Jeanette Winter. Wangari Maathai won the Nobel Peace Prize for creating the Green Belt Movement, with thousands of women planting trees across Africa.

Frida by Jonah Winter. A biography of the great Mexican painter Frida Kahlo.

The Other Side by Jacqueline Woodson. The homes of two girls, one black and the other white, are separated by a fence. Slowly the two girls come together and hope for a day when the fence is torn down.

Show Way by Jacqueline Woodson. The author takes her daughter through their African American ancestry and the cultural and familial role of quilts. Includes beautiful illustrations.

William's Doll by Charlotte Zolotow. Little William wants a doll, but his friends and his father think dolls are for girls. His grandma has a different view.

Appendix F

Graphic Novels and Graphic Nonfiction for Teaching Social Responsibility

Graphic novels and graphic nonfiction are not simple genres to define. Some of these books expand the boundaries of what we typically include in the graphic novel category and what is considered nonfiction. Many of these books—especially the nonfiction—were not written specifically for middle schoolers or young adults, but they can be good resources for teachers.

Graphic Novels

American Born Chinese by Gene Luen Yang
Anya's Ghost by Vera Brosgol
The Arrival by Shaun Tan
Bone by Jeff Smith
Daytripper by Fabio Moon and Gabriel Ba
The Eternal Smile by Gene Luen Yang and Derek Kirk Kim
I Kill Giants by Joe Kelly and JM Ken Nimura
Maus I & Maus II by Art Spiegelman
The Plain Janes by Cecil Castellucci and Jim Rugg
Pride of Baghdad by Brian K. Vaughn and Niko Henrichon
Robot Dreams by Sara Varon
Smile by Raina Telgemeier

Graphic Nonfiction

A.D.: New Orleans After the Deluge by Josh Neufeld
After 9/11: America's War on Terror by Sid Jacobson and Ernie Colón
Alan's War: The Memories of G.I. Alan Cope by Emmanuel Guibert
Around the World by Matt Phelan
Barefoot Gen: A Cartoon Story of Hiroshima (Volumes 1–10) by Keiji Nakazawa
Burma Chronicles by Guy Delisle
Clan Apis by Jay Hosler
Fallout by Jim Ottaviani, Janine Johnston, Steve Lieber, Vince Locke, Bernie Mireault, and Jeff Parker
Incognegro SC by Mat Johnson and Warren Pleece
The Influencing Machine: Brooke Gladstone on the Media by Brooke Gladstone and Josh Neufeld

It Was the War of the Trenches by Jacques Tardi

King by Ho Che Anderson

Laika by Nick Abadzis

Malcolm X by Andrew Helfer and Randy DuBurke

Nat Turner by Kyle Baker

A People's History of American Empire by Howard Zinn, Mike Konopacki, and Paul Buhle

Persepolis I and Persepolis II by Marjane Satrapi

The Principles of Uncertainty by Maira Kalman

Pyongyang: A Journey in North Korea by Guy Delisle

Radioactive: Marie & Pierre Curie; A Tale of Love and Fallout by Lauren Redniss

Safe Area Gorazde: The War in Eastern Bosnia 1992–1995 by Joe Sacco

Satchel Paige: Striking Out Jim Crow by James Sturm and Rich Tommaso

Stitches by David Small

Thoreau at Walden by John Porcellino

The United States Constitution: A Graphic Adaptation by Jonathan Hennessey and Aaron McConnell

Yummy: The Last Days of a Southside Shorty by G. Neri and Randy DuBurke

Appendix G

Thirty Children's and Young Adult Literature Blogs and Web Sites

A Fuse #8 Production	http://blog.schoollibraryjournal.com/afuse8production/
Bookshelves of Doom	http://bookshelvesofdoom.blogs.com/bookshelves_of_doom/
Bookslut in Training	http://www.bookslut.com/bookslut%20in%20training.php
100 Scope Notes	http://100scopenotes.com/
Cooperative Children's Book Center	http://www.education.wisc.edu/ccbc/default.asp
Voice of Youth Advocates	http://www.voya.com/
A Chair, A Fireplace & A Tea Cozy	http://blog.schoollibraryjournal.com/teacozy/
Educating Alice	http://medinger.wordpress.com/
Jen Robinson's Book Page	http://jkrbooks.typepad.com/blog/
Galley Smith	http://www.galleysmith.com/
I.N.K. Interesting Nonfiction for Kids	http://inkrethink.blogspot.com/
Bank Street College of Education Center for Children's Literature	http://www.bankstreet.edu/center-childrens-literature/
Interactive Reader	http://interactivereader.blogspot.com/
Guys Lit Wire	http://guyslitwire.blogspot.com/

Ms. Yingling Reads	http://msyinglingreads.blogspot.com/
Lee Wind	http://www.leewind.org/
readergirlz	http://readergirlz.blogspot.com/
Horn Book Magazine	http://www.hbook.com/horn-book-magazine/
Teen Reads	http://www.teenreads.com/
Reading Rants	http://www.readingrants.org/
Guys Read	http://www.guysread.com/
Book Nut	http://www.thebooknut.com/
Miss Print	http://missprint.wordpress.com/
Stacked	http://www.stackedbooks.org/
Richie's Picks	http://richiespicks.com/
Nonfiction Detectives	http://www.nonfictiondetectives.com/
Bookends	http://bookends.booklistonline.com/
bildungsroman	http://slayground.livejournal.com/
Kirkus Reviews	https://www.kirkusreviews.com/book-reviews/childrens-books/
School Library Journal	http://www.schoollibraryjournal.com/

Appendix H

Unit Brainstorming Sheet (front)

Before Reading	Topics, Themes, & Inquiry Questions	Small Activities
Projects	Book:	
		Mini-Lessons

Unit Brainstorming Sheet (back)

Questions for Journal Writing & Discussion:

Authentic Writing Assignments:

Appendix I

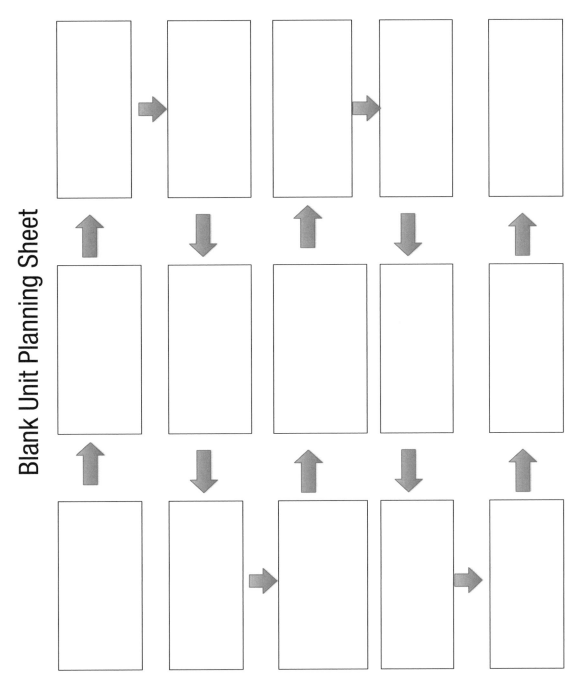

Blank Unit Planning Sheet

Appendix J

Technology Log

TUESDAY	WEDNESDAY	THURSDAY	FRIDAY
TV:	TV:	TV:	TV:
TM:	TM:	TM:	TM:
PH:	PH:	PH:	PH:
VG:	VG:	VG:	VG:
INT:	INT:	INT:	INT:
COM:	COM:	COM:	COM:
TW:	TW:	TW:	TW:
MO:	MO:	MO:	MO:
MU:	MU:	MU:	MU:
APP:	APP:	APP:	APP:
Other:	Other:	Other:	Other:

SATURDAY	SUNDAY	TECHNOLOGY LOG	MONDAY
TV:	TV:		TV:
TM:	TM:		TM:
PH:	PH:		PH:
VG:	VG:		VG:
INT:	INT:	Name:	INT:
COM:	COM:		COM:
TW:	TW:		TW:
MO:	MO:		MO:
MU:	MU:		MU:
APP:	APP:		APP:
Other:	Other:		Other:

TV = television / TM = text message / PH = talk on phone / VG = video games / INT = Internet /
COM = computer / TW = Twitter / MO = movie / MU = music / APP = appliance (put tally marks) / other?

Appendix K

Technology Log Graph

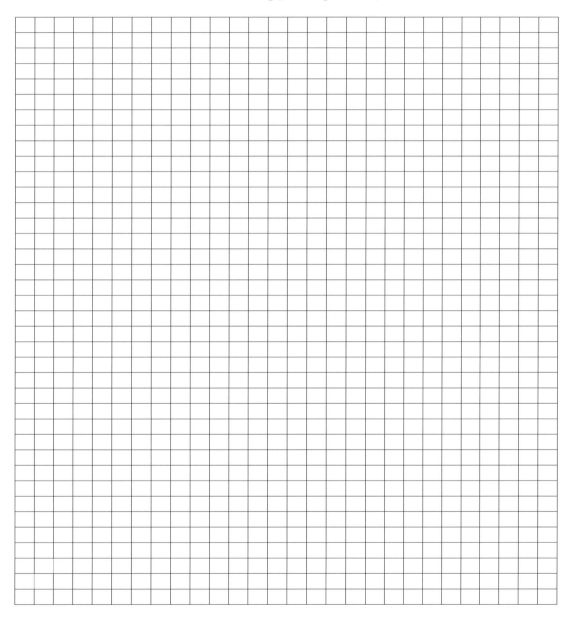

NAME _____ Appliance Use _____

Text Messages _____ GRAND TECH TOTAL _____

Appendix L

Planning Sheet for Picture Book Empathy Project

Book Title_____Author_____
Illustrator _____

Student Names _____
_____

• What are examples of empathy or caring in the story? Write in complete sentences! Is there more than one example?

• Is there a character in the story you empathize with? Who? Why? Is there a key page or part that touches your emotions?

• Write three good questions you will ask the younger kids about the story—but remember, they cannot have only one right answer!

1.

2.

3.

- Is there information you need to tell the kids before you read the book to them that will help them understand the story better?

- Write up to three words from the book that you think you should define for the younger kids before you read the book. If you need to, look up their definitions and write them down on an index card.

1.   2.   3.

- How will you explain what *caring* is to the younger kids? Write what you would say. Include an example of caring from your lives or their lives that would help explain it.

- How will you explain what *empathy* is to the younger kids? Write what you would say. Include an example of empathy from your lives or their lives that would help explain it.

Appendix M

Directions for Completing a Mind Map*

On the attached pages record notes as you read the novel. Keep the pages in your binder and update them daily. Your notes will help you with the final project, a mind map poster created by you and your group.

A mind map contains the following features:

1. A large, colorful picture of your assigned character, dressed appropriately for the setting and using specific details from the text as well as your own mind, and wearing an expression suitable for the mood of the text.

2. Objects that you associate with the character that are drawn, cut out of magazines, or printed off the Internet. You must be able to explain what these objects have to do with your character.

3. Important thoughts that your character was thinking throughout the novel. These are inferred by you unless your novel is told from the first-person point of view. If so, you must paraphrase in your own words. Put them in thought bubbles like this:

4. Words spoken aloud by your character in the novel. Choose only specific and important quotes that give us insight into the character and what he or she stands for. Put the quotes in speech bubbles. Have arrows coming from your character.

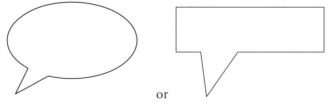

or

5. Words spoken aloud by others to your character. These comments will also be included in thought bubbles, but the arrows will point off the page. Make sure you identify the speaker(s).

6. Adjectives that describe your character.

Important Quotes by My Character

Page	Quote	What this says about my character/significance

Important Quotes Said to My Character

Page	Quote	What this says about my character/significance

What My Character Was Thinking

Words that go in thought bubble	Significance

*Mind mapping sheets were created by Mary Tripp.

Appendix N

American History + Family History Timeline Project

Name _____

Event	Who?	What?	Where?	Why?
Event:				
Dates:				
Event:				
Dates:				

References

Alexie, Sherman. 2007. *The Absolutely True Diary of a Part-Time Indian.* New York: Little, Brown.

Allen, Janet. 2000. *Yellow Brick Roads: Shared and Guided Paths to Independent Reading 4–12.* Portland, ME: Stenhouse.

Alvarez, Julia. 2006. *Before We Were Free.* New York: Laurel Leaf.

American Association of School Librarians. 2007. "AASL Standards for the 21st Century Learner." American Association of School Librarians. http://www.ala.org/aasl/guidelinesandstandards/learningstandards/standards.

Anyon, Jean. 1981. "Social Class and School Knowledge." *Curriculum Inquiry* 11 (1): 3–42.

Apple, Michael W. 1990. *Ideology and Curriculum.* 2nd ed. New York: Routledge.

Applebee, Arthur. 1992. "Stability and Change in the High School Canon." *English Journal* 81 (5): 27–32.

Appleman, Deborah. 2007. "Reading with Adolescents." In *Adolescent Literacy: Turning Promise into Practice*, ed. Kylene Beers, Robert E. Probst, and Linda Rief. Portsmouth, NH: Heinemann.

Aronson, Marc, and Marina Budhos. 2010. *Sugar Changed the World: A Story of Magic Spice, Slavery, Freedom, and Science.* New York: Clarion.

Association for Middle Level Education. 2010. "This We Believe: Keys to Educating Young Adolescents." Westerville, OH: Association for Middle Level Education.

Atkin, S. Beth. 2000. *Voices from the Fields*. New York: Little, Brown.

Atwell, Nancie. 1998. *In the Middle: New Understandings About Reading, Writing, and Learning*. 2nd ed. Portsmouth, NH: Heinemann.

———. 2003. *The Reading Zone: How to Help Kids Become Skilled, Passionate, Habitual, Critical Readers*. New York: Scholastic.

Beach, Richard, and Jamie Myers. 2001. *Inquiry-Based English: Engaging Students in Life and Literature*. New York: Teachers College Press.

Beals, Melba Patillo. 1995. *Warriors Don't Cry*. New York: Simon Pulse.

Beers, Kylene. 2003. *When Kids Can't Read: What Teachers Can Do*. Portsmouth, NH: Heinemann.

Berger, Ron. 2003. *An Ethic of Excellence*. Portsmouth, NH: Heinemann.

Berman, Sheldon. 1997. *Children's Social Consciousness and the Development of Social Responsibility*. Albany: State University of New York Press.

Bernstein, Sharon. 2010. "San Francisco Bans Most Happy Meals." *Chicago Tribune*, November 2.

Birkets, Sven. 2007. *Reading Life: Books for the Ages*. St. Paul, MN: Graywolf.

Broda, Herbert, W. 2011. *Moving the Classroom Outdoors*. Portland, ME: Stenhouse.

Campbell, Kimberley Hill. 2007. *Less Is More*. Portland, ME: Stenhouse.

Carroll, David M. 2004. *Self-Portrait with Turtles*. Boston: Houghton Mifflin.

Caskey, Micki M., and Vincent A. Anfara Jr. 2007. *Research Summary: Young Adolescents' Developmental Characteristics*. Westerville, OH: Association for Middle Level Education.

Chen, Milton. 2010. *Education Nation: Six Leading Edges of Innovation in Our Schools*. San Francisco: Jossey-Bass.

Christensen, Linda. 2000. *Reading, Writing, and Rising Up*. Milwaukee: Rethinking Schools.

Cole, Brock. 1989. *The Goats*. New York: Farrar, Straus and Giroux.

Coles, Robert. 1989. *The Call of Stories: Teaching and the Moral Imagination.* Boston: Houghton Mifflin.

Common Core State Standards. "Mission Statement." Common Core State Standards Initiative. http://www.corestandards.org/.

Costa, Arthur L. 2008. "The Thought-Filled Classroom." *Educational Leadership* 65 (5): 20–24.

Cowhey, Mary. 2006. *Black Ants and Buddhists.* Portland, ME: Stenhouse.

Crutcher, Chris. 1992. "Healing Through Literature." In *Author's Insights: Turning Teenagers into Readers & Writers*, ed. Donald R. Gallo. Portsmouth, NH: Heinemann.

Cushman, Karen. 2006. *The Loud Silence of Francine Green.* New York: Laurel Leaf.

Daniels, Harvey, and Steven Zemelman. 2004. *Subjects Matter: Every Teacher's Guide to Content-Area Reading.* Portsmouth, NH: Heinemann.

Daniels, Harvey, Steven Zemelman, and Nancy Steinke. 2007. *Content-Area Writing: Every Teacher's Guide.* Portsmouth, NH: Heinemann.

Darling-Hammond, Linda, et al. 2008. *Powerful Learning: What We Know About Teaching for Understanding.* San Francisco: Jossey-Bass.

De la Peña, Matt. 2008. *Mexican WhiteBoy.* New York: Delacorte.

Dewey, John. 1938. *Experience and Education.* New York: Collier.

DiCamillo, Kate. 2001. *The Tiger Rising.* New York: Candlewick.

Dorfman, Lynn R., and Rose Cappelli. 2009. *Nonfiction Mentor Texts: Teaching Informational Writing Through Children's Literature, K–8.* Portland, ME: Stenhouse.

Doyle, Kate. 2007. "The Atrocity Files: Deciphering the Archives of Guatemala's Dirty War." *Harper's,* December.

Duke, Nell. 2000. "3.6 Minutes Per Day: The Scarcity of Informational Texts in First Grade." *Reading Research Quarterly* 35: 202–224.

Edmundson, Mark. 2005. *Why Read?* New York: Bloomsbury.

Eisner, Elliot. 2002. "What Can Education Learn from the Arts About the Practice of Education?" *Journal of Curriculum and Supervision* 18 (1): 4–16.

Ellis, Deborah. 2001. *The Breadwinner.* Toronto: Groundwood.

———. 2007. *The Heaven Shop.* Toronto: Groundwood.

Engle, Shirley. 1960/2003. "Decision-Making: The Heart of Social Studies Instruction." *Social Studies* 94 (1): 7–10.

Fountas, Irene, and Gay Su Pinnell. 2001. *Guiding Readers and Writers (Grades 3–6).* Portsmouth, NH: Heinemann.

Freire, Paulo. 1970/1990. *Pedagogy of the Oppressed.* New York: Continuum.

Friedland, Ellen S., and Kim S. Truesdell. 2004. "Kids Reading Together: Ensuring the Success of a Buddy Reading Program." *The Reading Teacher* 58 (1): 76–79.

Friedman, Audrey A. 2000. "Nurturing Reflective Judgment Through Literature–based Inquiry." *English Journal* 89 (6): 96–104.

Friedman, Thomas. 2008. *Hot, Flat, and Crowded.* New York: Farrar, Straus and Giroux.

Gallagher, Kelly. 2004. *Deeper Reading.* Portland, ME: Stenhouse.

———. 2009. *Readicide.* Portland, ME: Stenhouse.

———. 2011. *Write Like This: Teaching Real-World Writing Through Modeling and Mentor Texts.* Portland, ME: Stenhouse.

Gallo, Donald R. 2001. "How Classics Create an Aliterate Society." *English Journal* 90 (30): 33–39.

Goleman, Daniel. 1995. *Emotional Intelligence: Why It Can Matter More Than IQ.* New York: Bantam.

Gorrell, Nancy. 2000. Teaching Empathy Through Ecphrastic Poetry: Entering a Curriculum of Peace. *English Journal* 89 (5): 32–41.

Greene, Maxine. 1988. *The Dialectic of Freedom.* New York: Teachers College Press.

———. 1995. *Releasing the Imagination: Essays on Education, the Arts, and Social Change.* San Francisco: Jossey-Bass.

Groenke, Susan L., Joellen Maples, and Jill Henderson. 2010. "Raising 'Hot Topics' Through Young Adult Literature." *Voices from the Middle* 17 (4): 29–36.

Haley, Alex, and Malcolm X. 1964. *The Autobiography of Malcolm X.* New York: Ballantine.

Harmon, James L. 2002. *Take My Advice: Letters to the Next Generation from People Who Know a Thing or Two.* New York: Simon and Schuster.

Harvey, Stephanie, and Harvey Daniels. 2009. *Comprehension & Collaboration: Inquiry Circles in Action.* Portsmouth, NH: Heinemann.

Haskins, Jeannette. 2011. "Making Magic with YAL." *English Journal* 101 (2): 101–104.

Hautman, Pete. 2006. *Rash.* New York: Simon Pulse.

Hess, Karin K., et al. 2009. "What Exactly Do 'Fewer, Clearer, and Higher Standards' Really Look Like in the Classroom? Using a Cognitive Rigor Matrix to Analyze Curriculum, Plan Lessons, and Implement Assessments." http://www.nciea.org/beta-site/publication_PDFs/cognitiverigorpaper_KH11.pdf.

Hinchey, Patricia. 2001. *Finding Freedom in the Classroom: A Practical Introduction to Critical Theory.* New York: Lang.

Hollander, Claire Needell. 2012. "Teach the Book, Touch the Heart." *New York Times*, April 22.

Hoyt, Linda. 2002. *Make It Real: Strategies for Success with Informational Texts.* Portsmouth, NH: Heinemann.

Ikeda, Daisaku. 2007. Foreword to *Educating Citizens for Global Awareness,* ed. Nel Noddings. New York: Teachers College Press.

Intrator, Sam M. 2003. *Tuned In and Fired Up: How Teaching Can Inspire Real Learning in the Classroom.* New Haven, CT: Yale University Press.

Ivey, Gay, and Karen Broaddus. 2001. "'Just Plain Reading': A Survey of What Makes Readers Want to Read in Middle School Classrooms." *Reading Research Quarterly* 36 (4): 350–377.

Joseph, Pamela Bolotin, and Sara Efron. 2005. "Seven Worlds of Moral Education." *Phi Delta Kappan* 86 (7): 525–533.

Keen, Suzanne. 2006. "A Theory of Narrative Empathy." *Narrative* 14 (3): 207–236.

Kilpatrick, William Heard. 1918. "The Project Method." *Teachers College Record* 19 (4): 319–335.

Kleibard, Herbert. 1987. *The Struggle for the American Curriculum: 1893–1958.* New York: Routledge.

Koningsburg, E. L. 2004. *The Outcasts of 19 Schuyler Place.* New York: Atheneum.

Konrath, Sara H., Edward H. O'Brien, and Courtney Hsing. 2011. "Changes in Dispositional Empathy in American College Students over Time: A Meta-Analysis." *Personality and Social Psychology Review* 15: 180–198.

Koss, Melanie. 2009. "Young Adult Novels with Multiple Narrative Perspectives: The Changing Nature of YA Literature." *The ALAN Review* 36 (3): 73–80.

Krashen, Stephen. 2004. *The Power of Reading: Insights from the Research.* Westport, CT: Libraries Unlimited.

Liptak, Adam. 2008. "Inmate Count in U.S. Dwarfs Other Nations." *New York Times*, April 23.

———. 2009. "Strip-Search of Girl Tests Limit of School Policy." *New York Times,* March 24.

LoMonte, Frank. 2010. "A. G. Cuccinelli's Go-Ahead to Search Student Cell Phones Raises Fourth Amendment Questions." Student Press Law Center. http://splc.org/wordpress/?p=1246.

Louv, Richard. 2005. *Last Child in the Woods.* Chapel Hill: NC: Algonquin Books of Chapel Hill.

Manguel, Alberto. 2006. *The Library at Night.* New Haven, CT: Yale University Press.

Mantle-Bromley, Corrine, and Ann M. Foster. 2005. "Educating for Democracy: The Vital Role of the Language Arts Teacher." *English Journal* 94 (5): 70–74.

Mar, Raymond A., and Keith Oatley. 2008. "The Function of Fiction Is the Abstraction and Simulation of Social Experience." *Perspectives on Psychological Science* 3 (3): 173–192.

McCormick, Patricia. 2006. *Sold.* New York: Hyperion.

McDonell, Terry. 2011. "In My Tribe." *Sports Illustrated,* November 28.

Moore, Kristin Anderson. 2008. "Teen Births: Examining the Recent Increase." The National Campaign to Prevent Teen and Unplanned Pregnancy. http://www.thenationalcampaign.org/resources/pdf/teenbirths_examincrease.pdf.

Muldoon, Phyllis. 1990. "Challenging Students to Think: Shaping Questions, Building Community." *English Journal* 79 (4): 34–40.

Murdock, Catherine Gilbert. 2006. *Dairy Queen.* Boston: Graphia.

National Assessment of Educational Statistics. 2011. "The Nation's Report Card: Civics 2010." Washington, DC: U.S. Department of Education.

National Council of Teachers of English. 1996. "NCTE/IRA Standards for the English Language Arts." http://www.ncte.org/standards/ncte–ira.

National Endowment for the Arts. 2007. *To Read or Not to Read: A Question of National Conscience.* Washington DC: National Endowment for the Arts. http://www.nea.gov/research/toread.pdf.

National Geographic Education Foundation. 2002. *National Geographic–Roper 2002 Global Geographic Literacy Study.* Washington, DC: National Geographic Society.

———. 2006. *National Geographic–Roper Public Affairs Geographic Literacy Study.* Washington, DC: National Geographic Society.

National Wildlife Federation. 2011. "Developing Healthy Kids Through Outdoor Play: The Whole Child Report." http://www.nwf.org/Get-Outside/Be-Out-There/Why-Be-Out-There/Special-Reports/Whole-Child.aspx.

Nobori, Mariko. 2011. "Ten Take Away Tips for Teaching Critical Thinking." *Edutopia.* http://www.edutopia.org/stw-kipp-critical-thinking-10-tips-for-teaching.

Noddings, Nel. 1992. *The Challenge to Care in Schools: An Alternative Approach to Education.* New York: Teachers College Press.

———. 1995. "Teaching Themes of Caring." *Phi Delta Kappan* 76 (9): 675–679.

———. 2003. *Happiness and Education.* Cambridge, UK: Cambridge University Press.

———. 2004. "War, Critical Thinking, and Self-Understanding." *Phi Delta Kappan* 85 (7): 489–495.

O'Brien, Andrea Maxworthy. n.d. The Power of One Voice: An Interview with Deborah Ellis. Cooperative Children's Book Center. http://www.education.wisc.edu/ccbc/authors/experts/dellis.asp.

Ohanian, Susan. 1994. *Who's in Charge? A Teacher Speaks Her Mind.* Portsmouth, NH: Boynton/ Cook.

Orr, David. 1994. *Earth in Mind: On Education, Environment, and the Human Prospect.* Washington, DC: Island Press.

———. 1995. "Educating for the Environment." *Change* 27 (3): 43–46.

Outdoor Foundation. 2010. "Outdoor Recreation Participation Report." http://www .outdoorfoundation.org/research.participation.2010.html.

Owens, Roxanne Farwick, Jennifer L. Hester, and William H. Teale. 2002. "Where Do You Want to Go Today? Inquiry–Based Learning and Technology Integration." *Reading Teacher* 55 (7): 616–625.

Partnership for 21st Century Skills. "Framework for 21st Century Learning." Partnership for 21st Century Skills. http://www.p21.org/.

Pearson, Mary E. 2008. *The Adoration of Jenna Fox.* New York: Square Fish.

Peart, Nicolas K. 2011. "Why Is the NYPD After Me?" *New York Times,* December 18.

Peterson, Bob. 2002. "The World Up Close." *Rethinking Schools.* http://www.rethinkingschools.org/ static/war/pdfs/clos162.pdf.

Petrone, Robert, and Robert Gibney. 2005. "The Power to Speak and Listen! Democratic Pedagogies for American Literature Classrooms." *English Journal* 94 (5): 35–39.

Pew Center on the States. 2008. "One in 100: Behind Bard in America 2008." http://www.pewstates .org/uploadedFiles/PCS_Assets/2008/one%20in%20100.pdf.

Pink, Daniel. 2006. *A Whole New Mind: Why Right-Brainers Will Rule the Future.* New York: Riverhead.

Pitcher, Sharon M., et al. 2007. "Assessing Adolescents' Motivation to Read." *Journal of Adolescent and Adult Literacy* 50 (5): 378–396.

Project H Design. "Design for Education for Tomorrow." http://www.projecthdesign.org/#studio-h.

Ravitch, Diane. 2010. *The Death and Life of the Great American School System.* New York: Basic Books.

Resau, Laura. 2009. *Red Glass.* New York: Delacorte Press.

Resau, Laura, and Maria Virginia Farinango. 2010. *The Queen of Water.* New York: Delacorte Press.

Rideout, Victoria J., Ulla G. Foehr, and Donald F. Roberts. 2010. "Generation M[2]: Media in the Lives of 8- to 18- Year-Olds." Menlo Park, CA: Henry J. Kaiser Family Foundation. http://www.kff.org/entmedia/upload/8010.pdf.

Riedelsheimer, Thomas. 2004. *Rivers and Tides.* DVD. Directed by Thomas Riedelsheimer. Mediopolis Films.

Rief, Linda. 1991. *Seeking Diversity: Language Arts with Adolescents.* Portsmouth, NH: Heinemann.

Ritchhart, Ron, Mark Church, and Karin Morrison. 2011. *Making Thinking Visible.* San Francisco: Jossey-Bass.

Rochman, Hazel. 1995. "Against Borders." *The Horn Book* 71 (2): 144–157. http://archive.hbook.com/magazine/articles/1990_96/mar95_rochman.asp.

Rodkin, Dennis. 2010. "Best Elementary Schools in Chicago and the Suburbs." *Chicago* magazine. http://www.chicagomag.com/Chicago-Magazine/October-2010/Best-Elementary-Schools-in-Chicago-and-the-Suburbs/.

Rogers, Carl. 1969. *Freedom to Learn.* Columbus, OH: Charles G. Merrill.

Romano, Tom. 2000. *Blending Genre, Altering Style: Writing Multigenre Research Papers.* Portsmouth, NH: Heinemann.

Rothstein, Dan, and Luz Santana. 2011. *Make Just One Change: Teach Students to Ask Their Own Questions.* Cambridge, MA: Harvard Education Press.

Ryan, Pam Munoz. 2000. *Esperanza Rising.* New York: Scholastic.

Rycik, Mary Taylor, and Brenda Rosler. 2009. "The Return of Historical Fiction." *The Reading Teacher* 63 (2): 163–166.

Saltzman, Paul. 2008. *Prom Night in Mississippi.* Directed by Paul Saltzman. Docuramafilms.

Samit, Jay. 2011. "All Politics Is Social: Social Media Engagement Will Decide Election 2012." Social Vibe. http://media.socialvibe.com/m/site/politicalsolutions/SocialVibe_Political_WhitePaper.pdf.

Sawch, Deb. 2011. "Asking and Arguing with Fact and Fiction: Using Inquiry and Critical Literacy to Make Sense of Literature in the World." *English Journal* 101 (2): 80–85.

Schmidt, Gary D. 2007. *The Wednesday Wars.* Boston: Houghton Mifflin.

Sepetys, Rta. 2011. *Between Shades of Gray.* New York: Philomel.

Shannon, Patrick. 1995. *Texts, Lies, and Videotape: Stories About Life, Literacy, and Learning.* Portsmouth, NH: Heinemann.

Singer, Jessica. 2006. *Stirring Up Justice: Writing & Reading to Change the World.* Portsmouth, NH: Heinemann.

Smith, Michael W., and Jeffrey D. Wilhelm. 2007. *Reading Don't Fix No Chevys.* Portsmouth, NH: Heinemann.

Smith, Patricia. 2011. "The 9/11 Dilemma: Freedom vs. Security." *New York Times Upfront*, September 5. http://www.scholastic.com/browse/article.jsp?id=3756395.

Sobel, David. 2008. *Childhood and Nature: Design Principles for Educators.* Portland, ME: Stenhouse.

Soto, Gary. 1998. *Petty Crimes.* Orlando, FL: Harcourt.

Spector, Michael. 2006. "The Last Drop." *The New Yorker*, October 23.

Spinelli, Jerry. 2003. *Milkweed.* New York: Scholastic.

Stallworth, B. Joyce. 2006. "The Relevance of Young Adult Literature." *Educational Leadership* 63 (7): 59–63.

Stavans, Ilan, and Lalo Alcarez. 2000. *Latino USA: A Cartoon History.* New York: Basic Books.

Stearns, Peter. 2008. "Why Study History?" American Historical Association. http://www.historians.org/pubs/free/WhyStudyHistory.htm.

Stone, Michael K. 2009. *Smart by Nature: Schooling for Sustainability.* Healdsburg, CA: Watershed Media.

Stott, William. 1986. *Documentary Expression and Thirties America.* Chicago: University of Chicago Press.

Strommen, Linda T., and Barbara F. Mates. 2004. "Learning to Love Reading: Interviews with Older Children and Teens." *Journal of Adolescent and Adult Literacy* 48 (3): 288–300.

Suzuki, David, and Wayne Grady. 2004. *Tree: A Life Story.* Vancouver: Greystone Books.

Swope, Sam. 2005. *I Am a Pencil: A Teacher, His Kids, and Their Stories.* New York: Owl Books.

Tavernise, Sabrina. 2011. "Poverty Rate Soars to Highest Level Since 1993." *New York Times,* September 14, sec. A.

Thoreau, Henry David. n.d. *Walden.* Boston: Beacon Press.

Tillage, Leon Walter. 1997. *Leon's Story.* New York: Farrar, Straus and Giroux.

Tovani, Cris. 2000. *I Read It, but I Don't Get It: Comprehension Strategies for Adolescent Readers.* Portland, ME: Stenhouse.

———. 2011. *So What Do They Really Know?: Assessment That Informs Teaching and Learning.* Portland, ME: Stenhouse.

VanSledright, Bruce. 1995. "'I Don't Remember—The Ideas Are All Jumbled in My Head': Eighth Graders' Reconstructions of Colonial American History." *Journal of Curriculum and Supervision* 10 (3): 317–345.

Vargas, Jose Antonio. 2008. "The YouTube Presidency." *Washington Post.* http://voices.washingtonpost.com/44/2008/11/the-youtube-presidency.html.

———. 2011. "Outlaw: My Life in America as an Undocumented Immigrant." *New York Times Magazine,* June 26.

Volponi, Paul. 2006. *Black and White.* New York: Speak.

Wagner, Tracy. 2003. "Forgive and Remember." *Rethinking Schools.* http://www.rethinkingschools.org/archive/18_01/forg181.shtml.

Wasserman, Selma. 2007. "Let's Have a Famine! Connecting Means and Ends in Teaching to Big Ideas." *Phi Delta Kappan* 89 (4): 290–297.

Wilhelm, Jeffrey. 2007. *Engaging Readers and Writers with Inquiry.* New York: Scholastic.

Wilhelm, Jeffrey D., and Bruce Novak. 2011. *Teaching Literacy for Love and Wisdom: Being the Book and Being the Change.* New York: Teachers College Press.

Wilson, Edward O. 1994. *Naturalist.* New York: Warner.

———. 1997. *In Search of Nature.* Washington, DC: Island Press.

———. 2002. *The Future of Life.* New York: Vintage.

Wilson, N. D. 2007. *Leepike Ridge.* New York: Random House.

Winerip, Michael. 2012. "Facing a Robo-Grader? Just Keep Obfuscating Mellifluously." *New York Times*, April 23.

Winkler, Adam. 2011. "The Secret History of Guns." *The Atlantic*, September.

Wolff, Virginia Euwer. 1993. *Make Lemonade.* New York: Henry Holt.

Wolk, Steven. 1998. *A Democratic Classroom.* Portsmouth, NH: Heinemann.

———. 2004. "Using Picture Books to Teach for Democracy." *Language Arts* 82 (1): 26–35.

———. 2008. "School as Inquiry." *Phi Delta Kappan* 90 (2): 115–122.

———. 2010. "What Should Students Read?" *Phi Delta Kappan* 91 (7): 8–16.

World Savvy. 2012. "Why Global Education?" http://worldsavvy.org/about/why–need/.

Zaki, Jamil. 2011. "What, Me Care? Young Are Less Empathic." http://www.scientificamerican.com/article.cfm?id=what-me-care.

Zevin, Gabrielle. 2007. *Elsewhere.* New York: Square Fish.

Zhao, Yali, and John D. Hoge. 2005. "What Elementary Students and Teachers Say About Social Studies." *Social Studies* 96 (5): 216–221.

Zindel, Paul. 1968. *The Pigman.* New York: Laurel Leaf.

Index

Page numbers followed by an *f* indicate figures.